About the Authors

BILL ROMANOWSKI lives in California with his wife, Julie, and their two children.

ADAM SCHEFTER, a former writer for the *Denver Post*, is a broadcaster with the NFL Network. He lives in Colorado.

PHIL TOWLE, M.A., is a performance coach who lives in California with his wife, Gail.

RO

MY LIFE O
LIVING DREAMS AN

HARPER

NEW YORK · LONDON · TORONTO · SYDNEY

M O

THE EDGE: SLAYING DRAGONS

BILL ROMANOWSKI

with ADAM SCHEFTER
and PHIL TOWLE

To my alter ego, "Romo," who became the symbol of my ceaseless drive for perfection. You are being retired, but you will always remain alive as my burning ambition to be the best in everything I do.

HARPER

A hardcover edition of this book was published in 2005 by William Morrow, an imprint of HarperCollins Publishers.

HarperCollins books may be purchased for educational, business, or sales promotional use. For information please write: Special Markets Department, HarperCollins Publishers, 10 East 53rd Street, New York, NY 10022.

FIRST HARPER PAPERBACK PUBLISHED 2006.

Designed by Iva Hacker-Delany

Library of Congress Cataloging-in-Publication Data has been applied for.

ISBN-10: 0-06-075863-5
ISBN-13: 978-0-06-075863-9

ISBN-10: 0-06-115217-X (pbk.)
ISBN-13: 978-0-06-115217-7 (pbk.)

06 07 08 09 10 ❖/RRD 10 9 8 7 6 5

CONTENTS

FIRST DOWN

December 22, 2003. The bright lights of *ABC's Monday Night Football*. Prime time, what every NFL player lives for. It is the showcase that brings the best we can offer in front of millions of adoring fans. And there I was, standing meekly on the sidelines, feeling like a loser while I stared numbly at the fierce battle in front of me.

Sixteen years in the league, 243 consecutive regular season wars, plus 28 straight playoff contests . . . and I, Bill Romanowski, aka Romo, was suddenly MIA. For the ordinary human being, it might seem absolutely normal to separate yourself from the brutality on display only a few yards away. Me? I felt strangely disoriented and empty inside.

How could I in good conscience watch my fellow Raiders in full-scale combat with the Green Bay Packers? I was always the one at the epicenter of the battle zone—and maybe too often at the center of controversy—but I'd never been relegated to the worthless role of observer. I can't tell you how ashamed I felt. While it was true that my trademark black war paint had faded lately, my unparalleled passion for football—a sport that had transformed me from an anonymous Bill Romanowski to the ferocious "Romo"—was as strong as ever.

My passion couldn't overcome my deteriorating body, though. Once my most reliable weapon, it was betraying me. The last of too many accumulative concussions had double-crossed the mind that ate, drank, and slept nothing but football since I was a twelve-year-old boy with a dream.

Anyone looking into my eyes that night could see not only the pain of a guilt-ridden teammate, but the gradually emerging pain of being forced away from the game I loved. It was the pain of a tired, worn-out, spent athlete clinging to illusions that his invincibility would run on forever.

As the game—and career—clock wound down inevitably to 0:00, I couldn't stop myself from the horrible thought that I had just lost my final game to the dragons I had fought so hard all my life to overcome. I was right back to square one.

I loved football with an unmatched intensity, driving myself to extremes and beyond so that I could excel as well as keep myself one step ahead of everyone else. My quest was always and only to be the best, nothing less. I fueled this obsession with ever-escalating expectations, trying to satisfy my childhood dreams to be somebody. The only way I knew how to get to where I had to go was to do more than the next guy, whom I perceived, rightly or wrongly, to be probably more talented than I was.

Even as I stood apart from the savagery on the sidelines, I was being hit by something else, a reawakening of my conscience. After all, I had to repress it to some degree if I was going to succeed at a career devoted to calculatedly administering pain to other people. Without an ounce of forethought, let alone concern for my victims, I had ruthlessly inflicted hurt on my opponents.

Was this a new morality? If it was, why had I ignored it for so long? Why had I allowed my obsession to compromise my integrity? Where was Bill Romanowski when Romo was winning four Super Bowls and chosen for two Pro Bowls?

Looking back on that Monday night game, I can see that I was actually beginning to let go of my career—and most importantly, Romo—allowing Bill to return to his rightful place. I couldn't do that fully or convincingly, though, without addressing who I was, the journey I'd been on, and who I'd become. I didn't conciously think about writing this book at that moment. Now I'm sure this was its opening kickoff.

Writing has been cathartic and therapeutic, a sort of cleansing, as well as an embracing of accountability. There were times, too, when I'd celebrate reliving the successes because you know that I never took time to appreciate them. When you're too afraid of losing what you have gained, you can't afford to pause even for a second for fear of falling behind.

Now, like many other athletes who may have put their families at risk, or treated them as a secondary priority, I must make up lost ground. But good intentions don't necessarily translate into immediate change. I'm still driven, even as I'm healing. I've come to understand that simply knowing isn't enough.

It's not hard to trace how I became who I am. From the time I strapped on my first helmet in Vernon, Connecticut, I found a purpose to living. Maybe it was the uniform initially. When you wear one, it's like you belong and you automatically are somebody. Even today, I revere my old, battered equipment, like a war hero his medals.

When I started to dream about the possibilities, I just wanted to make it to football's highest level. I thought that if I could just make it onto an NFL roster I would be satisfied. But I underestimated how hooked I would become.

When you're young, you are blind to the significance of

R
O
M
O

your dreams. You learn about reality *after* you've lived them, *after* you've accomplished, *after* you've made mistakes, *after* you've satisfied the cost of your ambitions. That's when your debts come due.

Back then, once I could feel myself making progress and see the relationship between effort and results, the visible rewards only fueled my desire, which in turn made me work even harder to get a greater payoff. Passion turned into fanaticism as I discovered that I had real potential. But my potential always seemed dependent on hard work, so rather than believe in whatever talent I had, I would always trust my work ethic.

There is no question in my mind that my success has always been directly tied to outhustling, outworking, and overachieving. I loved training so much because I was always competing—with myself. And, of course, I would always win that matchup.

In my impossibly demanding world, you never stop moving forward, and you absolutely cannot look over your shoulder. Our coaches use to constantly remind us, "If you're not always improving, you're falling behind." There's no such NFL reality as staying the same. Only better—or worse.

The average career in the NFL is roughly three and a half years. Imagine yourself finally reaching the zenith of your dreams, with only the briefest of moments to taste, let alone enjoy, your fantasy come true. Would you do it all over again? Would you do all it takes to get there, for a microsecond of satisfaction?

Whether I underestimated my talent or not, I decided early on that whatever the regimen prescribed by my coaches, it wasn't good enough for my precious dreams. I needed to do more, like a kid who needed to do extra credit in school to ensure a better grade.

Whatever it took, I was constantly exploring and pushing the limits of my performance and training methods to get me where I needed to go. I learned early on that coaches and trainers didn't necessarily have all the answers or weren't necessarily as dedicated as I felt they needed to be. When you discover that, you're sometimes left on your own to find your way, and you use fear to force yourself into the unknown, the unconventional, precisely because you are left alone to your own resourcefulness.

So I was alone, defending my precious dreams against those threatening, seemingly insurmountable dragons. I turned inside for my own counsel, learning to keep my most important personal feelings and thoughts as secrets. That's both a strength and a liability, of course. I was exceptional as a self-motivator, but weaker when it came to communicating with those around me. It felt much more natural to be a solo act, much more comfortable to live on my own terms.

And on my terms I relied on strategies borne of my extreme dedication to excellence. Fortunately, the teams I played for—the San Francisco 49ers, Philadelphia Eagles, Denver Broncos, and Oakland Raiders—paid me premium salaries to support these strategies. Over the course of my football career I spent more than $1 million on supplements, trainers, therapies, doctors, whatever I could do to improve myself and my teammates.

Ultimately, it all was done with the idea to keep winning. To keep playing. To keep surviving. To keep the dream alive.

In reality, I would have done this for free, that's how much I loved it. But I also believe I deserved every dollar I made and paid for every dime of it. I was left with a legacy of injuries—some ongoing, others permanent—that will accompany my accomplishments and memories until the day I stop breathing. (Take a look at the appendix section, "Injury History.")

Most of us peak in our twenties; the select few, like me, are fortunate to extend our NFL lifespan into our thirties. When retirement comes, and there are few graceful transition exits in sport, where we do we go with what we have done? We're not in our sixties, heading for golf carts in Arizona. We are cut loose into the real world, your world, where we can trade on our reputation for only a few more years.

But during my playing days, my problem was how much it bothered me when others didn't share my obsession for being the best, when I perceived they were settling for mediocrity. That, to me, is unacceptable, always will be. This is partly why I left a trail of ill will with teammates whom I judged as slackers, and coaches and trainers who didn't push me enough. This is part of my debt, but I accumulated them all along the way.

No question I injured some egos. No question I stepped over the line. No question I always provided leadership by example in a brutal sport that eats up and spits out anyone who allows himself to take even a millisecond break from the demands of excellence. But back then, the way I saw it was, anyone who didn't help me get where I was going became a dragon to my dreams.

Early on, I found out I could not relax any standards—or I would be putting my dreams in serious jeopardy.

When pure passion wasn't driving me, fear and insecurity were. Believe me, at times I still don't know which was more dominant. In football, there's no time to exhale, no time to think. No matter how well you do on one play, it isn't enough to help you on the next. The enemy is always reloading, the roster is always reshuffling, and it's hard surviving, no less thriving. Now I can admit I was afraid a lot; I just didn't take time to wrestle with my fears.

But through therapy and self-reflection, I've grown to understand that passion results in fewer side effects while fear pushes us over the line, leaving a trail of remorse and fallout from behaviors not well thought out in advance. From spitting in J. J. Stokes's face to shattering Kerry Collins's jaw to fracturing Marcus Williams's orbital bone, I sure had enough of those indiscretions.

People want to give me an out and explain my rage as a reaction to supplements. But over time, through therapy, I have grown to hold myself more accountable. I don't want to blame any performance-enhancing substances for anything that happened in my life or my career. I blame myself and, more specifically, my allegiance to fear.

It was fear of failure, as well as my obsession with fitness, that enabled me to train harder and smarter than any athlete I know. The idea the entire time was to achieve peak performance on Sunday. Come Monday and the rest of the week, I had to deal with the consequences of hitting and tackling enormous, powerful, or fast athletes. Those consequences led to more treatments, more supplements, and more doctors.

I always questioned them, as well as myself. Was I exercising the right way? Eating the right way? Basically, was I taking care of my body and my livelihood in the best possible way to handle the punishment, to recover quickly and be the linebacker that I lived to be? Training for most people was work, necessary drudgery. For me, it allowed me to get one step closer to my dreams.

But I also soon found myself walking the fine line between morality and proficiency, and took considerable pride in trying to outsmart the system. It wasn't about illegal; I was taking performance-enhancing substances they couldn't test for, like THG. As soon as I found out something could be tested for, I stopped taking it. I didn't want the embarrassment. But I clearly pushed the envelope ethically and morally, because if I could take something that would help me perform better and it wasn't banned, then hell, I was going to take it.

Ultimately, it wasn't about disrespecting the NFL. The NFL runs the greatest sport in the world, does it better than anybody

R O M O

else. But as urgent as I was feeling, as desperate as I was to make my ride last as long as possible, I wasn't going to depend on different people with their different agendas governing what was best for me and my dreams, let alone my body and well-being. When in doubt about right or wrong, I trusted myself and my cadre of professional experts.

Throughout my career, there never were discussions about what was best for the health of the athletes as much as about what was permissible. When you're up against the pressure to succeed or else, there is always some workout or supplement there to help. And once you feel the difference, you're addicted not to the substance, but to the excitement that you've just gotten that much closer to your goal. Now it becomes an insatiable hunger to find whatever it takes. Though I crossed the line, in retrospect, I was always an experimenter whose goal was exclusively to stretch my performance, not the rules.

I'm aware that many of you will explore these pages, scanning for revelations about illegal performance substances rather than more meaningful revelations about the man who took them. There will be something in these pages for everybody. But up front, know that I wanted this book to be deeper than sensational, so much deeper. I'm writing because I'm more interested in sharing the whys as opposed to purging the whats.

I want this book to be for people who share my drive, my passion, and my insecurities. It has represented a beginning for me. But as I restore Bill Romanowski the person, I know I'm coming from a place of increased integrity.

There will be no offloading of responsibility upon others. There will be no scapegoating of fellow athletes, coaches, or my beloved sport. This expression in your hands right now takes aim at my journey toward my truths. Along the way, I realized we all struggle with similar issues, especially those of us driven to the kind of perfectionism that challenges our values.

Face it: we are all addicted to something. We all have become seduced and overly attached to something or someone that we use as an excuse to justify our endgame. We all have become victims of our rationalizing behaviors, keeping our insecurities at bay, steering ourselves away from our real self and the real truth.

But the truth is, we shouldn't need any masks or manipulations to relieve our fears. We should believe enough in ourselves, and be strong enough ourselves, to do it.

It's easy for me to say now, sure. But for a long time, I was the self-proclaimed poster boy for disguise. With the public's help, I even created an alter ego, aka Romo, that followed me around as much as number 53. That was tough to let go of, that alter ego. But when you go behind the number and the man, that alter ego isn't even close to being the complete me.

This story is.

R
O
M
O

1 MY BODY'S LIKE AN ARMY

As a little boy, I was keenly aware of how my parents struggled with managing our family finances. There were too many nights when I would be sitting at the kitchen table, trying to make myself invisible as they wrestled with making ends meet. Even when I went to bed, I could hear them through the walls, worrying about how they were going to come up with the money to keep my four siblings, and our family, afloat. Maybe a second mortgage, maybe Mom would take on second jobs. Whatever it took to not only pay the bills, but also to put their five children through college.

Moments like those cut deeply into my view of my world and my future. Back then I was just anxious that they were troubled. Then, as I got older, I understood it more. There was nothing scarier than watching your parents, the foundations of our security, being rocked by whatever their problems were.

Dad suffered a stroke while he was at work. When I got home from school that day, Mom told me that Daddy was in the hospital with a brain aneurysm. Being nine years old, I didn't know what that meant. It wasn't hard to figure out once we went to visit him.

Doctors had shaved the hair off half his head, and he had a huge scar where they opened his scalp to go into his brain. It scared me and my mom. Even though Dad recovered well, I saw how afraid Mom was at the prospect of losing him. We all have our memories, and the scary ones seem to stay with us longer and follow us into adulthood.

One night some years later, probably around eighth or ninth grade, I remember being hit with the revelation that I could actually do something about my family's financial troubles and save my parents from at least a portion of their constant worries. I could earn a college scholarship. I didn't know whether I could make it baseball, basketball, or football. I didn't know whether I was actually good enough. But I knew if I made it my goal and worked hard enough at it, something positive would result. And if sports weren't enough, then I'd simply enlist in the military, like my dad did during the Korean War, and use the G.I. Bill to pay for my tuition.

Dreaming, I found, was the easier part. What was tougher was figuring out how to make it happen. I didn't have a road map to get from here to there. For whatever reasons, I didn't feel as if I had anyone to guide me. And I kept my intentions to myself. Looking back, I was afraid to share my dream out loud because I felt insecure about who I was and what I was capable of.

Sports were my logical ticket. I had my older brothers' role-modeling, but they also enjoyed hunting and fishing with Dad while I seemed more consumed with sports, or limited to that single passion. I wasn't sure what to do with that passion until I had an epiphany that would transform me forever. Instantly, I felt aligned with a purpose.

Even today, I remember picking up the October 4, 1982, issue of *Sports Illustrated* and reading an eight-page article on the then–University of Georgia running back Herschel Walker

R
O
M
O

titled, "My Body's Like an Army." Funny thing is, we didn't even have a subscription to the magazine. One of my friends, John Steed, did, and I stumbled across it by accident one day at his house. When I recently reread it, I realized not only did I remember the details, but I could feel the same excitement that I felt all that time ago.

When he was twelve, Herschel went to Tom Jordan, the local track-and-field coach in Wrightsville, Georgia, and asked him how he could get bigger, stronger and faster. Jordan gave him a simple game plan: push-ups, sit-ups, and sprints.

"During that first year Walker had done these exercises every day, unless rain kept him from sprinting along the road leading from his house down to the highway," the reporter wrote. "Jordan had never said how much to do, just to do those three things regularly. To Herschel, 'regularly' meant every single day, and by the end of that critical first year, he had done more than 100,000 push-ups, more than 100,000 sit-ups and had sprinted nearly half a million yards.

"He almost always did his push-ups and sit-ups in the evening, while he was either studying or watching television or, more usually, both. During every commercial break he would pump out a quick 25 push-ups and 25 sit-ups or would alternate the push-ups and sit-ups, doing 50 push-ups during one break, then 50 sit-ups during the next, until he had accumulated approximately 300 of each." Isn't that a great way to make use of that annoying commercial time?

This was inspiring stuff. Soon after, a little voice started speaking to me: *Here's somebody who succeeded in football and here's how he did it. Here's what he did to get stronger. Here's what he did to get faster. Here's what he did to become the best possible athlete.*

I wasn't startled by this voice. It was almost as if I was waiting for it, and it would come to me regularly throughout my life at times when I needed to hear it most—I came to think of it as my guardian angel. That first time it was comforting me, reassuring me, yet challenging me to do what it was telling me—or I would have to account to myself if I didn't. Here I was looking for a direction, seeking a road map, and now something spiritual, almost mystical, was taking over. Wherever this voice was coming from, I had to follow it to the letter. And between the article and the voice, I had my very first prescription: Push-ups, sit-ups, and sprints. Every day.

I immediately poured myself into the beginnings of my relentless pursuit of my dreams. Nothing would stop me. Nothing would deter me. My voice was telling me my life could be different, instantly and forever. The night I read it, I did eleven push-ups and twenty sit-ups, and I sprinted in the fields across the street from our house in Vernon, Connecticut. I had found meaning and purpose for the kid who didn't know where he was going.

Later I'd add pull-ups to the routine, ripping them off on the garage rafters. On the nutrition side, food became fuel, not pleasure. I quit drinking soda and started drinking milk. Other than ice cream, I stopped eating junk food, so out went the Fudge Stripe cookies and in came the vegetables grown in our backyard. Each morning, instead of eating a whole box of Cap'n Crunch, which I could do in one sitting, I would eat twelve pancakes, thanks to Mom. Whatever I needed, she would deliver.

There's something about when you have this new direction—it's invigorating. I remember thinking I had something I knew I wanted, and now I had a plan on how to get there. There was an energy inside me that made me feel reborn. And if over the course of my NFL career you strip away the questionable choices I made, I still became the hardest-working SOB on the planet. It was why I liked training so much. I could see how each step I was taking brought me closer to my dreams.

R
O
M
O

Little by little, I started getting stronger. My eleven daily push-ups increased to sixty, then eighty, then hundreds until I would fall face first on the ground, wiped. My twenty sit-ups jumped to fifty, then one hundred, then to the point where I just couldn't do them anymore. I'd sprint until my heart felt like it would explode. The more I did, the more I grew. My freshman year, I stood a real skin-and-bones five foot nine, 140 pounds. When I read the article in my sophomore year, I measured in at close to six feet, 175 pounds. Then my stomach started getting more ripped, my biceps more bulging. A year later, I was six foot three, 200. And for my senior year, I was a hefty, football-ready, six foot three, 215.

But more than just push-ups, sit-ups, and sprints, Herschel also emphasized the virtues of hard work and, just like that, I believed it. This great athlete was telling me, an impressionable high school kid, that the stuff nobody wants to do is the stuff that could make you a somebody. I was learning to discard mediocrity for greatness.

Then Herschel hit me with one more statement that made me reflect on my own mind set. "I keep hearing and reading about all this talent they say I've been blessed with," Herschel said in the article, "but I don't see it that way. For a long time I never understood I was blessed, except for having such a good family and all. But I do see I have been blessed, though not in the way people think." Then Herschel pointed to his head. "This is where I've been blessed. Not in my body. My mind's like a general and my body's like an army."

As I absorbed this, I realized I thought that same way, with only a slight difference. I believed then, as I believe now, that my heart was bigger and stronger than anybody's. My heart was my general. My drive came from within.

What I also had was support. My mom and dad, Donna and Bill Romanowski, were always there for me. When I read the *SI* article, they'd been married for nearly twenty-seven years. They first met on, of all things, a blind date while they were students at Ohio University, set up by their friends, Bill Brown and Margaret Warmeling. Mom and Dad went to some movie whose title they still don't remember, something about people riding around on pink elephants. It was awful, so they left the theater. But not each other. On December 17, 1955, they got married at St. Mary's Catholic Church in Mentor, Ohio, where they live today.

For their honeymoon, they drove back to Athens, Ohio, and began plotting their future. Before financial reality and Mom's hysterectomy smacked them in the head, their plan was to have ten children—enough for a baseball team. As they like to joke, they were Catholics living in Ohio's brutal winters, what else were they supposed to do? They didn't waste any time. Not even a year after they were married, they had their first child, Mike. Three years later, Joe. Three more years later, Suzie. And then, on April 2, 1966, they had me.

It also happened to be the same day of the funeral for my father's mother, Rosella Romanowski, who lost her life to breast cancer at the age of fifty-six. Talk about an emotional day. Dad spent the morning at his mother's funeral in Glouster, Ohio, then flew home in time to rush Mom to Manchester Hospital, since by then the family had moved to Vernon, Connecticut.

When I finally popped out, kicking and screaming like the linebacker I became, I was the largest of the five children that my parents eventually would have, the last one being my little sister, Tricia. At my first official weigh in, I tipped the scales at eight pounds two ounces. Mom wanted to name me William, and Dad wanted to name me Thomas, so they compromised—William Thomas Romanowski.

They brought me home to a small chocolate-brown, split-level house right across the street from Skinner Road Elemen-

R
O
M
O

tary School. Our address was 18 Leona Drive, as it was for the rest of my childhood. In 1962, they'd moved to Vernon, a nice town fifteen miles northeast of Hartford, ten miles west of the University of Connecticut, and halfway between Boston and New York. There were hilly fields and white birches and plenty of farm land, with the Hockanum River running through town, where we used to catch turtles and toads. Nobody locked their doors, nobody locked their cars. It was near United Technologies Corporation in Hartford, where Dad landed an engineering job. He designed fuel cells and even would attend most of the space shuttle launches. Smart man, Dad; a great man.

While Dad worked, Mom cooked and cleaned and played happy homemaker. Every meal was homemade, whatever we wanted. Pancakes, spaghetti, steak—we ate like kings. Though we were middle-class, we ate like we were rich. By that I mean that our furniture and furnishings, our cars and our possessions, were really ordinary. But my parents always made eating the best food the most important family time of the day. Mom and Dad insisted that nothing ever come from the can, nothing ever be frozen. I became conscious of what I put into my body. Everything was home-grown in our backyard, lettuce, green beans, peppers, cucumbers, and rhubarb galore. When I look back on it now, I can't believe what my mom did for all of us. She was a slave to her children, yet never begrudged it. Mom's single-minded devotion to excellence was an ideal role model for me.

The greatest gift Mom and Dad ever gave us was being there. Unlike so many parents today, they were always there: think Norman Rockwell. We had a blue Ford station wagon and an old green Dodge. We picked blackberries that Mom baked into her pies. For vacations, the seven of us took ten hour drives to visit family in Ohio or short trips to Vermont for skiing outings. Great times, those trips.

But mostly we were a full house. At the time Mom and Dad bought our house, it had only three bedrooms. But over the years, they added on bedrooms for each child, until eventually, there were six. Wasn't easy, though. Dad would get home from work and do all the exterior foundation work, the sheet rock work, the electrical work . . . every night up until midnight just to save us some money.

A unique touch was the wood stove in the middle of the living room. Neighbors used to congregate there all the time, especially in December 1973, when Connecticut's most famous ice storm slammed into the state. A half-inch-thick coat of ice covered everything, damaging trees and homes, shutting down roads. For almost two weeks, approximately 650,000 houses in Connecticut were without power. It seemed like all the neighbors who didn't have heat came to our house, where they were always welcome. Our wood stove became priceless. It practically heated a neighborhood.

When the weather thawed, it allowed us to do what made us happiest. After school or on weekends, we would get on our bikes and ride to the other side of Vernon, or Manchester, or to South Windsor, or Ellington. My friends and I would be gone all day, riding for miles at a time when nobody ever worried about children being taken. When we weren't riding bikes, we were playing something else. Sports always matched the season. Football in the fall, basketball in the winter, baseball in the spring.

Baseball was something I got from my dad. We both played catcher, only I don't think I played it as well as him. I could never match up with the old man. Back in his day, Dad had a choice to play baseball for the Zanesville Indians, one of the Cleveland Indians minor league teams, or accept a scholarship to Case Western Reserve from the Chicago Cubs, who wanted him to play for one of their minor league teams. Dad took the

R
O
M
O

Cubs up on their offer, only he flunked Case Western's entrance exam. He was so ashamed that he quit baseball altogether and got a job as an engineer, doing surveying work, much of it in coal mines.

Dad helped me with basketball, too, but in a different way. For my ninth birthday, he dragged an old light post home from a nearby garbage dump. What was great about the post was that the top of it curved, providing some needed space between the hoop and the pole. On my friends' baskets, the pole was directly beneath it, and we'd run into it. But not on mine.

Dad also installed a floodlight that illuminated the whole court and a spotlight that shined directly on the hoop. From daylight to sunset I would stand in my driveway for hours, first pretending I was John Havlicek, then Larry Bird, always shooting hoops. Always dreaming.

Football was something I wasn't allowed to play until I was ten. I guess my parents were afraid I would get hurt. But I remember them taking me to my brothers' Pop Warner football games (Mike is ten years older than me, Joe seven), then their high school games. Watching Mike play guard on offense and end on defense, and Joe play offensive and defensive tackle mesmerized me. Going to their games was a big deal to me. It made me want to play football. Everybody called each of my brothers a "Romo." Eventually, the legacy would extend to me, little Bill. To be a "Romo" was, as you'd expect, the biggest compliment little brother could ask for.

When I got to play football for the Shamrocks, coaches put me at running back and free safety. Even then, what jumped out was my innate ability to know where the ball was going. I was always around it and always making tackles. I wasn't a hitter so much as I was a tackler. But what I liked was that I was doing what my brothers were, and I was good at it.

Not that they were overly impressed. They considered me

more of a crybaby than anything else. Whenever they would walk by me, they would smack me on the head. Or stick dirty socks in my mouth. Or pull dirty underwear over my head. And I would always go running to Mommy. Honestly, they didn't think I was all that tough, and through all of this I guess they were trying to toughen me up. After all, when I was nine, I threw a pitch near the head of a player who then flung his bat at me and connected. I needed fifteen stitches in the side of my head. As a kid, I never fought back.

I wasn't interested in my family's macho activities either. On the days my father and brothers would go hunting deer, rabbits, and pheasants, I didn't bother going with them. I wanted to stay home to ride my bike or play basketball. When my brothers would skin muskrat in our basement or hang deer in our garage, I preferred to play Scrabble with my friends. This is part of the reason why to this day, in what would probably surprise people who have followed my career, my sister Suzie calls me "the biggest softie I've met in my whole life." Me.

She knows how much I loved animals. Why would I want to kill them when I wanted to take care of them? Our dog Copper, an Irish setter, followed me everywhere and slept in my room every night. We wouldn't go anywhere without each other. When I was eight, Copper struggled with some kind of hip injury and started having accidents in the house. That wasn't like her.

Mom and I took her to the hospital and when we left her there, I was crying. She told me that maybe Copper would be all right. The next day, when she told me Copper wouldn't be, I cried even more. How does an eight-year-old boy learn how to deal with that? Normally, your mom or dad would talk you through it, but that wasn't how we did it in my family. My parents came from the generation when people didn't always talk about their feelings, their dreams, their hopes and goals. I don't

ROMO

fault them for that. I just realized I had to turn inside and work on my feelings by myself. And when I didn't know how to deal with something, I soon let it go unresolved in favor of what was next. I would pursue another area of interest even more.

To this day, my mom and dad try to figure out their issues on their own. They don't ask, "Well, how do you feel?" That didn't happen in my house, and I crave it now. That's why it's so important for me to understand what I'm feeling at a given moment, so I can relate better and communicate better with the people around me. Football never helped me in that area. In football, it's all about the next game, the next workout, the next practice, trying to be good enough. There's rarely time to take the next breath. There's rarely time to realize, "This is hard, this is tough." There aren't a lot of people sympathizing, saying, "Man, you really worked hard, and I'm sorry you didn't make that play." There's no sympathy in football. While I was becoming the toughest, most disciplined athlete, I was inadvertently lowering my level of consciousness.

As a little boy I wasn't thinking about any of this, of course. I was too caught up in losing Copper. My older brother Mike helped with the kindest gesture—he gave me his dog Charlie, a half Irish setter, half black Labrador. Until the time I left for college, Charlie became my best companion. Like Copper, he slept in my room, too.

He could not have liked the hours I kept, though. In high school, I would be up at four-thirty in the morning to do the best non-football job I ever had—milking cows. Six days a week during the summer and on Sundays during the school year, I would drive twenty-five minutes to Luginbuhl Farms and watch the sun rise with the cows. Then an electric fence would push the cows from their holding pen through two retractable gates into a parlor the size of a three-car garage. Once they got inside, it was milk time. We would spray them down, clean them off, grab their teats, attach the automatic milkers, and milk them. When they were done, we'd take off the milkers, clean off their teats, and out they would go. We would milk 250 cows a day and make what I would call something better than milk money—thirteen dollars a morning, twenty-six dollars a day. And each day I would bring home a gallon of milk to drink over breakfast.

The cow I most remember was Number 48, whom I loved like Copper and Charlie. Each morning when I arrived, she would wake up, walk right up to me, and start rubbing her head into my chest. I would pet her and milk her and send her on the way until we met again the next day. If nothing else, when I was feeling low, I will always have fond memories of cow Number 48.

Another job I liked was bussing tables for a caterer on weekends. I got to eat watermelon and honeydew and big ripe strawberries that you couldn't find anywhere else in the winter. Otherwise, though, working was pretty unbearable. For two straight summers starting when I was fourteen, I worked in a tobacco field in Ellington, Connecticut, picking leaves, sweating like crazy, listening to the bosses screaming, "Go faster, work harder." Not much fun. Nor was my next summer job at a construction yard, where it seemed like there were snakes or hornets' nests under each piece of plywood I picked up. I didn't like my job stocking toy shelves at the local Caldor, a major chain retail store back east. There was also a part of me that was starting to understand something about jobs and how important they were—and how I wanted something different, something more out of my life. Maybe I just wanted a way out of Vernon. I felt blessed being raised there, but I just felt like I had a calling, that there was something bigger and better waiting for me. That voice in my head was saying, *You can be more. Go be more.*

For the last football game of my freshman season at

ROMO

Rockville High School, they allowed me to practice with the varsity. At the time, I was still the scrawny kid whose body was better suited to basketball. As I looked out at the varsity players, all I could think was, "These guys are huge!" It was a little different from the junior varsity team I was on. I was scared to death of getting pummeled by them.

Back then, not much scared me. I had a real wild side and I'd try anything. I would drive my rusty pickup truck along Abbott Road with ten kids hanging out of it. I would skip school if I felt like it. There were daredevil day school ski trips to Vermont, where I would go nuts on the slopes. Over time, though, I started thinking about what I was doing and I realized, *This isn't for me.* But drinking, for a brief period, was.

On weekends, my high school buddies—John Steed and Glen Schmelter—and I would drink some beers. During halftime, the big question wasn't "What's the score?" but "Who's going to the keg party after the game?" Invariably, almost all of us did. We went to the parties and we drank, but for as long as I can remember, I always had this little voice cautioning me. *Is this going to get you where you want to go?* it would ask. Usually, the answer was no; stop whatever you are doing, now. So starting my sophomore year of high school, I stopped.

My few drinking experiences tell you how different I was back then, before Herschel and others spoke to me. In between my freshman and sophomore years, when I joined a health club and started lifting weights three days a week, I quit lifting, because I hated how sore it made me. At first, I actually thought I didn't need to lift to succeed in football. There was enough evidence to support it. During spring drills for football between my freshman and sophomore years, I remember running around on defense with a blocking dummy and just knocking the crap out of people. Coaches looked at me like, "Not bad."

It was the same thing in the summer, when we reported to

what we called "Hell Week," one week of two-a-day practices to get ready for the season. The same traits that were obvious for the Shamrocks were obvious now. I could read plays, find the football, and get to the runner—enough so to win a starting job on varsity. That was a big deal as a sophomore, and it meant a lot to me. It also made an impression on others, especially my high school coach, Tom Dunn.

"You know, Romo, you've got something special," Coach Dunn told me. "You've got a gift." He took it upon himself to develop it. He goaded me into the weight room, if you could call it that, located in our gym, where we had an old multistation Nautilus machine. It was a big deal to bench the stack, but during sophomore and junior football seasons, I couldn't even come close to doing it. Still, I spent my summers in there, going into the weight room after morning milk sessions with the cows. Coach Dunn would be waiting for me, and I'd have cow manure all over my shoes; I reeked. In hot summer air that could make you puke, we would spend two hours lifting weights, pumping up, getting stronger for the upcoming football season.

Now I didn't have just an article inspiring me. I had a real person, Coach Dunn. Until he came along, I didn't have anyone else mentoring me in football, telling me that I had a special gift. I've always believed that Coach Dunn directly, and Herschel Walker indirectly, were pivotal in helping me achieve my dreams.

By the time I returned for my senior season, after all that summer training, I was lifting more than I ever had. I'd put the pin on the bottom of the Nautilus machine, the maximum weight—I'd love to know what it was, but there were no numbers to tell me how much—and I'd rack the stack. That was a nice accomplishment, but there was more to do. Back near the end of my junior year, a few months earlier, after hearing

R
O
M
O

smaller colleges expressing some concern to him, Coach Dunn gave me a pep talk about lifting my grades.

"Romo, I'm a little worried that your grades aren't good enough to get into a major college program," he told me shortly before finals. Up until then, I had done pretty well, but I never put much effort into it. I maintained a C average, but Coach Dunn gave me a wake-up call: "If you don't pull your grades up, the chances of your getting a scholarship are not very good."

That's all I needed to hear. A scholarship was the reason for all this and to not get one . . . well, that was unacceptable. From that point on, my focus was not only on working out and doing great in sports, it was doing well in school. There were plenty of mental push-ups, sit-ups, and sprints to go along with the physical ones. The grades in my senior year speak for themselves: Modern algebra II-96. College chemistry-92. College English-83. Mechanics II-91.

Just about straight A's.

My grades on the football field were even higher. After playing outside linebacker my sophomore year and middle linebacker my last two years, Coach Dunn also used me at fullback, tight end, offensive tackle, and punter. "During his senior year, we had to bring four different jerseys with us so we'd be prepared for all of Billy's possible position changes," Coach Dunn said to my hometown newspaper. "If we ever decide to retire all his numbers, we won't have enough uniforms left."

One thing I realized in high school was that, somehow, I could absorb an enormous amount of pain. I would get neck stingers on a regular basis, but I never wanted to come out of the game, and I never did. Even when I had a real bad stomach virus, this nasty flu, I wouldn't come out. I just hoped I could make it through the game without going in my pants. So what I did was, I padded my butt with towels, just in case I did go, and never missed a play. All along, I had this fear that if I didn't play in that game, or any game, it would affect my chances of getting a scholarship. To this day, Coach Dunn still makes fun of me with those towels. But that game set the tone for the rest of my career. I never missed a game in high school, and I don't remember missing many tackles. Colleges noticed.

Near the end of my junior year, but especially at the start of my senior year in the summer of 1983, letters rolled in from schools across the country. The three schools I decided to visit were Boston College, Notre Dame, and Miami. Mom and Dad drove me up to Boston College for my first visit, the first weekend of September 1983. BC was playing Morgan State and I don't remember the game so much as the performance that the school's band put on. It was incredible. As a guy who liked to play the guitar, a habit I picked up in high school, I loved watching this band. My overall impression was very positive. The year before, BC had lost to Bo Jackson and Auburn in the Tangerine Bowl, and quarterback Doug Flutie was headed into his junior season. It seemed to me like the program was on the rise.

My visit to Notre Dame was not scheduled until after the season. That trip was a bit more adventurous. I never knew that there are different time zones. How was some high school kid from Vernon, who had never been on an airplane, supposed to know that there is a central time and a mountain time and a pacific time? After I landed in Chicago, I spent so much time hanging around and admiring O'Hare, I missed my connecting flight. Couldn't believe it. I called Notre Dame and said, "This is Bill Romanowski and I don't know what to do." They fixed it, not surprisingly. Notre Dame could do anything.

As soon as I got there, they showed me a film, *Wake Up the Echoes*, a fifty-three-minute movie about the magic of Notre Dame football with spotlights on the Fighting Irish's legendary coaches Knute Rockne, Frank Leahy, and Ara Parseghian. Then

R O M O

they gave me a Notre Dame jersey with a list of everyone who had worn the number at the school. They walked me into their state-of-the-art weight room and all I could think was, *Unbelievable*. I had never seen anything like it.

On Super Bowl Sunday, head coach Gerry Faust invited me to his house for a party to watch the Raiders beat the Redskins 38–9 in Super Bowl XVIII. When I walked into his house, I was amazed by the television: I'd never seen such a big one. Everything was so nice and new, so unlike the town in which I grew up. I remember calling my parents from South Bend with a message that terrified them.

"I'm coming to Notre Dame," I told them.

"Come home and let's talk about this," they told me.

They convinced me to be more open-minded and to take my last trip to Miami, which I wanted to do anyway. I grew up a huge Miami Dolphins fan, with a Bob Griese poster in my room, and, of course, I'd never been to Florida. So the next week, I flew down there, this time not having to worry about any time zone stuff.

At Miami, there was no *Wake Up the Echoes* film. We were just lucky to wake up. There were no strippers or hookers, like there seem to be on some college recruiting visits these days. But players were out all night, smoking pot, partying. The recruiting host the school assigned to me took me to this bar right off campus where players drank free. Guys were doing shots as if it were another drill for them to go through. I drank one melon ball before I snuck out, found a payphone, and called a friend. One of America's top party schools, where alcohol apparently was a part of each football scholarship, wasn't for me. "I'm really turned off by this school," I told my buddy. "I need a place where I can focus on my classes and play ball."

After I returned I talked with my parents, Coach Dunn,

everyone I trusted. When it came to my final decision, I remember saying to myself, *If I get hurt and can't play football anymore, where would I be happiest? Notre Dame, out in the middle of nowhere? Miami, where every night is like New Year's Eve? Or Boston College, a small Jesuit school six miles outside of Boston and a two-hour drive from home?*

On Tuesday, February 7, on the night our high school basketball team was playing the Windsor Locks Raiders, I made my decision about where I was going to accept the scholarship I had envisioned.

The next day, two articles appeared in the local newspaper, the *Journal Inquirer*. Neither was as in-depth as the Walker article, and only one carried any significance.

The larger story was headlined, "Romanowski's foul shooting lifts Rockville." The article reported how I had hit both ends of a one-on-one with :05 seconds left to give our school a 45–44 victory. There was also a sidebar:

ROMANOWSKI SAYS HE'LL ATTEND BC

VERNON—He'll try to make it in Massachusetts.

Rockville High linebacker Bill Romanowski, one of the top high school linebackers in New England, has announced that he'll be attending Boston College in the fall.

The 6-foot-3, 230-pound senior had narrowed down his choices to Boston College, Notre Dame and the University of Miami before deciding to stay in New England.

"He's excited about it," Rockville Coach Tom Dunn said. "He had many opportunities, but he decided to stay close to home. He likes the New England area."

Romanowski played offensive tackle, end, fullback

and linebacker in his three-year career at Rockville High. He was recruited as a linebacker, however, by Boston College.

"They consider him their top linebacking recruit," Dunn said. "They had four or five players on their list, but Romanowski was their No. 1 choice.

"I think Boston College is getting one of the best players in New England, if not in the entire East. I think he'll do very well."

Upon accepting my scholarship to Boston College, there was a sense of accomplishment. The idea of it brought me to tears. I had set my mind to something, and here was proof that I could attain it. I set a goal, I had a dream, and after four years of work, that dream was coming true. Now it was time for big-time college football.

That just reinforced how powerful goal-setting was. And now it was time to set higher goals with loftier dreams. I was beginning to like this thing called success, becoming more attached to the idea that if I applied myself, my determination could carry the day.

As I packed my bags and said my good-byes to my family and friends in Vernon, there was no way I could realize that the larger the dream, the more obsessed I would become.

2 BOSTON COLLEGE: A MAN ON A MISSION

For some people, college is about drinking, pulling pranks, partying, dating, having fun. Not for me, though. I treated school like a job. There was work to do, and any fun was the reward for any success achieved through all the hard work.

The setting was just right for it. Boston College is a beautiful 116-acre campus spread across Chestnut Hill, adjacent to Boston, where a gothic architectural style mixes with newer buildings. It is a Jesuit school, home to more than 100 Jesuit priests, religious referees who became ideal support for an 18-year-old who had already set in motion his own spartan regime for self-control.

While my friends were out until four or five in the morning, my self-imposed curfews would be designed to ensure eight hours of sleep, minimum. While my buddies were chugging beers in Boston, I was guzzling more milk in my dorm room. If they lacked intensity in practice, I made up for it. I treated every practice the same—like Armageddon.

I knew I was different from the rest of my freshman class

when we reported to Chestnut Hill in August 1984, five days before the rest of the team. My new teammates were talking about how happy they were to be at Boston College or how they were happy to redshirt. I began to feel disconnected from them because they seemed too ready to settle. And I was like, *I belong here. I'm not over my head.* I just had to prove it to everyone else.

During my first college practice, my very first Oklahoma drill—where you take on an offensive lineman and a running back—I lowered my head, took on sophomore guard Steve Trapilo, and plowed into running back Ken Bell. My first college tackle. I thought, *that'll show them I belong.* Coach Jack Bicknell noticed me right away. But not exactly the way I wanted. "Get your head up, Romo!" he screamed. "You're going to break your neck!"

With every drill, every lap, every sprint, I had to be first. At every practice, I ran and threw around my body as if redshirting were the last thing I'd want to do. And still, it wasn't enough. The week before our September 1 opener against Western Carolina, our team gathered at Alumni Stadium for its usual mock game, when coaches stick all the players who won't travel or play in yellow jerseys on one side, and all the players who will travel and play in maroon Boston College jerseys on the other. They ordered me to the far sideline—into a yellow jersey.

Imagine the utter humiliation I felt. The pain shot straight into my core. There I was with all the freshmen, all of them joking around, having fun. I was so embarrassed, so crushed, I started to cry. I was so hurt that I wasn't on the other sideline, with the starters, wearing a red jersey. The coaches were telling me right then, "This kid might help us one day, but not this year." And I couldn't handle the rejection.

I had to walk away so that nobody would see me crying.

What flashed through my mind was, *Is this what caring about something too much gets you? Embarrassment and pain?* As I stared across the field at the starters, across the fifty yards that may as well have been fifty miles, I told myself: *I don't know how long it's going to take—maybe a week, maybe a month, maybe six months—but however long it takes, I'm going to be over there. I will be there.*

From that moment on, all hell broke loose in practice. I was relentless, blowing up anybody in my way. The offense was like, *What's wrong with this guy?* What was wrong was that I was in a yellow jersey, which is good if you're racing in the Tour de France, but not if you're competing for a job on the Boston College football team. After making play after play, assistant coach Frank DeFelice began to see my determination and the error of the coaching staff's decision. "You're one mean mother, aren't you?" I remember Coach DeFelice telling me. "You're going to be a hell of a player." His words brought me back to Coach Dunn's. Here was a coach who believed in me, and man, I thrived on that. He would get me so fired up, guiding me, believing in me, helping me. He donated his time to me, and he did it because he loved the game as much as I did. Coach DeFelice gave me conviction. He pushed me, and in turn I pushed myself harder.

In the week leading up to our September 1 opening game against Western Carolina, I managed to change the coaching staff's mind so much, they inserted me on the kickoff coverage team. Another goal achieved. Now I had something else to prove—I deserved to stay on the traveling team.

Now let me say this: When I reported to Boston College, coaches clocked my 40-yard dash time at 4.87 seconds. But when I stormed down the field on the opening kick against Western Carolina and looked out of the corner of my eye to see if anybody was keeping up with me, there was nobody in my peripheral vision. I'm telling you, there was nobody within 10 yards of me. On pure desire and focus, I had to be running the 40 in 4.3 seconds.

I was so out of control, I ran right past the guy I was supposed to hit. The only thing I hit was the ground, a real wicked face plant. When I returned to the sideline, Coach Bicknell was waiting for me again. "Romo, I have *never* seen anybody run down on one kickoff so fast in all my life," he said. "Just hit the guy with the damn ball!"

Anything to impress the coaches, I would do. On the night of October 7, when I was at the Roberts Center to watch game film of Temple, Coach Bicknell called me over again. I was worried because the only times he'd talked to me was when I was in trouble. "Romo, we need you to move to fullback," Coach said.

Fullback? I was stunned. I had played fullback at Rockville in short-yardage situations, when we needed a big block for small distances. But I didn't want to play fullback. Unfortunately, our regular fullback, Jim Browne, had been suspended. Coach Bicknell thought I was big enough and tough enough to handle the position. "Well," I told him, "if you need me there I'll do it." Anything to help the team win. Anything at all.

Fortunately, my career at fullback did not last very long. Two of our starting linebackers, Andy Hemmer and Ted Gaffney, got hurt, creating a need at my favorite position. Hemmer got hurt in the first quarter against Penn State on the first Saturday in November. As soon as he did, coaches yelled for me to get in the game. At first, I was like, *Me?* I knew I was going to play, but against Penn State? Penn State is the school you always hear about growing up, especially back east. It is "Linebacker U," and it has spit out linebackers like Jack Ham, John Ebersole, Matt Millen, and Shane Conlan. And here I was, a linebacker, getting my first extensive playing time against them.

I had a little motivation when I ran on to that field. Penn State didn't recruit me. I was going to show them they'd made a mistake. I was going to show them that when they were mining the country for linebackers, they forgot somebody they shouldn't have. Right away, I got a sack. Then some tackles, thirteen in all. Coach Bicknell remarked, "He's got that knack of rolling his hips and just sticking you. Other guys hit you. Romo just smacks you." Unfortunately, Penn State smacked us around, 37–30. Still, I knew my reckless performance meant I was going to have to be fitted with a full-time maroon jersey. Sooner rather than later.

"You could tell from the first that he had ability," my linebacker coach Red Kelin told the local press. "He has the three most important physical requisites: the ability to run, size, and he's a good athlete. But more important he has the intangibles. Football is fun to him. He likes contact. The game is all-important to Bill. He bleeds inside if things don't go right."

After speaking with the press, Coach Kelin had his own message for me. On the Saturday morning before our game against Army, he knocked on my hotel room door at the hotel we stayed at in Newton, Massachusetts. "Romo," he said, "you're going to be starting today."

I was overcome with emotions. I shut the door behind him and tears just filled my eyes. I couldn't stop crying. Everything I set my mind to was coming true. Each one—receiving a scholarship, getting into a game, winning a starting job—was like a little gift from God. I'd set a goal, achieve it, and then think about what would be next. It became an obsession. Nothing—and I mean, nothing—was going to stop me. There wasn't a party that was going to keep me from being the best I could be. There wasn't a class that was going to interfere. Not even a girlfriend. I was obsessed, even down to the details of my uniform. I insisted that everything fit just right. My shoes had to be clean,

R O M O

my gloves had to fit perfectly, my pads had to be the same way. Our equipment man must have hated my compulsiveness, even though he helped me whenever he could.

What also helped me my freshman year was that BC had a bunch of guys who were making something out of themselves. Quarterback Doug Flutie, fullback Steve Strachan, tight end Scott Gieselman, nose guard Mike Ruth, linebacker Ted Gaffney, split end Gerard Phelan. I looked at the players who garnered respect, and number one, they were great people. Number two, they were not big partiers. They busted their ass in school, just like they did on the field. I watched my teammates who combined would play more than one hundred NFL seasons, learned from them, and tried to do more than just replicate them.

My free time was spent in the weight room. After practice, while other players left, I went right back to the bench presses or leg squats or bicep curls. It got to the point where our trainers couldn't get rid of me. Our head trainer, Randall Shrout, would tell me, "Time to go home, Romo." Our assistant trainer and strength coach, Wes Emmert, would be begging for a reprieve, too. "Please, Romo, enough already," they'd say.

"You've got to be kidding me!" I would tell them. "Here's somebody that wants to spend an extra two hours after practice in the weight room, after everybody has gone, and you're not going to stick around? That's bull."

Once I tasted some success, it drove me even more. There were sixteen tackles in my first start against Army on November 10, a game we won 45–31. An interception during a 24–16 victory over Syracuse. Another interception the next week against Miami. But more than any other, the one play I most remember from my freshman year is one of the top three most famous plays in college football history.

It came in the first game I ever played on national television the day after Thanksgiving of my freshman year. Both offenses were unstoppable that day. Miami's quarterback, Bernie Kosar, threw for 447 yards and two touchdowns while running back Melvin Bratton ran for 134 yards and four touchdowns, including a 1-yard touchdown run with :28 seconds left that gave Miami a 45–41 lead.

After the touchdown run, I walked to the sideline, upset that our defense had allowed an apparent game-winning touchdown. I sat down and lowered my head over the shame and humiliation I felt. Something stirred inside me though, so right before the last play of the game, I figured: *You know what? I think I'll get up. That's the least I could do.* I stood up on our sideline and watched our quarterback Doug Flutie drop back and run around and heave a football about as far as he could throw it, from our 37-yard line, about 65 yards into the Orange Bowl air, down into the arms of our wide receiver, Gerard Phelan. We had a 48-yard touchdown and a 47–45 victory.

All I could think as I went running on the field, waving my helmet, was, *Holy moly! Holy moly!* The game cemented the Heisman Trophy for Doug and caused a celebration in our locker room the likes of which I had never before seen. For an hour, guys were dousing each other with Gatorade and water. Nobody could believe we had pulled it out. The game sealed a bid to the Cotton Bowl in Dallas, which was perfect for me since by that time both my older brothers, Mike and Joe, lived in Dallas. My whole family arranged to travel to the game, as did most of Boston. It turned out to be the biggest airlift out of Boston since World War II. That was the great thing about college football. It brought our campus, and more important, my family, together. It almost got to be like I was turning into the big brother. I could provide something for my family that was meaningful to them.

When we got down there, Coach Bicknell told our team we

R
O
M
O

deserved the invitation, this was our reward, we were going to practice hard in Dallas and we were going to party hard. Guys were all for it. They were going out all night, throwing up during practice the next day, taking in the full college experience. Our fans and players actually drank the hotel dry. I never heard of something like that before, but it happened. By the end of the week, you couldn't even get a shot of cough syrup there.

Me, I stuck to myself that whole week. No drinking, no clubbing, not much socializing. Nothing was going to interfere with my preparations for the game. When I would go to bed at 8 P.M. each night, I would visualize playing a great game and winning the Cotton Bowl's Defensive MVP. I played that game so many times in my head, and I made so many big plays, that when the game actually kicked off, I knew what was going to happen before it actually did.

On the game's first series, I deflected Houston quarterback Andre Ware's pass. Then I nailed one of their running backs for a 3-yard loss. I finished our 45–28 victory with eleven solo tackles, thirteen overall, and, just like I pictured, the Cotton Bowl Defensive MVP. After the game, Boston College's receivers coach and recruiting coordinator Barry Gallup pulled me aside for an important lesson. "Here you are, Romo, you've had all this success," Gallup told me. "The best recommendation I could give to you is this: Be humble. Be humble with the press and be humble with your teammates. You'll be liked that much more if you are."

It was something I tried to do. After all, I prayed regularly and I believed that God had a hand in the amazing year I'd been having. I used to slip away regularly to the chapel on the main part of our campus. From then until the time I graduated, the visits were as regular as those to the weight room. None of my friends ever knew I went, but after class, four times a week, I would walk in to my private sanctuary, sit down, and pray for five minutes. I could see a pact developing between me and God. He gave me talent, and I gave back every drop of myself. Prayer helped me realign myself internally, helped me focus on my spiritual mission to give back my best. I'm not overly religious, never have been. Going to Catechism, Communion, and confession never felt good to me. But prayer to me is important. Prayer to me is hoping that life gives you more of what you're focusing on, or investing in.

Invariably, my prayers at Boston College were almost always the same: "Dear Lord, help keep me safe. Help me be the best I can be. And help me realize where I want to go." Straight to the National Football League.

Think about how many people go through college and don't know what they want, even after they finish it. Too many. My case was just the opposite. From the time I got to school, football filled my mind. But in life, as I've learned, when something becomes so important as to become an obsession, everything else fades into the background.

At Boston College, I shortchanged my classroom education, and I regret it. Division I football placed tremendous demands upon all student athletes. Aside from the obvious time-management challenges, we were forced to deal with the excessive pressure of performing in front of 40,000 to 70,000 uncompromising fans where all of our successes and failures were exposed without any emotional protection. I learned to use pressure to my advantage. I seemed comfortable with the responsibility of doing my best. But the energy I poured into football left me lacking it for my studies. It was hard to focus on school when I was training until seven every night.

I would come home physically spent, emotionally depleted, and then on Saturday, game day, I was wounded. I just didn't

R
O
M
O

have enough left for school. At some schools that devalue education, you always could drop two or three of your classes and keep your minimum workload to stay eligible. At Boston College, if you got one class down, they were watching you; two, probation; three, you were out. You never had that luxury of lightening up on your course load. Nor did I want it. I knew school was important, but it always came second to football. It was evident in the way I approached classes.

During an accounting class my sophomore year, when I was totally lost yet again and looked over at my neighbor and asked, "Do you know what this professor is talking about?" she did. She always did. That was one of the things I grew to like best about Tiffany Burris.

She was an accounting major who steered me through that class and through all the other tough ones, and there were plenty in the business school of management. On a deeper level, she really helped get me through college.

Eventually, when I needed to talk to somebody about something, I went to Tiffany before I went to anybody else. She heard about my family, my life, my passion, my drive, my problems in the classroom, my successes on the football field. She understood me in ways others did not.

Not that it was hard to understand me. Every waking moment, everything I did revolved around making it to the NFL. Not a single day passed without me thinking about it, and it showed in my lifestyle. By now you should know that if my teammates would head out for pizza and beer, I'd have pizza and milk. When they headed out to parties after games, I stayed behind to take care of my body and dream about the NFL.

For the rare party I did go to, there was this little voice in the back of my head saying, *Is this going to keep you from making it to the NFL?* And a lot of times, the answer was, *Yes. Yes it will,* so

I'd slip out. When my friends used their meal plan at the dorm dining room for cheeseburgers and French fries, I skipped that, too. Instead, I headed to the grocery store across campus, where I could use my meal plan money for the freshest fruit, the greenest vegetables, the healthiest items.

Sometimes I'd take out some of my teammates, guys like flanker Darren Flutie, running back Jimmy Bell, and quarterback Mike Power. "Dad," they would tease me, "where are you taking us?" I took them to buy pasta, granola, fruit. We'd come home and I'd cook up these high carbohydrate meals so we could all get bigger. For dessert, I would allow them to splurge. I would take out the Häagen-Dazs vanilla ice cream, mix it together with milk, bananas, and strawberries, and come up with the healthiest milkshakes.

Some of the guys came to rely on me, though I'm not sure if it was because of my nutritional guidance or my car. During our sophomore and junior years, I was the only one with wheels, a dreary dark brown 1977 Toyota Sport Coup with holes in the floorboard. We'd still all pile in—me, Mike Power, the Widell brothers that played offensive line—and I'd drive everybody to and from our summer bouncing jobs at Faneuil Hall. On the way back, after we had worked until three in the morning, I would insist that we drive to Boston's North End so I could wait for the boats and trucks to come in with the fresh produce.

While my teammates moaned that they were tired and wanted to go home, I spent thirty minutes sifting through the produce to find the best-looking watermelons and berries and heads of lettuce. The longer I looked, the louder their cries became. "Romo!" Mike would shout. "We want to go to bed!"

One thing about me, though. I always made sure I got my eight hours of sleep, every night. No matter what time we

R O M O

returned home, I insisted on giving my body the sleep it needed to perform at the optimum level the next day. It was too important not to.

Each day turned into another training session. When we went on our spring break to San Juan, Puerto Rico, during my senior year, other guys would be sitting around, lying in the sand, drinking piña coladas. Not me. I'd be running wind sprints in the surf, in three feet of water, like there was a game that week.

Back home at BC, my favorite running path was not exactly the most orthodox one. It was at St. John's Seminary, just outside our campus. There was this steep eighty-yard long hill, the perfect climb, with an eight-foot statue of Mary at the top. The grass there was perfectly manicured. It reminded me of the videos I had seen on television of the Chicago Bears running back Walter Payton, running hills. If it worked for him, I wondered, why couldn't it work for me? When I first found it, I showed it off to some of my teammates, like it was my newest and proudest possession. "Romo, you can't train there," Mike Power told me. "That's sacred ground."

"Oh yeah?" I said. Needless to say, we ran there. Ran hard and ran often, probably three times a week, ten to twelve sprints up the hill per visit. We wouldn't stop until we got to the top of the hill and touched the statue of Mary. Priests would be walking by us in elaborately draped robes, staring at these topless BC boys ripping up their lawn.

Different summers brought different methods of training. Before my junior year, I worked at a football camp outside of Boston, helping teach younger kids the game. What I didn't expect was that I'd be learning something, too.

Ron Burton, the Patriots' first-round draft pick in 1960, delivered a speech to the camp and it couldn't have impacted anybody more than it did me. He told us how we had to be willing to do the things that nobody else was. When other players were out partying, we should be sleeping. When other players were sleeping, we should be out training. He reminded me that it came back to hard work. Nobody, I decided, was going to out-work me.

That was tough to accomplish in the summertime, though, with my jobs. After each of my freshman and sophomore years, I drove a Coca-Cola truck from 7:00 A.M. to 5:00 P.M., then trained from 5:30 to 10:30. What Burton said lingered in my mind. After my junior year, I decided I would commit myself to training, and I was able to find a low-maintenance job as a bouncer twice a week in Boston. Mom, meanwhile, supplemented the family income with the homemade pies she was selling to the Valley Fish Market and Restaurant in Ellington, Connecticut.

I began working out extensively and taking karate classes. Kung Fu was something I had always wanted to do and never had the time for. It really helped with my flexibility, focus, quickness, and speed. It also had occurred to me that Herschel Walker had taken martial arts. Enough said. If there was something that could help me play better, I was going to do it. That became my mantra for success and, later, some of my struggles.

"There's a tendency when a guy gets that early success to think he's got it made, that they don't need to keep working," Coach Bicknell told some Boston reporters before my senior season. "But he's kept working at it. He stayed here all summer and prepared. It's a work ethic that comes from his family background. He works extremely hard."

It wasn't that I was trying to be a saint. On the rare occasion, I could let myself break from my spartan lifestyle. On the night of my twenty-first birthday—April 2, 1987—I went with my pals Darren Flutie, Mike Power, and Jim Bell to Boston. In my adult life, this was really the only time I completely let go. We

R
O
M
O

did shots of tequila, Wild Turkey, then more shots of tequila and Wild Turkey. Until I threw up everywhere.

Never before had I drunk so much that I didn't know where I was or what was going on. Now I had. It was a very scary feeling for me. About the only thing I can remember after getting sick, other than promising never to do that again, was putting my arms around Mike and having him help me to my room. "Please help me," I kept saying to Mike, hoping words would wipe away the drunken misery. "Help me, Michael. Help me." I remember being frightened even in my fogged stupor that I was throwing away my future. When I woke up the next day, I vowed I would never again allow myself to compromise my dreams.

Just like I pictured winning the Defensive MVP for the Cotton Bowl, I did the same for the Hall of Fame Bowl in Tampa, Florida, against Georgia my senior year. In my mind, I knew I was going to win the Defensive MVP. The only problem was, with one minute left in the game, we trailed and the ballots were cast. Voters did not wait until we had pulled out the victory in the closing seconds, 27–24. They already had given the award to one of Georgia's players, despite the 19 tackles I had that day to go along with the 123 I had that season.

But that was all right. My focus was on having the best senior season and positioning myself as best I could for the NFL. Slowly, recognition was starting to come my way. Before my senior season, *Athlon's Eastern Football* magazine led its Boston College preview with a write-up of me. "On the field," I was quoted as saying in the magazine, "I like to tear people's heads off." That was my attitude. In a game, I hated to see a back go down easy. I wanted to see him punished. The most fun in football is tackling someone. People were telling me they couldn't believe the difference in me on and off the field, like a Jekyll and Hyde. On the field, my best friend could be my worst enemy. Others outside the program started noticing it.

The *Boston Herald* featured me in its September 25 issue, under the headline, "BC's unknown hitter—'Romo' among the best."

Contentiousness comes naturally to William Thomas Romanowski, who is, after all, a linebacker.

"He's a good kid and an intelligent kid," Boston College football coach Jack Bicknell said. "But when he does interviews I cringe because he just says what's on his mind."

One day Romanowski tells a reporter, "Some guys use steroids. I don't"—thus implicating his teammates, who were understandably displeased. On this day, a reporter asks him why he doesn't wear his hair spiked or crew cut like linebacker/crazyman Brian Bosworth.

"Why should I look like an idiot?" Romanowski replies. "You don't have to promote an image off the field. You don't have to be a crazy nut. What counts is what you do on the field. You've just got to like to hit."

My comments weren't the type that other guys would make or like. And while I did have my close friends, clearly my lifestyle distanced me from other people. So I wasn't surprised when, during my senior year, our team didn't vote me captain. Instead, it selected tight end Peter Casparriello, nose guard Dave Nugent, and fullback Jim Turner. I would have plenty of college honors and national honors, but being captain at BC

ROMO

wasn't one. It bothered me more than I let on. As I look back on my development as a person and a football player, I can see that the former was getting the short end of my effort. I wanted to be appreciated, liked, even loved, but I didn't invest in what could make that happen. I was focused on a larger mission: to produce the best possible senior season and to leave a legacy at BC while making a mark with NFL scouts.

Our nationally televised game at USC, where Keith Jackson and Bob Griese called the action, had to help. USC had one of its most famous alums, O. J. Simpson, address the team before the game with a little pep talk. It had Rodney Peete at quarterback, and I was matched against Trojans guard Dave Cadigan, who went on to become a first-round draft choice with the New York Jets.

It was one of those games where I felt like I couldn't be blocked. The stat sheets credited me with a college-high twenty-six tackles. Later, I obsessively reviewed the videotape. It was twenty-seven, actually. I can see now how nothing was quite enough. After I corrected the number of tackles, I played back every play and beat myself up for not making even more. Still, ABC selected me as the player of the game, and Coach Bicknell made me feel even better. "He deserves everything he gets," he told the media. "This kid comes and works his butt off. He didn't go out and come back all bloated up like some players. He's the first one at practice and the last one to leave."

The whole season went the way the game at USC did: no captaincy but plenty of tackles. There was a school-record 156 for the season, breaking the mark I set my sophomore year with 150. All together, in my forty starts at Boston College, there were a school-record 488 tackles, not bad for a guy who didn't crack the defensive lineup until the seventh game of his freshman season.

The interesting thing was, after our senior season ended,

I started seeing guys working out harder than they ever had before. They wanted a tryout in the NFL or the Canadian Football League. I remember looking at these same guys that thought I was out of my head for treating football like a job and saying to myself: *Where were you four years ago, when I wasn't going to those parties and I wasn't getting drunk? Where was this drive then? Where was this focus then? Had you been working out like this all along, had you been treating your football career with the seriousness you have now, who knows where you would be going.*

Not long ago, I spoke with my former BC roommate, quarterback Mike Power. He told me that, over the years, he has had numerous conversations with some of our former teammates, each of whom expressed a similar sentiment: "We wish we had it all over again," my former teammates would tell Mike. "We wish we had done what Romo did. We wish we had listened to him when he told us to train harder. We were at school for a good time, and he was there with a mission."

I headed out to the all-star game for some of college football's top prospects, the East-West Shrine game in Palo Alto, California, on January 16, 1988. My coach for the game was Jack Bicknell, and what he saw at those practices didn't surprise him in the least. Me flying around. Me outworking everybody. Just before the game, Coach Bicknell called together our team to vote for a captain. To my surprise, they elected me. As we walked off the field, Coach put his arm around me and whispered: "Congratulations, Romo. The guys at BC didn't elect you captain, but the best players in the country did."

Validating any success I had was the invitation I received to the NFL's annual scouting combine. I studied for those tests harder than I did any in school. Of course, that came at a price, too. That final semester was a nightmare. With the East-West Shrine game in January, the combine in February, the draft in April, and traveling back and forth for mini-camps and the like

R
O
M
O

in May and June, I still had to finish up schoolwork and prepare for my finals.

When it was time to take my management and operations final, a class in which I had maintained a B-plus average, I knew I was not as prepared as I needed to be. I had gone to all the classes, not missed any, but my mind, my focus, all my thoughts were on the future, not school. To help salvage the situation, I wrote a letter of apology to the professor after taking the final exam.

> *Dear Professor,*
>
> *I think you can probably understand where my head has been the past month. I have spent four years focusing with the goal, the drive, the determination to make it to the NFL. And that dream is coming true. I'm truly sorry, but I was not able to prepare in any way for your final. Please take that into consideration when you give me my final grade . . .*

Thankfully, he did. In my management and operations class, I finished with a B-minus. Talk about your morality. Clearly, I was chipping away at my principles. It was another precursor to winning at all costs, where dishonesty was the price to pay. I'm not proud of that, not at all. It's embarrassing how I put football in front of everything else, especially my values.

When I arrived at the Scouting Combine in Indianapolis that February, there were a ton of good linebackers entering the draft. Chris Spielman and Eric Kumerow from Ohio State, Marcus Cotton from USC, Dante Jones from Oklahoma, and Ken Norton from UCLA, to name some. As we gathered for the start of our 40-yard dash, I looked up in the stands and felt nervousness creeping down my body. Sitting there were some of football's coaching legends: Dallas Cowboys coach Tom Landry, Miami Dolphins coach Don Shula, New York Giants coach Bill Parcells, Washington Redskins coach Joe Gibbs, San Francisco 49ers coach Bill Walsh. The same faces I had watched on television were now watching me.

They were there to see how fast we could run, how many times we could bench press 225 pounds, how high we could go on the vertical jump, how quick we were in the shuttle run. As I looked up at those coaches with tears welling, I remember saying to myself, "You can test somebody in the bench press, you can test somebody in the 40-yard dash, but there's one thing you don't have a test for." And I put my hand on my heart. Then I whispered to myself as much as to them, "I promise you. I will outwork, outperform, outshine, and outlast every one of these linebackers on this field today."

F rom my parents' house in Vernon on April 23, we watched the 1988 NFL draft. It was a big party, at least twenty people, my family and friends. We sat in front of the television, waiting, and waiting, watching linebackers go off the board. California's Ken Harvey to the Phoenix Cardinals with the twelfth overall selection. Ohio State's Eric Kumerow to the Miami Dolphins, my favorite team, with the sixteenth overall selection. Florida's Clifford Charlton to the Cleveland Browns with the twenty-first. USC's Marcus Cotton to the Atlanta Falcons with the twenty-eighth. Ohio State's Chris Spielman went to the Detroit Lions with the twenty-ninth. Our draft party began to die down. The same linebackers I worked out with in Indy, the same ones I vowed to outperform, were going before I did. My brother, Joe, was telling me not to worry. My dad was telling me

R
O
M
O

to relax, my time was going to come. Just then, the phone rang. The Dallas Cowboys. They had the forty-first overall pick.

"Bill, we wanted you to know we're making a decision between you and Ken Norton," one of the Cowboys' officials told me. When they did, Norton was their man. Then Mississippi Valley State's linebacker Vincent Brown went to the New England Patriots with the forty-third selection, which was fine with me. In general, New England had not had good luck with BC guys, and I was ready to get out of New England. I wanted a change. But where? Purdue's Fred Strickland went to the Los Angeles Rams with the forty-seventh overall selection. Oklahoma's Dante Jones went to the Chicago Bears with the fifty-first overall selection. Our phone rang again. The Indianapolis Colts. They had the seventy-sixth overall selection.

"Hang on, Bill," one of the Colts' officials told me. "We're going with either you or Washington quarterback Chris Chandler." When they made their decision, Chandler was their man. On the very next pick, Indiana linebacker Van Waiters went to the Browns with the seventy-seventh overall selection. By 7 P.M., midway through the third round, our party was basically over and so was ESPN's. Unlike these days, when every pick is televised, ESPN ended its draft coverage early. And then, just before pick number eighty, our phone rang again.

"Bill, John McVay, San Francisco 49ers general manager," he told me. "We've just selected you in the third round. Congratulations." When I hung up, I couldn't allow myself to enjoy the moment and say, "Wow, how incredible is this! I just got drafted by the San Francisco 49ers!" Everyone around me did, though. The party at my house picked up, right along with my anxiety. They were cheering, shouting, celebrating like it was New Year's Eve in April.

"You lucky sonofabitch," my best friend, John Steed, told me. He knew how the 49ers had established themselves as one of the NFL's glamour franchises, one of the top organizations in sports. Everyone did. San Francisco had won Super Bowls during the 1981 and 1984 seasons, had been to the playoffs in each of the past three seasons, and had established a standard of excellence.

"You're going to have a chance to win a Super Bowl," my agent Tom Condon, a former BC offensive linemen who played twelve years for the Kansas City Chiefs, told me when he called.

My friends and family were giving me more information about San Francisco than I knew. It was a lot to process. All I could think, with my first NFL minicamp scheduled for the following weekend, was, *I've got to make this team.* It was my next dream, though it felt even more like a dragon. It was more pressure than I ever had felt in my life. It wasn't about a scholarship anymore. It was about my livelihood.

The weird part was, I could have been picked by any team. But it was the 49ers, where the stakes and expectations were greater than anywhere else, except my own. To me, it represented another roadblock I had to get around, another obstacle to get me one step closer to where I wanted to go—to the big time.

When I signed my first contract with the 49ers I received a $125,000 signing bonus. I was so proud of it, I photocopied the check and mailed home copies to my mom and dad. I thought I was the richest man on the face of the earth. Obviously I had a lot to learn.

R
O
M
O

3 SAN FRANCISCO 49ERS: ONE GOAL AND ONE GOAL ONLY

A silver-haired man with steel-blue eyes, Coach Bill Walsh looked like he easily could have been a history professor at Boston College. I found out soon enough though that instead of teaching it, Coach was intent upon making history.

Before our first minicamp started, Coach Walsh walked into the meeting room inside our new training facility. By the time he reached the front of the room, silence ruled.

"Congratulations to everybody in this room and everybody on this team for being part of this," Coach Walsh told us. "Everybody here has earned the right to be a San Francisco 49er. Now we have one goal and one goal only. And that goal is to win a world championship. Anything less is unacceptable to this organization."

That was the first thing he said, the very first thing. Finally, a coach who affirmed my expectations. His message stood out not only for its content, but for its contrast to what other coaches emphasized. To be clear, every coach's pledge is to win.

But here was a man who essentially said that winning wasn't enough. Only a championship would do for him. I couldn't remember Coach Bicknell ever saying anything like that at Boston College, nor Coach Dunn ever saying anything like that at Rockville High School. They were great motivators, my former coaches. But I always felt like I craved success more than anybody else; not in San Francisco.

Coach Walsh spoke a different language—my kind of language. It was about being the best. Period. He told us about a standard that was held by all the champions who sat around me: Joe Montana, Jerry Rice, Ronnie Lott, Roger Craig—some of the greatest players of all time. Then Coach told us to look around the room, at the players sitting next to each of us.

"These men are not your competition for jobs," Coach said. "You're not competing with the guy next to you. You're competing with yourself. You need to do everything you can do to make this team. I don't want you to spend training camp worrying about what the guy next to you has done. If you do that, you'll put too much pressure on yourself and not perform to the best of your abilities. We want everyone here performing to the best of his abilities."

Taking charge, fostering friendships, working together—all of Coach Walsh's principles. With each one, it was reinforced to me that I had gained entry into NFL heaven. Life in San Francisco was not good, it was great. Rookie defensive tackle Pierce Holt and his wife Deana took me into their home, like I was a member of their family. Life was easy. I was living a dream, and anybody could hear it in my voice. When I called my friends back in Boston, they could hear an enthusiasm that exceeded what I had in college. Linebackers coach Bill McPherson even nicknamed me "Smiley" because nobody could wipe the smile off my face—even when we were going through two-a-day practices, even when they handed us a playbook thicker than

R
O
M
O

the Bible. I had so much excitement each and every day I showed up to work.

My feeling was and always has been, if you love what you do, then you don't have to work a day in your life. Now that I was in training camp with the two-time world champion 49ers, with an organization as successful as most of those on the Fortune 500 list, I wasn't working. I was playing.

Let me tell you how much I loved it. During minicamp, we would use our hotel room to change. Each night, we returned from practice and I would carefully place my gold and cardinal red 49ers helmet atop my dresser, well within view from my bed. The helmet, to me, was its own work of art. When I lay in bed at night, I would marvel at it, until I drifted off into another dreamland.

As I've already mentioned, surrounding me was an incredible collection of players. We're talking legends of the game. To be a rookie in May 1988 and be on the same field as Jerry Rice and Joe Montana and Ronnie Lott was better than being in the world's most prestigious private school. Each offered his own lessons.

Jerry Rice was smoother than any player I had ever seen. To see how fluid and graceful he was in his routes truly reminded me of watching a ballerina. Every one of his steps was beautiful. What really jumped out to me was that, whenever he caught a ball in practice, he ran with it to the end zone. Every time. Always maximum effort.

Then there was Joe Montana, whose presence constantly loomed over everybody. He had what I call "The It"—something so few athletes do. Broncos quarterback John Elway was the only other player I ever played with that had The It. But Joe combined The It with great coaching and a great team to take it to another level. Whenever he walked on to the field, his team believed they would win. Every time. He was Joe Cool, but he was also Joe Confidence.

Another thing about Joe: He really knew the value of keeping a team loose. At our training camp at Sierra College in Rocklin, California, players would scoot around campus on bicycles they had rented for the summer. We would ride them to practice during the day, to meetings at night. Well, one night when our defense walked out of meetings, every one of our bikes was gone. Not one of my defensive teammates had a bike left. We looked all around, but couldn't find anything.

Then somebody spotted the bikes—hanging in the top of huge maple trees, like they were Christmas ornaments. Thank you, Joe Montana.

Ronnie Lott, to me, personified toughness. His attitude, his style, his demeanor reminded me of the way I acted at Boston College, only at a much more sophisticated level. From the moment we reported to camp, Ronnie had a profound effect on who I am and the player I became. He trained me like an apprentice, never worrying about how much he might embarrass me. He didn't wait long to do it.

In our second preseason game against Oakland in the Los Angeles Coliseum in August, I wound up scrapping with Raiders' tight end Ethan Horton the whole game. At some point, Horton pushed me in the back without my realizing it. When our defense reviewed the game film the next day, Lott did—and he made sure everyone else did, too. Right in the middle of our game film review, Lott stood up, walked to the front of the room, flicked on the lights, and barked out a command to our defensive coordinator, George Seifert.

"Shut off the film," Lott ordered. Once it was off, Lott looked over at me with some of the intensity I learned from him.

"Romo," Lott shouted. "If I ever see anybody push you in the

R
O
M
O

back and you don't do something about it, I will personally kick your ass." A little rookie, I was too terrified to even answer him. Lott said what he had to, shut the lights, told Seifert to put the film back on, and went back to his seat. From that point on, I swore that nobody was going to hit me without getting hit back harder.

Every day I showed up to work and saw Ronnie, that was all I could think of, that verbal challenge. Every day. Here was one of the greatest players ever to play the game challenging my manhood and saying not only do you play that play, but there is a certain way to play the play. And for Ronnie, it all started and ended with respect.

Ronnie always taught the game of respect. Whenever he pulled together the team, whenever he called somebody out, he lectured them on how important it was in the game of football. It was important to be respected by your teammates and, of course, your opposition. When he verbally undressed me in front of our team, it represented the beginning of "Romo."

His stern message was one of those events that shape you, not necessarily as a man, but as a way of conducting yourself on the field. He watered the seeds of the player I was growing into. Essentially, Ronnie gave me permission to unleash myself, to be on the attack, to play football the way the most feared men in the game played it.

It was the piece of motivation I needed as a professional, trying to create a name and identity in a locker room full of Hall of Fame players. I wanted everybody's respect, and I wasn't going to just hit people to earn it. I was going to pummel them.

But a part of me also was torn because, at heart, I was the smiling nice guy who showed up as the happiest guy in the world. In the end, I had to give up some of my natural innocence. The same smiley guy realized he had to not just stand his ground, he had to take it.

Our defensive end, Charles Haley, should have realized this. But he was having too much fun tormenting rookies, like he did every summer. Each year Charles would pick out a different rookie to abuse. This year it was lucky me. I'd like to think there was something he saw in me, something he liked. Maybe he just wanted to see if I had what it took to play in the NFL. Or maybe it was his way to figure out if he could respect you. Charles was one of the best pass rushers to ever play in the NFL, and he knew how to raise rookies the tough way.

We'd be in the locker room and Charles would be trash-talking me the way he would an opponent. "Romo, you wimp," he'd say. "You can't play. You're trash." You name it, he'd say it. At first I listened to him without responding. I didn't know how to handle it. But he persisted until my response changed.

"Well, why don't we walk outside, Charles?" I finally told him one day. "We'll see real fast who's a wimp. And I guarantee you, I'm going to be the one who walks away." Through a good five verbal exchanges, our animosity kept building until one day, just before the season kicked off, he lined up directly opposite me on our punt team. I manned the left guard, he manned the right defensive tackle. He was just going to try to not let me off the line of scrimmage. Before he touched me, I launched a preemptive strike. Punched him five times—*Pow! Pow! Pow! Pow! Pow!*—in rapid-fire succession. This time, I fought back before I got hit. Charles never bothered me again.

I had passed one test, but there were plenty others my rookie year. An NFL rookie's job before every road game is to bring the chicken—Popeyes or Kentucky Fried. And don't forget the biscuits. If we ever forgot the food, there was hell to pay because the other veterans always counted on having their chicken meals.

Before one road game, a fellow rookie safety Greg Cox and I stopped to pick up chicken, which put us way behind schedule

R
O
M
O

for our four-thirty flight. We rushed to the team plane, boarded it, and stepped inside at about four twenty-eight. When we stepped on the plane and turned the corner, the whole coaching staff was already seated in first class staring at us. In a subtle but certain way, Coach Walsh made an important distinction to us: Chicken can wait. The plane can't.

My rookie year provided other valuable lessons. For starters, there were the terrible reminders of how brutal this game can be. During the first week of training camp, I was standing next to our starting linebacker Todd Shell when he ran outside to defend a sweep play, engaged a tight end, and then suddenly fell to the ground, limp. The play didn't look like anything out of the ordinary, and the hit on Todd didn't look particularly savage. But he broke his neck. Just like that he never played again.

With the unexpected loss of our outside linebacker, the 49ers issued me another test and changed my position. They switched me from the inside linebacker position, which I had played since I joined the Shamrocks back in Connecticut, to strongside linebacker, where my chief responsibility was to guard the opposing tight end. Up until then, I never had guarded the tight ends. The experience was totally new, totally different. I did whatever I could to distinguish myself. During the first training camp, I would repeatedly battle our tight ends Brent Jones, John Frank, and Ron Heller, who didn't always like our competitive confrontations.

"The guy's intense, that's for sure," Heller said to a reporter. "But sometimes he's a little overaggressive. My main complaint is that he likes to head-butt, which isn't illegal but makes it really tough to block. I'd have to say he should be a great player in this league."

Our coaches, thankfully, agreed. Without Todd and with outside linebacker Keena Turner still rehabbing the torn anterior cruciate ligament he suffered the season before, the coaches surprised me. They named me a starter for my first NFL game against the New Orleans Saints. Not much about the game stands out to me now, other than a couple of tackles I made. But what happened after the game does. Coach Walsh called the team together after our 34–33 victory.

"This game ball," Coach Walsh said, "goes to Bill Romanowski." He tossed me the football and I thought, *I am now a part of the team, I belong.* But I also learned it doesn't always last long. Two games later against Atlanta, there were two plays in which running back John Settle started up the middle and bounced outside, right to the spot I was supposed to be. Only I had run inside to chase him down. Each time he gained extra yards because of my eagerness, my mistakes. There was a lesson: Don't try to do too much; take care of your responsibility. If you don't you quickly discover what happens. The next Sunday, I was not a starter.

This is life in the NFL. One day you're a starter, the next day you're not. To help me get through my first season, my parents moved out to the Bay Area for six weeks around Thanksgiving time. Mom cooked and cleaned for me while Dad looked for a place for me to live. It was like we were back in Vernon, nothing much changed. Our old home in a new city. With my support system in place, I found my way back to the starting lineup, back on to the field.

Even though I never had missed a game for the Pop Warner Shamrocks, Rockville High School, or Boston College, in the NFL I learned I was not indestructible. On one play against the Saints, I tried to single-handedly break up their counterplay. I went low to take out the Saints' Pro Bowl guard Brad Edelman, as well as the New Orleans offensive tackle, and instead got kneed right in the back of my head by Edelman. Right away, I could feel something was bad, real bad. I was dizzy, disoriented.

ROMO

I never liked having people come out to take care of me—ever—so I forced myself up. Once I did, I felt as if I was going to fall right back over. My equilibrium was way off, my balance all messed up. Our trainers came to get me, and with their assistance I staggered to the sideline. Up until then, I had never had a feeling of anything close to this. I had had upset stomachs and sprained ankles and neck stingers, but this was scary, the scariest thing that had ever happened to me on the football field.

After halftime, at the start of the third quarter, I ignored the pain, shrugged off any symptoms, and told our trainers I felt good enough to go back out there. *Sure I did,* I told myself. I never would have told myself anything different. This became standard practice for me. I refused to pay attention to my head and my body. There was nothing that was going to keep me off the field. The sidelines always reminded me of failure.

Only later did I realize exactly what had happened. I read about it in my 49ers medical report.

11 Dec. 1988

Dr. Klint/e

Forty Niner dressing room, Candlestick Park, game against the New Orleans Saints. Late in the 2nd quarter of today's game was kicked in the right occipital region and was transiently stunned. Did not lose consciousness. Thereafter he noted that he was lightheaded and slightly ataxic, so removed himself from the game. He did return in the 2nd quarter. He was examined in the locker room at the half, at which time his symptoms had already begun to improve. He had total recall for the first half's events. No headache although slight discomfort in the right occipital area. He had no visual symptoms. He describes a sensation of "being slower than normal."

I didn't realize it at the time, but "being slower than normal" meant that, for the first time in my NFL career, my brain had been bruised. My first NFL concussion. Concussions result from a trauma-induced change in mental status and can occur when the head hits, or is hit, by an object, or when the brain is jarred against the skull. Over the course of my career, that happened a lot.

What followed were varying symptoms that included headaches, disorientation, confusion, dizziness, a blank stare, incoherent or incomprehensible speech, lack of coordination or weakness, amnesia of events that led up to the injury, nausea and vomiting, double vision, and ringing in the ears. Those are just the short-term symptoms. Longer term effects can include mental problems, sleep disturbances, a low-grade headache that persists, sensitivity to bright lights and loud noises, light-headedness, and ringing in the ears.

Despite the effects of my first NFL concussion, I still wanted to play. Up until that game, I never before experienced an injury that would remove me from a game. Each play meant so much to me that to miss even one was like a death sentence. It was something I could not accept. So this time, like so many more in my career, I went out and played the entire second half. I was a young, wild, reckless linebacker, determined to help bring more wins to San Francisco. Of course, I didn't know at the time that this mentality would lead to at least twenty more concussions over my sixteen season NFL career, but I'm not really sure of the exact number. Most never were documented. In the NFL, many aren't. Players hide concussions from trainers out of fear for their job. Now I fear trying to add up all the concussions I suffered. I can't remember them all.

■　■　■

With the heavy physical toll, I discovered quickly enough that players are always searching for ways to help deal. One of the first treatments I was introduced to as a pro was Motrin and Supac. Prescription strength Motrin is like a wonder pill, the equivalent of four Advil. It is not like the type anybody can buy over the counter now and it works by pushing an enzyme that makes anti-inflammatory chemicals instead of more inflammatory ones. Perfect.

Supac is a combination of aspirin and caffeine. This is a straightforward and fairly smart drug. As I learned in my ever-evolving education, caffeine increases energy production in your body by affecting an enzyme involved in the process called cyclic-AMP or cAMP. Each time cAMP goes around it increases your energy production, and caffeine keeps cAMP spinning, which gives you the boost. Making energy, though, also creates damage and inflammation. The makers of Supac knew that and put an anti-inflammatory, aspirin, in it.

This was all very new to me, these anti-inflammatories. Back at Boston College, there were tight reins on anything and everything we put into our bodies. When I would get regular stingers in my neck, pinched nerves in that same area from hitting with my head, we'd take some Tylenol or Advil. If I took one anti-inflammatory in my four years at Boston College, it's one more than I remember.

But college was one type of education, San Francisco another. What I learned right away in the NFL is that, whatever you need to play, whatever you need to get you going, it's there for you. Before my first practice I grabbed my Motrin and Supac, even though I had no idea what I was putting into my body at the time, that these pills could lead, without warning, to ulcers or internal bleeding. I chugged them with some water.

After my first experience with anti-inflammatories, I realized right away how great they are. You don't feel sore after practice. That never happened before. Soreness was something I lived with. Now I had found a way to neutralize it. I thought they were so amazing that I shipped a big jar of it back to the boys at Boston College. I figured if some caffeine and aspirin could help them a little, why not?

Meanwhile, our strength coach Jerry Attaway preached the benefits of Gatorlode, a high-carbohydrate energy source for rapid muscle glycogen restoration. As soon as I would finish a workout, Jerry would have me drink Gatorlode, which would replace the glycogen I had just burned. I Gatorloded that rookie season. It was so new to me, so different, finding out that there were wise ways to train, intelligent ways to treat your body. And they didn't stop there.

During the first week of training camp, I tweaked my groin and nearly freaked out. Here I am, trying to make my mark, trying to make the team, and I'm slowed down. My groin was throbbing, so our trainers handed me some Indocin, along with the knowledge that, in the NFL, there were treatments for just about any ailment. There were other nonsteroidal anti-inflammatory prescription-strength pain killers, like Feldene, Naprosyn—the group is usually associated with the AARP, not the NFL. These anti-inflammatories were powerful and dispensed on an as-need basis. Throughout the NFL, the symptoms are always one step ahead of the cure. And frankly, we're also just putting out fires, one after another.

Whenever one of my muscles or joints began aching, there was a jar of DMSO cream—dimethyl sulfoxide—stashed away in a training-room cabinet. This cream, banned in some states but legal in the NFL, worked really well. A dynamo molecule, DMSO is so small and dense it can penetrate almost any surface you put it on. Once I was told that if I spilled DMSO on a table and left it there it would seep through the wood and drip onto the floor. I don't know about a table, but it sure penetrated my

R
O
M
O

skin. I used it to reduce inflammation and recover from work-outs and games. The S in DMSO stands for sulfa; your body uses sulfa to detoxify tissues and reduce inflammation. One day I had another little hamstring problem and I rubbed some DMSO into it. What do you know? The next day, the problem was gone, just like that.

There were treatments not only for ailments but also for performance enhancement as well. Some of the guys used to rave about the powers of Creatine, an amino acid that is an important store of energy in muscle cells. Most athletes, at one time or another, have supplemented with Creatine. Today it is a popular nutritional supplement, finding acceptance even among younger athletes at the high school level. It is easy to understand why. I watched one of my teammates go from bench pressing 315 pounds once to pumping it up five times. So what did I do? I tried some Creatine. When I noticed somebody taking the minerals chromium piclonate, I took some to give my blood sugar level a quick adjustment. Chromium helps insulin work. Insulin drives sugar into cells, the basic process of starting the energy-producing chain of events. No insulin, or worse, having too much insulin because you don't have enough chromium is a sure way to run out of energy, and forget about growing. To keep my insulin working efficiently, I took a few hundred micrograms of chromium a day.

When the perfectly legal brewers yeast went around the locker room, I tried some of that, not even realizing it was intended as a source of B-vitamins, amino acids, proteins, minerals, enzymes, and nucleic acids.

When players in the locker room passed around vials of the herb ginseng, I wanted to try it. It was like a weak cup of coffee compared to some of the other stimulants I had begun taking. But it worked. An herbal extract that helps your brain and body, ginseng helps nerves function better and supports your adrenal glands in making the two hormones that enable you to respond to and recover from stress: Cortisol and DHEA.

Now, you want your adrenal glands to work just right; too much Cortisol breaks down muscle and adds fat, and too little results in fatigue and increased soreness. DHEA declines as Cortisol rises in the stressed person, compounding the problem. Too much Cortisol breaks down muscle, and not enough DHEA prolongs the effect. Taking ginseng, especially when it comes from aged ginseng roots, can really help you work hard and recover fast. Ginseng was there for us every Sunday, every game, all we wanted.

Eventually before games, our team doctor would administer injections of vitamin B-12 in my glute, which I was told would help my energy levels. You can take B-12 in supplement form, but it is not always absorbed. B-12 requires a substance made by your stomach to accompany it into the intestine where it gets absorbed. You don't always make enough of that chaperone substance to absorb all the B-12 in your supplement or meal. So I took it with an injection.

Injecting anything into your body gives you pause. But just looking at the color and clarity of B-12 tells you it's probably good for you, and it really is. If you're depleted you really feel the beneficial effects of B-12. A former NFL veteran had told me about this practice, saying he knew about some guys who used to inject B-12 while also taking amphetamines back in the 1970s. Later, amphetamine use in the NFL stopped completely. But the B-12 injections didn't—with good reason. Your nervous system burns B-12 like a Porsche burns gasoline, making it one of the most valuable and necessary vitamins for neuromuscular activities, like working out and playing and keeping your cool before and during the excitement of games.

You need to replace or stock up on as much B-12 as possible if you're going to ask your nervous system to do a lot of work

R
O
M
O

with your mind or your body. And when you play football, you work with both. Vitamin injections right into my bloodstream became a pregame routine throughout my career, up until I unbuckled my chin strap for the last time.

My eyes were being opened to a world I never knew existed, a mix of Western and alternative medicine.

Before games, an incense-like scent invaded our locker room. The first time, I was glancing around, trying to figure out what the hell was going on. I was thinking I had just been time-warped back to the 1960s in Haight-Ashbury. And then I realized what it was. A couple of the veterans were burning sticks of Moxa, an ancient form of Chinese heat therapy designed to loosen your joints and help you run faster. Perfectly legal, nothing wrong. Roger Craig told me that ancient Chinese mailmen would use Moxa and then run fifty miles without stopping. The sticks were about as thick and long as cigars, and the guys would light them up and press them as close to their knees as they could without burning themselves, then move it around to different acupuncture points.

Did I try it? Are you kidding? Something that would make you run faster and have more endurance? Absolutely. Eventually, it seemed like everyone in our locker room was using it. Did it work? Hell, I don't know. But let's put it this way: If you think it's going to work, chances are it does. The mind is powerful. It believes what you train it to believe.

But I'll tell you what did work. Halcyon, one of the most powerful prescription sleeping pills out there. Some of our players were so wired and nervous the night before a game that they could not sleep without a little help. The 49ers used to set up a ballroom for late-night snacks, maybe a beer or two, and any type of last-minute medication that was needed. Usually guys would need something for a headache, a cold, the flu, or some stomach cramping. But every now and then, they needed some Halcyon to get the sleep that is so important to performance. Sometimes the Halcyon—or what the players called "hammers"—came along with some laughs, too.

Every now and then, a couple of guys would wash down their Halcyon with beer. Their big thing was to see if they could take their Halcyon, drink their beer, and still make it back to their hotel room before they fell asleep in the hallway. In retrospect, it doesn't seem that funny, but back then it was hilarious.

I usually didn't have a problem with sleep. Our team was so good, so talented, I slept like a baby.

C oach Walsh always knew which buttons to push. He would keep us loose by doing things that to this day would bring a smile to any 49ers face. During our run to the Super Bowl, Coach would always turn to our defensive assistant coach, Tommy Hart—once a standout defensive end for the 49ers from 1968 through 1977—for a little team-wide counsel. The Thursday before each of our games, Coach Walsh would ask Coach Hart, in front of the whole team, "Green light or red light?" Green meant the players could have sex in the days leading up to the game; red meant they could not. It lightened up the mood at the training facility and became something all the guys looked forward to hearing every Thursday. Would we be green lighted? Or red lighted? Let's put it this way: Coach Hart wasn't stupid. He enjoyed having his players' support.

Coach Walsh also knew how to make us think. He compared each regular-season game to 1/16th of a 16-round fight, a tactic that now has become a cliché with coaches all around the NFL. When we reached the postseason, in what would turn out to be his final games as the 49ers coach before the team owner Eddie

R
O
M
O

DeBartolo decided to hire our defensive coordinator George Seifert instead, Coach Walsh surprised me even more.

After we beat the Chicago Bears 28–3 in the NFC Championship game and returned to San Francisco to prepare for Super Bowl XXIII in Miami, Coach Walsh insisted to us that we were doing nothing more than playing an away game in Miami against the Cincinnati Bengals.

"You think about the Super Bowl, and you lose track of what you did to get to this game—and that's playing great football and doing your job and taking care of your responsibilities and winning," he said. "We're gonna play an away game against Cincinatti in Miami."

How brilliant was that? It reminded me of that scene in *Hoosiers,* when Coach Norman Dale, played by Gene Hackman, walks his Hickory High School basketball team into Hinkle Field House for the Indiana State Tournament, and knows just what to do to wipe away the awe his small-town players feel. Hackman pulls out a measuring tape and sizes up the distance between the free throw line and rim of a big-city arena. He shows his players that no matter how large the stakes are, the court on which they will play for the state championship is exactly the same size as their own back home.

Miami did throw a little craziness into Coach Walsh's plan. On the night of Monday, January 16, in Overtown, a policeman shot and killed a speeding motorcyclist. Another man, a passenger on the same motorcycle, died a day later from the wounds he suffered. Overtown turned into America's most unsafe neighborhood, with rioting and looting spreading to Liberty City, only eight miles from our hotel, the Miami Airport Hilton and Marina.

My own mental focus technique was visualization. I reverted back to before the Cotton Bowl of my freshman year at Boston College, playing the game in my head before I ever played it on the field. I pictured myself at the forefront of the action in this Super Bowl. I pictured myself making a big play.

This one was a bit different, though. I didn't start. Played plenty—I went in after the first series, but didn't start. By the time Super Bowl XXIII rolled around, Keena Turner was not fully healthy, but he was ready, as he proved in the pre-game huddle when he told us, as he always did, "The play is coming to you! Be the one to make the play! Expect to make the play!"

But it was hard to make plays when you weren't on the field. It drove me crazy, standing on the sideline, watching the game start without me. Right in the beginning I would tug on Coach McPherson's shirt. "Hey, Coach, Keena's hurting," I pleaded with him. "You've got to get me in there. Please!"

Keena was coming off knee surgery, and halfway through the season he suffered a pinched nerve in his shoulder, so he wasn't full strength, and I was. But mentally, I was nowhere close to where Keena Turner, a ten-year veteran, was. He was a great leader and a great linebacker. Still, he was incapable of playing the full game. Once I got in, the game turned into just what I envisioned. I was at the forefront of the action, making the big play I pictured. Late in the third quarter, with Cincinnati ahead 6–3, Bengals quarterback Boomer Esiason threw a pass along the left sideline to wide receiver Tim McGee. I just happened to be drifting underneath, so I leaped up, tipped the ball, and caught it.

Right away, I looked up to the sky and yelled, "Thank you, thank you." I'm telling you, I knew that play was coming. I knew I would deliver. I could picture it, even if the opposition couldn't. "It wasn't that Boomer didn't see me," I was quoted as saying in that week's issue of *Sports Illustrated*. "It's just that I don't think he figured out I could jump that high."

R
O
M
O

The play helped swing the game's momentum. But we were still down 16–13 when our offense took the field late in the fourth quarter. I stood on the sideline with my fingers crossed, watching Joe Montana lead us down the field, just praying. I was pacing back and forth. It was in Joe's hands, yeah, but in a way, I wanted it to be in mine. It drove me nuts that I couldn't be a part of the game at its most decisive moment. Fortunately, as was almost always the case with Joe, one of the most clutch athletes in the history of sports, it worked out. He completed eight of nine passes for 97 yards, including a 10-yard strike to John Taylor with 34 seconds left. We were 20–16 winners and the world champions—not a bad way to start your NFL career. As I walked off the field, arms in the air, screaming and yelling, I realized it had happened again: being in the big game, making a big play that helped determine the outcome, winning the game I wanted more than any other. This had to have something to do with my guardian angel. Everything I set my mind to, I got. All I could keep repeating to myself was, "World Champion! World Champion!"

You picture a moment like that as a little kid, dream about it, but even then it's not as good as the actual feeling. It's a feeling you never forget. Add to this the honor of having been named first-year All-NFL Rookie, and I was flying high.

In our locker room after the game I enjoyed sharing the moment with my great teammates, knowing all the energy and effort it took us to get here. We basked in our victory and savored our accomplishment—for about 60 seconds.

Then, as all the players huddled in the middle of the locker room, Ronnie Lott started chanting, "Re-peat! Re-peat! Re-peat!" Soon enough, our whole team joined him. It echoed in my head that night and through the off-season.

How remarkable it was to see the attitude of this unique collection of champions who would literally celebrate the biggest moment of their football lives by immediately promising another title next year. I knew I belonged. It didn't take but one win, and I could tell—I was addicted to the incredible feeling of being the best in the world. I would chase it for the rest of my career.

R
O
M
O

4 DON'T EVER TELL SOMEBODY YOU'RE NOT ALL RIGHT

Two thoughts consumed me as I prepared for my second season with the 49ers. (1) How to win a starting job. (2) How to hit people with the maximum possible force. The two, in my mind, went together like dreams and dragons.

I was obsessed with becoming the starter for the San Francisco 49ers. Not part-time, like I was during my first season when I started ten games and then was on the bench when Keena Turner recovered from his injury. Full-time. Keena had been a leader for us, and the team and community respected him. I learned a lot from him. But I wanted his position and couldn't do enough to get it.

In the opening week of training camp, I stepped into the line of scrimmage and hit our running back Roger Craig with a blow that told him and the coaches exactly how much I wanted it. Roger didn't like it, not one bit, especially since we had spent a portion of my first off-season in San Francisco training together, running impossibly steep hills again and again. He had helped create this fitness monster. Now he was paying for it. And he let me and everyone else know how much he disapproved of it.

"Romo, what the hell are you doing?" he yelled, jumping up after the hit. "This is practice."

"Screw you," I shouted back, turning to head back to the defensive huddle. "This is football."

I had a lot of respect for Roger, a phenomenal athlete and a terrific teammate. But during my second camp—with George Seifert our head coach and new impressions to be made—my world revolved around winning a starting position. Even if it meant sticking my own teammate.

Nothing could slow me down. I would be out at practice and all I wanted to do was be noticed. I wanted everybody to see my desire to be a starter, to be a player, to be something special. I knew coaches were going to watch Jerry Rice on film and I figured if they were watching him, they were going to see me, too. So every time Jerry would catch a pass and run to the end zone, I would chase him down from behind. Every practice, everyday. Whenever you would see Jerry running to the end zone with the football, you would see me right there behind him, in full pursuit.

Coaches might have liked this, but I don't know if Jerry always did. During one practice that summer, I came off a block and violated the 49ers unwritten rule of practice: no one touches No. 80. Well, I stuck my forearm into Jerry's chest, knocking him right on his ass. Jerry didn't like that too much. He got up and came after me. He hit me; I hit him. After a couple of these exchanges, there was pushing and verbal sparring until the offensive linemen came to Jerry's rescue and broke it up.

This actually happened in three straight training camps, an annual rite of summer there for a little while. The second time I

R
O
M
O

did it, I head-and-shouldered Jerry and he dove at my ankles. Coach Seifert jumped in to try to break it up and he slipped and fell on his rump.

Coaches cautioned me to be careful. They advised me to tread a little lighter on my accelerator. In August 1989, after smashing Roger and clobbering Jerry, they even had to pull me aside to give me my own little pep-down talk. "Relax," Coach McPherson, my former linebackers coach who had been promoted to defensive coordinator, told me. "Relax, Romo. Just play."

I ignored Coach and everyone else who tried to offer similar orders. I couldn't afford to take that part of myself away, not if I wanted to compete with players who I had come to believe were stronger and faster and more talented than me. I felt like I had to play at a higher level of intensity, to use my rage like a weapon.

To make it in the NFL, a player needs all the weapons he can get. Speed, strength, smarts, and relentlessness. Without them, I always felt my job was in jeopardy. Actually, even with them it was. My nagging insecurities, which followed me from city to city, really were no different than any other NFL player's. We love to project this image of tough guys, and plenty are, but we all also realize that it could be gone in a flash. Teams are always trying to find someone better. The pressure to perform every minicamp, every training camp, every practice, every preseason game, every game, every year grows all the time and it doesn't leave you alone. I have never stepped on a practice field or played a game without my performance being thoroughly critiqued by what seems to be a zillion cameras just waiting to expose my flaws.

Do you know how unsettling that is? How stressful? Some people in other professions rise to a certain level where their jobs are safe, if not tenured. Not in the NFL. In the NFL, they—

GMs, coaches, younger players, injuries—are coming after you all the time. Just like they came after Ronnie Lott and Joe Montana and Roger Craig and Jerry Rice—players the 49ers eventually got rid of. And if players of their caliber are affected, well then everybody's fair game. It plays with your mind. The real challenge for players, and the ones that go on to become champions, is overcoming their own doubt. The real key to success is having the confidence to play every play at your highest level.

Heading into my second season, the 49ers invested their first-round pick on Tennessee linebacker Keith DeLong, their sixth-round pick on California linebacker Steve Hendrickson, their ninth-round pick on LSU linebacker Rudy Harmon, and their twelfth-round pick on North Carolina linebacker Antonio Goss. Their message was implicit: The 49ers felt like they needed help at linebacker.

At that time, I remember self-doubt temporarily getting the best of me. I told myself: *If I can just find a way to hang on to the roster and make it in the NFL for six years, I'll be happy. I'll have more money than I'll know what to do with and I can walk away from the game proud.* My short-term goals were more pressing. Heading into my second year, they consumed me, to unhealthy levels. No matter how hard I worked, I didn't feel I was working hard enough. No matter how hard I trained, I wasn't training hard enough. Whatever I was doing, it wasn't enough. My second year, I started only two NFL games.

My contributions came primarily on special teams. Our special teams coach, Lynn Stiles, handed out T-shirts to his special teams players that said, "Bruise Crew." I figured if I couldn't make an impact at linebacker, I would do my best to make one on special teams. While bruising as many kick and punt returners as possible, I finished second on special teams in points, but first on big hits. We called big hits "pancakes." And I liked pancakes as much as a pro as I did when I was a kid. At the end of

R
O
M
O

the season, Coach Stiles rewarded me with a video camera and television.

But I should have known it would not be the type of season I wanted, nor expected. The season even started out with a learning experience that stayed with me the rest of my career. During our opening-game 30–24 victory at Indianapolis, I tackled Colts running back Eric Dickerson along our sideline. It was one of those tackles where it didn't look like he got the best of me, but he did. My teammate and fellow linebacker Matt Millen (who is now in charge of the Detroit Lions front office) came running over to me as soon as he saw I was down. "Romo, Romo, you all right?" he asked.

Now, a football player's natural reaction, his predictable reaction, is, "Yeah I'm fine." But I wasn't. I could hardly breathe. I let my guard down for an instant. "No," I told Matt, gasping for air. "I'm not all right."

Well, the rest of the season and every time I saw Matt after that, he never let me forget how young and stupid I was. "Romo," he would tell me, "don't ever tell somebody you're not all right on the field." That's the attitude football players are taught to adopt. You've got to play hurt and never admit pain. All around the league were examples of players that would.

Buffalo had an All-Pro guard, Jim Richter, who, to this day, was the best guard I ever played against. Jim could not move his neck and he wore the thickest protective strap I've ever seen to cover it, but he played as if it didn't matter. When he hit you, he hit you so hard it would shock your senses—a football version of shock and awe. Running into him felt no different than running into a tree trunk. We had the satisfaction of beating Buffalo 21–10 that December, but I went up against Richter, and that hurt. That really hurt. Not that I would ever have admitted that to Matt or my other teammates.

Sometimes the blows were too much for any player to overcome. During our seventh game of the season at Stanford Stadium against the Patriots, on the second play from scrimmage, I watched our safety Jeff Fuller charge up from his position to take on running back John Stephens. Head on, Fuller drilled Stephens in the chest, then fell limp to the ground, unconscious, like he had been shot. "I never saw a man's face look like that," our linebacker, Michael Walter, told reporters after the game. "It looked like he was in shock. His eyes looked . . . huge. You just wanted to look at him and go, 'Oh, God.' "

Over the years, you see it so many times on the football field, a player lying there, motionless. Heck, it had happened just the year before with Todd Shell when he broke his neck, ending his career. Each time you hope and pray it's nothing serious. But this time, there seemed to be little that hope and prayers could do. Fuller was removed from the field on a stretcher and rushed by ambulance to Stanford Hospital, where he was admitted to the intensive-care unit.

After Fuller was in the ambulance, the game started right back up again, as if nothing had happened. This is how it works in the NFL. If a player goes down during practice with a severe injury, teams just move the drill to another part of the field, away from the scene of the accident. During a game, the whistle blows, the quarterback gets under center, and away we go. Sure, the game goes on, but a little piece of everyone's warriorlike invincibility diminishes.

During the course of the same game, as is the case in so many NFL games, players continued dropping. Our fullback and special teams captain Harry Sydney was lost for the season with a fractured left forearm. Our linebacker Jim Fahnhorst sustained a stress fracture in his right foot. Joe Montana sprained his left knee.

But Fuller's injury was the most serious. After we beat the Patriots 37–20 in what was clearly a hollow victory, our players

R
O
M
O

were so shaken by Fuller's injury that the 49ers had our doctor, Michael Dillingham, address the team. Dr. Dillingham told us that the force of Fuller's hit ripped apart the nerves that connected his neck to his right arm and he also suffered three compressed vertebrae. His football career was over. Dr. Dillingham stressed that Fuller's injury was not life-threatening, but, he added, Fuller "may not recover the full use of his (right) arm," and added that, "in general," the nerves that Fuller severed "will not regenerate."

Hearing that scared me and scarred me. When a doctor talks in those terms, you can't help but realize how brutal this game is. It's not something you're thinking about when you're on the field, though, with 75,000 fans screaming, "Kill him, Romo!" When you're on the field with your armor on, there's a feeling of being invincible. And then when these events unfold right in front of you, you realize that you're not. It reminds me of the time of the great gladiators, how when one won, he stayed alive; when one lost, he also lost his life. Working in that environment, with that mentality, you better spend time with the right chiropractors, undergoing the right training routines, putting the right things in your body, or your career can take a wrong turn real quick. Every doctor I visited, every supplement I ingested all revolved around being able to handle that trauma better than anybody in the league.

Yet even when you do everything possible to build up your body, to maximize your resistance, to become fast enough and strong enough to reduce the chances of an injury striking you down, there are no guarantees of survival in the NFL.

Dr. Dillingham knew what he was talking about when he offered our team his prognosis for our fallen teammate. To this day, Jeff Fuller has failed to regain the use of his right arm.

■ ■ ■

It's not always popular to have fun in the NFL because people tend to think it means you're not working hard. But the season can be such a grind that you need to have some fun. Fortunately, I could escape from the NFL's pressures, mostly with the help of my fellow linebacker and mentor, Riki Ellison. Both curious and intensely competitive, we trained together, hung out together, and every few months, Riki would take up a new activity and try to beat me at it. He would take golf lessons for a month straight, invite me out to some course, and if he won, he would ask me to golf with him again; if I won, he would quit playing.

From golf it was on to fly fishing. But Riki hadn't realized that I had fished a lot as a kid. He could take all the lessons he wanted, he wasn't going to catch a bigger fish than me. When I shamed him there, he put down his rod for good.

So it was on to tennis, a sport Riki was sure he was going to whip me at. What he didn't know was that I played a great deal of tennis at BC. When I beat Riki at tennis, he never played it again, either.

Even in defeat, Riki looked after me like a big brother and remains a key mentor in my life, even today. Riki became someone I looked to, someone I respected.

And in a way, that was how it should have been. He used to tell me that when he first came into the league, he learned from the great former linebacker Jack "Hacksaw" Reynolds. He'd tell me stories about him. One was about how Hacksaw used to show up at meetings with twenty to thirty sharpened pencils and refuse to give any to his teammates. Anybody who asked him to borrow one would be told, "Would you go to a football game without a helmet? No, so don't come to meetings without a pencil."

He was so intense that for the 49ers' first Super Bowl in 1981, he showed up for the team breakfast at 7 A.M., dressed

R
O
M
O

head to toe in uniform. Riki inherited Hacksaw's intensity and attention to detail, and he tried to pass down some of it to me. Riki also passed on his passion for surfing.

On one of our off days, Riki, who grew up in Southern California, asked if I wanted to join him and some of his buddies for the day in Santa Cruz—surfing. "Absolutely," I told him. "I'd love to go."

As a kid, my childhood friend Glen Schmelter and I discussed living in California one day and surfing. The idea of following through on it fired me up, though at first I wasn't sure if I made the right decision. Riki's version of teaching me to surf was taking me out into the waves and saying, "Follow me." I followed him and got completely crushed. A six-foot wave came crashing down on me and I nearly drowned in my first attempt to surf.

Wish I could say my other attempts were better, but that would be a flat lie. Surfing is hard enough to learn, but when you're six foot four and 242 pounds, it's easier to squeeze into a magnetic resonance imaging machine. It took me six months of surfing before I finally caught my first wave. Six months! Riki definitely shamed me there. But it didn't matter to me. On those rare occasions when he would actually defeat me, did I quit? A loss only pushed me to get better. (P.S. Guess who's the better surfer now?) Surfing had a spiritual side to which I felt completely connected. It reminded me of the feeling I had when I skied mountains in Vermont and Massachusetts as a kid, or played football now. I felt as if I were put on this earth to do it. Out on the water, peace would seep into me and stress would seep out. Surfing touched my heart in ways I never would have imagined.

After my buddy Glen moved out West and into my house in Milpitas, California, in the spring of 1989, I would take him along with me and Riki. We would tie our surfboards to the top of the car, load up the cooler with food for afterward, blast Beach Boys music from the radio, and take off.

"Lenny, Lenny, number two," I would yell out to him when we were in the water, knowing damn well that wave number one was the perfect one to ride in. Glen would start paddling out to wave number two and, in the meantime, I'd be on the better wave, laughing at him the whole time.

The following Christmas, I bought Glen a new surfboard. As soon as he opened it, he looked at me and I looked at him and we thought: *To hell with the rest of the presents. We're going surfing!*

This was how our San Francisco holidays went. On Easter, when our friends were going to church, we would go to our sanctuary in Santa Cruz, praying for an endless succession of heavenly waves. What a great lifestyle we uncovered out in northern California. On one day we could go skiing at Lake Tahoe and on the very next day, be back in Santa Cruz, surfing. How many places in the world can you do that? Even better, we had a small circle of friends to share it with.

On draft day 1989, as I was lifting in the 49ers weight room, Coach Seifert popped in to bounce a scouting question off me. "Hey, Romo, what do you think of Jimmy Bell?" he said, referring to my roommate at Boston College, the six-foot, 205-pound running back. The 49ers were toying with the idea of drafting him. Another BC boy heading west.

"If you can get him in the late rounds, he would be a phenomenal pick," I told Coach Seifert.

Sure enough, in the eleventh round, with a selection the 49ers had acquired from the Raiders, they drafted Jimmy, a pick that worked out better for me than San Francisco. For the one year he spent out in the Bay Area, Jimmy moved into my house.

**R
O
M
O**

He did it almost at the exact time Glen did. Suddenly, there were three New Englanders trying to make it out West, in addition to my rookie friends Keith DeLong and tight end Wesley Walls.

While Jimmy and I went to practice, Glen ran a deli in San Jose and served as our personal shopper. When he got off work at about 3 P.M., he would buy salad, chicken, corn, and broccoli and come home to start prepping it for dinner. Each night we walked in from the 49ers training complex, and Glen would be standing in the kitchen chopping vegetables. With all the chopping he did, we nicknamed him "Chopper." Once Chopper did his job, I was ready to do mine. I was the house's personal cook, preparing our healthy, nutritional meals.

We ate right and lived right. And as happy as I was during my first season in San Francisco, I was much more comfortable my second season. How could I not be? Riki mentored me on and off the football field and advised me on a whole host of subjects, including money. At the time he was making $400,000 per year and I would say to myself, *If I could ever make $400,000 a year, I'd be the richest man on the face of the earth.*

In a different way, I was already rich. My friends had turned my house into a home. Even my other teammates began welcoming me in ways they had not the first season.

Our new nose guard Jim Burt, who had spent the 1981–1988 seasons helping the New York Giants win a Super Bowl, worked with me every day after practice. Even though he played nose guard, he had studied Lawrence Taylor, Harry Carson, and Carl Banks play linebacker in New York and he passed along the nuances that he had observed. All of which was extensive. He showed me how to use my hands, how to turn my feet at certain angles. Most important, he taught me how to tape down my pads. He would always tell me, "If they can't hold you, they can't block you."

I'd have my jerseys tailored to where they fit as tight as spandex. Even then, I had laces stitched into the sides of my jerseys so I could pull them as tight as possible. As if that weren't enough, I used two-way adhesive carpet tape between my pads and jersey. While most players arrived in the locker room two or three hours before each game, I would get there four hours in advance. Eventually, it became a spiritual exercise for me. And forget about pinching an inch off me, you couldn't pinch a millimeter. It was so tight-fitting, I had to have two or three people help force my one-piece contraption on to me. It was one of my secret weapons until the day I left the game.

I also noticed that the 49ers' offensive and defensive linemen used to spray their jerseys with silicon, so as to make their jerseys so slick that nobody could hold on to them. At the time, there was no rule against the silicon, so before each game, I had our defensive assistant coach, Tommy Hart, help me out by spraying me down with silicon.

These were just added advantages that gave me more of an edge, which I would use to help myself on the battlefield. Guys couldn't grab me; if they tried to hold me, their hands would slip off. But that's how I always conducted myself, doing things to extremes—I always felt if I couldn't be held, I couldn't be blocked. Thank you, Jim Burt, wherever you are.

Later, after I arrived in Denver, Broncos offensive line coach Alex Gibbs took the tricks to another level. Before the game, he would gather together all of his linemen outside the shower and smear them with Vaseline from the big jars of it that he always kept around. Alex would take gobs of it and rub it onto his players' jerseys. It was his way of showing his guys that he really wanted them to start with an edge. When I heard about that, I got right in line and got myself smeared with the stuff, too.

Eventually, the league caught on to it, and banned any use of silicon or Vaseline, threatening $50,000 fines to the teams or players who continued using it. I still kept doing it, just not

ROMO

nearly as much. I would put on surgical gloves and apply the slightest amounts of Vaseline to the areas where I knew offensive linemen, tight ends, and running backs always tried to grab me. Then I didn't view it as cheating; I viewed it as pushing the envelope. There were referees on the field to enforce the rules and any one of them could have caught me at any time. Fortunately, none did. Or maybe, in retrospect, too bad they didn't.

These were some of the game's little secrets. Turned out there were other ones, too.

For all the prescription medications I noticed around the 49ers, there was one I didn't. It never occurred to me why certain players would get especially jumpy before games, or why others would throw up. I thought it was related to an extreme case of pregame nerves, nothing more. Then, on our October 1989 trip to New York to play the Jets, I discovered the secret culture of Phentermine, an appetite suppressant with amphetamine-like effects. It was not banned in the NFL until the start of the 2001 season, shortly after my trial for fraudulently obtaining it.

Phentermine is the most commonly prescribed medication to treat obesity. From what I know, 1.2 million prescriptions are written for it each year. Doctors don't know exactly how Phentermine works, but somehow it increases the level of adrenaline in your nerves and, ultimately, in your brain. The more adrenaline in your system, the faster thoughts become actions. The more adrenaline, the more nerves get involved in an action. The more nerves involved—a phenomenon exercise physiologists call "recruitment"—the more strength and power. And strength and power are what the NFL is about, which is why Phentermine was so popular before it was banned.

Before the game against New York, I was handed half of a

long, thin, white tablet with blue polka dots on it. I didn't even worry about what it would do to me, how it would make me feel, what it might do to my body. Again, I thought if it was good for another player, it's good for me. Half a tablet of Phentermine gave me more quickness, strength, and power. It did so by amplifying the adrenaline in my brain. I thought it was great. It seemed safe because it was common. Doctors prescribed it for ladies my mom's age, so how harmful could it be?

Over time I realized that the real advantage I got from taking Phentermine was not the power, the quickness, nor the strength. It was the feeling that I had a secret weapon, some kind of edge or advantage the other teams' players didn't have. Sure I felt the drug and I was quicker and more energetic, but it also made me fuzzy sometimes and jumpy. Thinking back on it I might have played a little worse when I took it, but you couldn't convince me of that back then.

What Phentermine did for me right away was put me in the zone. I truly wanted to run into a brick wall as hard as I could. You cannot believe how good it felt to hit somebody. It was like, "Give me more of this, give me more of the hitting, give me more of the contact, give me more of the pain." I'd even hit my own guys. I remember when we were hosting New Orleans during a Monday night November match-up, a game we won 31–13, and our defensive tackle Pete Kugler—who had a really dry sense of humor—shot the gap between the center and guard to make the tackle in the backfield. I ran up to him and jumped on him, slapping his helmet and high-fiving him, my energy overflowing. "Hey, Romo, don't get too excited," Pete told me. "It was just an accident."

But there was nothing accidental about the way I felt on Sunday. My mind set was different, my state altered. No matter how hard I flew into somebody, I could not fly into him hard enough. Even better, if something hurt on my body, the Phentermine dulled my pain and allowed me to inflict it on others instead.

The first time I took it I managed to land a hit on Jets running back Roger Vick, the type I spent the entire off-season dreaming about. Well, after we flew back to San Francisco, my teammate Kevin Fagan and equipment manager Ted Walsh called to tell me that they had just been watching television and they had seen that my hit on Vick had made the Schick Razor Hit of the Week.

That was big stuff to me. I was all excited about it, trying to find it on television. I spent the rest of the week glued to my TV, hoping to see my Schick Razor Hit of the Week. In between, I was calling people, telling them I had won this award and asking them to call me if they saw it. Funny but nobody did, all week. The only call I got was from Kevin and Ted, and they were joking. Ah well.

Now, were there side effects to the Phentermine? Of course. What action doesn't have a reaction? It led to irritability, hyperactivity, insomnia, and changes in personality as drastic as the ones I experienced on and off the field. I went through it all. But what I really hated most about the Phentermine were the comedowns. What a cruddy feeling. You'd take it on Sunday and, by that night, you were still wired, yet tired and physically and emotionally drained. I mean, wiped. It hurt to speak. Your stomach was in knots. You couldn't sleep that night. You struggled to sleep the next night. It was two straight days of eyes wide open. Each week, I couldn't wait for the season to end to not have to do it anymore. I began to both hate it and love it, if that is possible.

But while the seasons lasted, I took more of it. After my first experience with it against the New York Jets, I didn't want to walk on to the field without it. Taking Phentermine became as much of a pregame ritual as taping your ankles, putting on your helmet, smearing your eye black. I never wondered whether it was right or wrong, whether or not I should be doing it. I just felt like it was a prescription diet pill, so why shouldn't I be able to use it?

Almost always, there were thirty Phentermine tablets in the prescriptions I got. Now understand, players do different things to get ready. I was always the type of guy where if it was good for me, I wanted to share it with teammates. But with Phentermine, we're talking about a prescription medication. What if I had given it to somebody and he suffered a heart attack? Think about that.

Having taken Phentermine is embarrassing now for a lot of reasons but most of all because it reminds me that as hard as I trained, as diligent as I was in preparing, I still needed a "secret weapon" to feel like I was invincible on the field, when in fact what would really have made me a great player was the supplementary work. I didn't need Phentermine to play my best, and I wish now that I hadn't felt I did. Who knows what damaging side effects it was having on my body and my brain.

There is no greater rush than the one you get in January, in postseason football. Just like I thought we would, we stormed through the playoffs and right into Super Bowl XXIV in New Orleans against the Denver Broncos.

Following form, I visualized that I was going to make a play to change the game. So I wasn't totally surprised when, in the third quarter, Broncos quarterback John Elway threw a ball into the end zone to his tight end Clarence Kay. I jumped in front of the pass and intercepted it. Only problem was, there was a flag on the play. Officials called me for face guarding. The interception was wiped out, but the memories of the day were not.

Jerry Rice scored three touchdowns, fullback Tom Rathman

two, and Joe Montana earned his third Super Bowl MVP award. We blew out the Broncos 55–10, cranking out our second straight Super Bowl victory. Sure enough, after the game, Ronnie Lott gathered together the team just like he had the year before and started chanting: "Three-peat! Three-peat! Three-peat!"

But it was okay to enjoy the feeling of a repeat. All season long, it felt like a foregone conclusion we would. What set apart any great team I played on, including the two that won Super Bowls in San Francisco, was the energy that charged the locker room. If you play for a champion, you can feel it, all season long.

We knew that if we played the way we were capable of, nobody was beating us, period. Forty-Niners football meant victory. Do you know what that does to a team when you go into a game like that? When you know the question is not whether you're going to win, but just how badly you're going to beat the other team? It was a feeling that returned to me later in my career in Denver, but it is tough to duplicate.

Around the league, coaches, general managers, and owners are constantly trying to capture that feeling. Only they can't. There's no way to *get* it. It just *happens*. With a certain mix of guys, with a certain mix of chemistry, it moves into your locker room and invades the air. It's the attitude of winning, and it's highly contagious. It makes players better, and it makes people better.

And here I was, all of twenty-four years old, with two Super Bowl rings and two meetings with President Bush. I thought this was how it was supposed to be. Of course, I'd come to realize these were huge achievements. I think about John Elway, who had to wait until he was thirty-seven to win his first Super Bowl. Then there are so many other great players who accomplish so much yet never get to carry the Lombardi trophy. Man, I was blessed.

Following our first Super Bowl win, I had written a thank you note to the 49ers owner, Eddie DeBartolo. I thanked him for being allowed to work for a first-class organization, thanked him for the classy ways he treated his team, and promised I would work my ass off to help him become the NFL owner with more Super Bowl trophies than any other. He replied with a hand-written note of his own, saying he never had received a letter like mine from any of his players, which felt pretty special. But that was the way DeBartolo always made his players feel—special.

Typical of DeBartolo, he put together an annuity for Jeff Fuller to take care of him for the rest of his life. Then, after we had beaten the Bengals in Super Bowl XXIII, DeBartolo had chartered a plane to fly the organization back to his hometown in Youngstown for a party that defies description: lavish gift baskets waiting in our hotel rooms. An incredible cocktail party at his house. Jeffrey Osborne singing in his backyard. Then another huge party at the hotel.

DeBartolo outdid himself after our latest Super Bowl win. He flew our whole team to the Westin Kauai for a four-day, all-expense paid retreat. All the golf we wanted. All the spa treatments the women wanted. Players could have left their wallets home—you couldn't spend a dollar if you tried.

Over the years, some of the players grew close to DeBartolo, primarily Montana, Craig, Lott, Tom Rathman, and Harris Barton. They would go on weekend junkets to Las Vegas, usually when Mike Tyson was fighting there. What happens in Vegas stays in Vegas, but there are certain things I can share with you.

We would be sitting at the blackjack table, my pocket stuffed mostly with $5 chips, and DeBartolo suddenly would flip me a

R
O
M
O

$1,000 chip. The first time he did it, I just about fainted. But as he flipped me another and another it became a regular occurrence.

Well, a thousand bucks was a big deal to me. So I would take the chip, put it in my pocket, and replace it with the few $25 chips I had. Then when DeBartolo walked away—after playing $5,000 hands that blew me away—I would pull the $25 chip off the table and replace it with my $5 chip. By the time the weekend was over, I would head back home with $5,000 in my pocket—enough spending money to last me through the whole off-season. Off-seasons afforded me some time to wind down from the previous season, to go surfing, to sleep better, to visit family, to spend some time with my friends. And to golf.

Something about golf relaxed me. It had ever since I started playing it as a little kid in the schoolyard across from our house with my parents' old golf clubs. I remember when I first picked up the sport and decided to give up baseball, my dad looked at me as if I were crazy. "You sure you don't want to play baseball?" he asked, more of a suggestion than a question. "You sure?"

I never concentrated on golf, but I maintained enough of an interest that I could always shoot a respectable score, sometimes even more than respectable. During one off-season tournament, the NFL Golf Classic, Jim Burt and I actually won the tournament, which carried along the prizes of two Cadillac Sedan Devilles. When I won my car, it triggered a great idea. Back when I was a junior in high school, we played a game against New Britain High School under the Friday night lights. To play at night, under the lights, was a huge deal. Our team felt we had reached the big time. It was always a dream to give other players the excitement every Friday night that I experienced on the one Friday night.

To help achieve it, I created the Lights On Foundation, my way of giving back a little something to Coach Dunn and

Rockville High, which gave so much to me. I sold raffle tickets back home, auctioned off my Cadillac, and raised $60,000—enough to install lights on the school's fields. I loved helping them, giving those kids some opportunities I never got.

During my first off-season in the NFL, I purchased a bunch of weight-lifting equipment—squat racks, incline benches, military benches, free weights—and donated it all to Rockville High to replace that junky old multistation Nautilus machine that I had used. Then, during my second year in the league, I found out Rockville was playing the state championship game on artificial turf. So I went around the 49ers locker room and collected turf shoes from my teammates. By the time everyone tossed in some barely used turf shoes, I had seventy pairs mailed back home to the players.

I especially loved to go back and talk to all the kids. When I was at Boston College, I would tell them that I would trade the Cotton Bowl victory for a chance to be back in high school, playing for the state championship. That was the one thing I always wanted that I never got, a state championship. But they did. They won one. And I couldn't have been any happier for Coach Dunn and his team when they did.

Donations to my old high school were always different—weights, turf shoes, my time—but the ideas were the same. Helping people perform the best they could was something that always meant a lot to me. But nothing gave me any more pleasure than when the lights went up at the school. Those high school kids constantly would feel the excitement that I did only once during my days at school. That meant more to me than winning back-to-back Super Bowls.

**R
O
M
O**

5 HOW COULD THEY LET THEM GO!?

Sucking in all the air I could, I braced myself for the kick. Ronnie Lott delivered it. Right to my solar plexus. Moments later, I braced again, this time for Charles Haley, who teed off on me, just like he wanted to my rookie season. They took turns pummeling me and I stood there and absorbed every kick.

Eventually, I got my chance to kick back. But not until our instructor, George Chung—who eventually became the 49ers training advisor—gave me the okay. George is a five-time World Karate Champion and member of the Black Belt Magazine Hall of Fame. He has taught more than 30,000 students and promoted more than 1,000 of them to the black belt level. Back in 1990, we were his three newest—and I would venture to say meanest—students.

George would put us through intense full-body workouts, kicking and punching until we felt as if we had just gone through a football game. We would be bruised, sore, drenched in sweat, but we loved it. Anything we could do to refine our football skills, to make ourselves better players, appealed to us more than any day off would.

This is how it was. My off-seasons were designed to uncover new ways to help me improve during the regular season. To make my weaknesses a strength.

Our cornerback, Eric Wright, used to tell me in his usual sarcastic way, "Romo, you jerk, you're going to play thirteen, fourteen years, make all kinds of money. I only wish I had trained like you from the beginning." It reminded me of what the guys back at BC would tell me after watching me run myself ragged. And that was a compliment as good as any. That was recognition of my respect for the game, the hard work it took to play it and prepare for it. So it's not surprising that I was always open to trying new training methods. Almost all proposals merited careful consideration. The best ones endured.

During an off-season autograph session at Moda Italia Uomo, located in Los Gatos' Vasona Station just outside of San Jose, a big burly man waited me out and introduced himself. "Udo Magel," he said, extending his hand and shaking mine. Right away, I could feel the power in his hands. They were thick and strong, not unlike his six foot two, 220-pound frame. I could also tell he knew his profession. He explained that he was a physical therapist from Germany, who had spent eight years in the air force hospital where he became a certified nurse and paramedic rescue worker. When his physical therapy and sports training degree didn't transfer to the United States, he got certified in massage therapy here.

On the afternoon I met him, Udo explained how much more meticulous German athletes are in their training. He described how the German philosophy is to get massage every day, like Americans eat breakfast, lunch, or dinner. It's part of the workout, part of the recovery. It's taking care of yourself.

R
O
M
O

Udo also told me about hot and cold tub contrasts, how I should spend two minutes in a 35-degree cold tub and then go right into a 112-degree hot tub for one minute. Muscles reacted to this favorably. This was a practice I liked so much, I kept it up my entire career, adding time. By the end of my career, I was spending forty minutes hopping from a 35-degree cold tub to a 112-degree hot tub. Try it some time. Your muscles will thank you.

Udo's other recommendation was to always finish your showers in cold water. With a long cold splash. To this day, like with the cold- and hot-tub treatments, I do. His stories and knowledge intrigued me enough that I agreed to visit him for a $50 massage session at his Santa Clara home. The first area he worked on was my quadriceps. As he dug his meaty hands into the top of my legs, he said, "Oooh, you have so many knots in your quads."

Udo was killing me, but what made it feel better was that he told me how much this would help my performance and my recovery—to improve them I'd put up with anything. If it would have helped me catch a running back, I would have been willing to drink gasoline. At first, I would visit Udo once a week. When I realized how much better I felt in my karate workouts with Ronnie and Charles and my hill runs with Roger and Riki, I started going twice a week. Soon enough, twice a week turned into an every day massage. Finally I decided to put him in pen in my day book. Like the electric bill, Udo became a regular part of my monthly expenses. I hired him full-time, paying him $1,000 a month.

Wanting to spread the word, I turned other guys on to him. Pierce Holt, Kevin Fagan, and Jerry Rice began using Udo, too. More players discovered Udo and the powers of massage. I wanted everybody else to receive the same treatments, to be at their best. Everything I did, I tried to help everybody. It reached a point where Udo was treating so many players that I figured it would be easier to simply set up an office for him at the 49ers training complex. I went to ask permission from our general manager, John McVay.

I told McVay how common massage therapists were in Europe, how they were key components of teams, like a medical staff. Every European team had one, so why isn't that the case here in the States? This was something I thought could really help us. "And," I added, "it would make it easier, where the guys don't have to travel all over the place, if right after practice we could get worked on here."

McVay agreed, and Udo became a regular at the 49ers training facility. Not coincidentally, I became a regular in the starting lineup for the 1990 season, when I led the team in tackles. For the first time, the starting job was all mine. What helped propel me into the role, I believe, were my intense off-season training sessions and my work with Udo. The more I did, the more I achieved.

In my daily talks with Udo, I learned that massage should be administered after a game, when all the lactic acid that built up in the muscles could be worked out. So that was what I did. After every home game, I would drive one hour south from Candlestick Park, back to our training facility in Santa Clara, and meet Udo.

The 49ers security guards already had gotten to know Udo, so they would let him in. Usually, I would arrive by 11 P.M. to meet him, and we would work together until after one in the morning. In the middle of the night, in the darkness of the 49ers training complex, Udo would break up the lactic acid that had built up in my muscles. He would undo the damage that had been wrought earlier that day. He would massage me until I left the training facility feeling as if I could have played another game right then. I'd stay around the training facility

R
O
M
O

until three or four in the morning, studying video tape of the game we had just played, trying to get ahead of the work week before it even kicked off.

I'd see Udo again on Monday, and this became our routine throughout my career in San Francisco. He would meet me at our team hotel the night before games for a pregame massage, meet me at the training facility for a postgame massage, be there during the week for constant massage.

Physically, I felt as good as I could possibly feel, and there always seemed to be a solution to any challenges my body faced. But spiritually, there was a part of me that wanted to share my life with a woman, a partner.

In May 1991, I continued playing in all the charity basketball games that I did around Northern California with my 49ers teammates. I lived off these games, earning $200 a pop, playing as many as five times in a week. During one of them against the Los Angeles Rams at Selland Arena in Fresno, this long-haired, knockout brunette walked in and I was mesmerized. She stole my attention away from the game.

I never got to introduce myself to her at the game: The crowds were too large and I lost her. But fortunately, when I walked into the nightclub Beethoven's after the game, I noticed her again. I thought, *Wow! Who is that woman?*

She thought, *Who is this guy wearing a white sweatshirt, Madras shorts and Tevas in a nice nightclub?* It took me a few minutes to muster the courage to introduce myself. But once I did, I found out her name was Julie Lagrand. She was from Fresno, a nutrition major at Fresno State. Needless to say, we had a lot to discuss.

"What business are you in?" Julie asked, which told me how much of an impression I'd made on her earlier in the evening, when she hadn't even noticed me at the game.

"I play football."

Julie, as it turned out, was a big football fan—another big plus.

"What position?" she asked.

"Linebacker."

"Inside or outside?"

That was all I needed to hear—she knew the difference between an outside and inside linebacker. We hit it off. She was beautiful, smart, funny—and she pushed my buttons. Fifteen minutes into our conversation, she nonchalantly asked, "Do you have a light?"

When she saw that my stomach had just about dropped to the floor over the possibility that she smoked, she laughed. I exhaled. She had a great sense of humor.

After we closed out the bar, I gave her a piggyback ride to her car and we made plans for the next morning, breakfast at the Fresno hotel where I was staying. I didn't tell her I was supposed to be going back to Milpitas that night and instead stayed over with the sole purpose of spending time with her. She wasn't sure what type of guy she would encounter in the morning, but when she showed up at my door and went to knock on it, she noticed a room service tray on the floor. On it were the remnants of a hamburger and a virtually empty glass of milk instead of a bottle of Jim Beam. Of course. Milk. Her gut instinct was validated. This might work.

We had breakfast, talked all morning; we fit together like San and Francisco. We connected. There was chemistry. We both knew we had found somebody important, somebody we wanted to see regularly. Over the next eighteen-plus months, Julie and I went on only six dates. There was only one hang-up—a battle within myself about whether I would be able to share my career, my football, and my training with a woman. I knew society's high divorce rate, and I knew the struggles that my brothers and sister had gone through in their marriages. For some reason, I

R
O
M
O

was always around a lot of divorces, and it made me concerned, fearful even, especially with the life I lived. I didn't have much room for people, especially those with normal lives. I knew it would take somebody different and deep inside. I always hoped I would meet somebody who could capture my heart the way football had.

Fortunately I always had my family. During the off-seasons, I would try to do some hunting with my two brothers who lived in Dallas and my dad, who had moved with Mom back to Ohio. While I was opposed to hunting when I was younger, now I saw it as a good break from training, but more important, a better reason for all of us to get together: some male bonding.

During April 1990, Glen and I flew from San Jose to Dallas to meet up with the Romanowski men for a little hunting trip. We rented a cabin about four hours west of Dallas and set out to drive there at 6 A.M. Not more than a mile from our place, Joe looked along the road and started shouting, "Boar! Boar!" Fifty yards away, there they were—three wild boar. Huge ones.

Being that you're not allowed to shoot roadside, Joe pulled the truck to the side of the road and Glen and I jumped into the back. I grabbed my AK-47 and my 30 clip, Glen grabbed his Uzi and his 20 clip, and we took aim. We knew that at the sound of a single gunshot, the boar would take off. "Lenny," I said, "you get the one on the left, I'll get the two on the right. And we'll shoot on the count of three."

One . . . two . . . and then, well, I started firing away. Me—always wanting to get the edge. We unloaded 50 rounds at these boar, filling the trunk of the truck with shells and the bodies of the boar with bullets. Before they could even move, they were dead. Lenny and I jumped out of the truck, ran to our prey, and began pulling them by their hoofs toward our truck. Just when we got them there, a heavyset woman pulled up and started screaming at us.

"What are you idiots doing?!" she yelled.

"What are we doing?" my brother Joe said. "We're killing wild boar."

"Those aren't wild boar! Those are Martha Cash's prize pigs!"

Prize pigs that were best in show at last year's Cotton Bowl.

That explained why the animals never moved when the shots started ringing out. That explained the nipples we noticed when we dragged the animals back to the car. They were pigs as much as they could be pigs. And we were the pigs who killed the pigs.

Moments later, the sheriff's deputy arrived on the scene and brought us to the town's police station. But we got real lucky there. When the sheriff's deputy brought us in and explained to the sheriff what happened, he and the rest of the policemen were more interested in getting my autograph. I signed as many as they wanted and got off relatively easy. We wound up paying $800 so Martha Cash could buy herself some new pigs. For the rest of our hunting trip, every time someone in town saw us, they would say, "Uh-oh . . . better lock up your pets."

The same could have been true back in the Bay Area. On our bye week, me, Kevin Fagan, Pierce Holt, Jim Burt, Wesley Walls, Mitch Donahue, and Keith DeLong would go on hunting trips. We shot rifles, hunted birds, but mostly, we bonded and laughed and escaped the pressures of the game. But hunting never was something that felt good to me; it was all about being around my teammates, or my brothers and Dad. Any time I've done it since then, and there haven't been many, it hasn't left me with a good feeling about myself. But back then, I was in a different place.

R
O
M
O

• • •

Back on the football field, even though I now was a full-time starter, San Francisco no longer was Shangri-la.

During one practice, my own teammate Bubba Paris pushed me in the back after I had beaten him on a play, something he did as regularly as eating. Bubba had mastered cheap shots on players. Others might have stood for it, but I didn't. I went right back at him. Belted him in the head with a punch that Coach Seifert witnessed. He threw me out of practice for hitting one of my teammates, the first but not the last time it would happen.

Our season did not go much better, especially against the New York Giants. The Giants had the toughest tight end tandem in the league, Mark Bavaro and Howard Cross. Bavaro's arms were bigger than my thighs. When I lined up against him, every play was like wrestling a steer. After the first play, it felt like the fourth quarter. All I could think was, *How am I going to make it through this game against this ox?*

And when Mark wasn't in the game, Howard was. Whereas Mark had bulk to his arms, Howard had length. He had the longest arms of anybody I've ever seen. They practically hung down to his ankles. He could use those arms to shield me in a way no other blocker I've gone against could. I would be fully extended, fighting him like mad, and it was like he was toying with me, effortlessly, his arms cropped close to his body. I never had to worry about Howard catching the football, but I couldn't stop worrying about how he was going to embarrass me with his blocking.

In our first game against New York in December, a 7–3 victory, neither of those tight ends turned out to be my biggest concern. My biggest concern was that I had suffered another head injury, according to my medical reports.

3 Dec. 1990

Dr. Klint/e

Late in the 4th quarter of tonight's game was transiently stunned while making a tackle. He was dazed for a brief period of time. Walked off the field on his own. He had no amnesia and except for some immediate light-headedness had no other neurological symptoms. He was allowed to return and finish the game.

Cc: Lindsy McLean, SF49ers, 4949 Centennial, Santa Clara, CA 95054

Must have been something about the Giants. In our January 1991, NFC Championship game rematch against them, I got hit hard and felt the effects of the blows long afterward. It happened midway through the fourth quarter, on a third-down play. I got the wind knocked out of me, but I don't remember how it happened, since I took so many hits from Mark and Howard. But I do remember that I virtually crawled to our sideline, sucking in air, unable to talk. I tried to, but nothing came out of my mouth. I knew I was supposed to stay in the game on the punt return team, and I tried to motion to our special teams coach Lynn Stiles to tell him. Only he didn't notice me waving at him.

On the ensuing punt, when we had only ten players on the field—with me being the guy that was supposed to be out there but wasn't—the Giants called for a fake punt. Their linebacker, Gary Reasons, took off and ran 30 yards with the ball in the play that swung the momentum of the game. The Giants converted my mistake and their fake punt into a 38-yard Matt Bahr field goal that trimmed our lead to 13–12.

Later in the quarter, Giants defensive tackle Erik Howard plowed into Roger Craig, producing the fumble that Lawrence

R
O
M
O

Taylor recovered and New York converted into a game-winning 42-yard field goal on the final play of the game.

Everyone around San Francisco blamed Roger for the loss. They should have blamed me—the guy who wasn't where he needed to be. Had I not gotten hurt, had I been on the field when the Giants ran the fake punt, they would not have been able to build the momentum they did. We would have had a chance to win our third straight Super Bowl.

Losing never goes over big anywhere. But it was especially despised in San Francisco, where Super Bowls were the standard. The 49ers reacted angrily and accordingly. In the off-season, they jettisoned both Ronnie Lott and Roger Craig, cut them as if their prior contributions meant little. This did not go over real well with the players, not at all. Everybody knew that any of us could be next. Pressure and insecurities only grew. Mine especially. Maybe it shouldn't have been a surprise, but with their second-round pick in the 1991 draft, the 49ers drafted the incredibly fast Clemson linebacker Johnny Johnson. They picked him to take my position, no questions about that. More fear set in. No matter how well I played, it never seemed to go away.

Our frustration really boiled up the next season when our record dropped to 2–3 after we lost to the Raiders, the team that had signed both Ronnie and Roger. In our locker room after the game, Charles Haley just went berserk. Throwing chairs. Kicking lockers. Screaming curses. "How could they let them go!?" Haley yelled, again and again. Near the end of his rant, he stuck his fist through a window. Blood splattered across the locker room. There was so much of it, and Charles was in such bad condition, our trainers had to call the Raiders trainers for assistance to get stitches in his arm. Our guest locker room had to be cleaned up.

Shortly after the game, Coach Seifert called a number of the top guys on the team—Jerry Rice, Steve Young, Pierce Holt, Kevin Fagan, me—into his office. He looked at each of us and told us, "I need more out of you." Even though I was giving him everything I had, I understood his message. We weren't getting it done. We needed some more leaders to step up: At times when the atmosphere was tight, these were the players who knew how to lighten the mood in the locker room.

One time, we pooled together money and told our trainer, Lindsy McLean, that if he took off his wig—a sight none of us had ever seen—we would give him $2,000. No one ever thought he would do it. But he went into the back room, came out bald as a basketball, and our entire locker room erupted. I've never heard so many people laugh so hard. The laughter was so loud—guys standing on taping tables and clapping, players slapping their lockers in hysteria—that the coaches actually had to come downstairs from their offices to tell us to quiet down. Lindsy got his money, and we got a little relief.

Others also knew how to cope with the tension that stifled the building. It was so refreshing to have a linebackers coach like Bob Zeman, who'd replaced Coach McPherson when he was promoted to defensive coordinator. In the early 1960s Coach Zeman had played defensive back for six seasons in Los Angeles, San Diego, and Denver, so he was one of the only assistants who understood what it was like to be a player.

When other coaches would get stressed out during practice, Coach Zeman always would provide some calmness. He would just say, "If you're supposed to be perfect in practice, and you can't make a mistake, then why are you even practicing? Isn't that why we're practicing—so we can get it right?" Eventually

R
O
M
O

that season, we did. What happened was everybody stopped worrying about who was not there and started worrying about himself. Once that happened, we went on a run in which we won our final six games.

In our last game of the season, we blew out the Chicago Bears 52–14, just kicking the crap out of them. By then we were playing better than any team in football. But the shame of it was we didn't make the playoffs, not even with our 10–6 record.

Though the mood improved at the end of the season, it still wasn't anywhere close to what it was when I showed up as some naïve rookie. The pressure was mounting, the stress elevating. Some players were being shipped out. Others simply wanted out.

THE JOYS OF FATHERHOOD AND THE PERILS OF PHENTERMINE

While our team was slipping, my relationship with Julie was growing. More and more, I found, she dominated my thoughts. Sometimes I wondered if it was too good to be true because the closer I got to make a decision about uniting our futures, the more my fears cropped up.

I worried that with a family, I wouldn't be able to give both it and my career the time each needed. One, if not both, would have to suffer, I figured. I didn't believe or think that I could be the best husband when I already was having a big-time affair with football. Balance was something that never really existed for me. It was all or nothing. And at the time, I was head over heels in love with football, and I didn't know if I could share the love with anybody else. Football was my dream, and now I was being asked to divide my loyalties.

But it became clear from the moment I met Julie that she was a remarkable person. She knew about my sport and didn't seem to be awed by it. We had hours and hours of conversation on the phone. We talked about spirituality, we talked about life and our dreams. As I think about it, I realize all I was doing was putting her through a test like I put myself through a test to get ready for a season. On some level, I never felt good enough, and I'm sure on some level I was scared that she wasn't going to be good enough. Unconsciously I was probably trying to find enough wrong with her so I could bail before I got too close to her or got hurt.

But the more I got to know Julie, the more she seemed so sincere, so ideal. It forced me to admit that I was falling in love and I had found the person I was looking for. So I did the best I could. I continued asking Julie for her patience, for her consideration, for our future. "I'm like a CD," I promised her. "I will mature."

On November 22, 1992, in a road game against the Rams, Los Angeles' tight end Pat Carter kicked my ass all over the field. Even if I knew the play that was coming, he still reached me before I could reach the ball. When the football went outside, I could not escape his blocks. Five times I got turned around, abused, whipped. A friggin' embarrassment, that's all I can say.

One of the worst parts about playing a poor game in the NFL is that the next day, your teammates see it. They have no idea as the game is unfolding that you've embarrassed yourself on the field. But they see it the next day in the film room, and it's a horrible feeling. Imagine if your mistakes are reviewed in living color with public critiques from your bosses.

Worse, when I played a bad game—which fortunately wasn't that often—Coach McPherson would be so disgusted that he wouldn't even talk to me. He wouldn't call me Smiley, wouldn't call me Num-Nuts, wouldn't call me anything. When

I needed him most is when he punished me with avoidance. He would just cut me off, like I had wronged him. I loved that man; he was the one who stood up for me on draft day and convinced the 49ers to select me. He was the one who first taught me the technique that became such a part of my game. I had a special bond with him, like I did with all my linebackers coaches. But at times like those, when I felt the pressure strangling me, I also hated that man. He knew how to play with my mind and my emotions. When he wouldn't talk to me, it hurt me deeply.

To say I was mortified wouldn't be exactly right. I was more petrified. It goes back to the insecurities that every player feels. Now mine were heightened. A million thoughts were popping into my head. Julie . . . my future with my contract scheduled to expire after the season. But most of all . . . was I regressing as a player?

With so many thoughts swimming in my mind, I violated one of my basic principles to never let anything or anyone distract me from my priorities. Maybe it should not have been any surprise that the game I played against the Cowboys in the NFC Championship on January 17, 1993, was not much better than the one I played earlier in the season against the Rams. Again, I was just ordinary—missing some tackles, botching some plays, costing our team. A linebacker bred to be so strong felt unbelievably weak.

When some athletes get beat the way I did that season, they find an excuse and never accept that the opponent was better. Not me. In November, Pat Carter was better than me, much better than me, and in January, some Cowboys I faced were. This told me I had to work harder. I had to become more intense. I had to find other training methods.

In the interim, I had a problem. At the time my production was down, my contract was up. I was free to sign with another team. But outside of Washington and San Francisco, there

R
O
M
O

weren't many teams that wanted me. I visited Washington, talked with San Francisco, debated my future. And here was my bottom line—read into the situation: My life already had enough going on without introducing a move to a new city for a new job with a new team.

So, I re-signed with San Francisco—then sought to sign off on my biggest move yet.

On February 7, 1993, I called Julie to share my heart: her CD had matured. It was now, finally, ready to be cashed in. Since the night we met about twenty-one months earlier, we each had endured a torrent of emotions, but we knew it would be worth it. With plenty to discuss, I flew her from Fresno to San Jose for a candlelight dinner that I spent all day preparing: salad, baked potato, bacon-wrapped filets, and a bottle of red wine. We talked for a long time. I asked for her understanding and told her this was what I wanted all along. I wanted her to be an even more meaningful part of my life than football.

Soon after, our romance wasn't on the fast track. It was on the Bullet Train. The next weekend, we went away with John and Amy Steed to Bodega Bay. We visited Julie's family in Fresno together. We spent every weekend together. We went ring shopping together. We could not get enough of each other.

On March 16, the night we returned to my house after another charity basketball game, we walked out back, where flickering lights surrounded the East Bay. Facing the water and the stars, I asked Julie, "Will you make me the happiest man in the world and marry me?" Crying, she nodded yes.

The first call went to Julie's mom. "Hey, Mom," I asked her. "What do you think about us getting married in Hawaii?"

"That sounds great!" she answered. "Give us about a year to plan it."

Only there was a problem. Julie refused to live with me until we were married. And I did not want to go through another football season without her, no way. We flipped open the calendar and realized May was for minicamps, June was for passing camps, July was for training camp. That left April, only April. Suddenly, happiness turned into sheer craziness. Julie's mom stepped in and was an enormous help in the wedding planning. We located an idyllic setting—Kapalua Bay, in Hawaii, at sunset. We found a free date—April 24, 1993, a little more than five weeks away.

Ordinarily, planning weddings presents its own inherent set of stresses. But ours was even more complicated. Our wedding in Hawaii marked the first time that Julie would meet my family. My family was taken aback slightly by the pace at which I was proceeding, but I knew what was right. Julie was right.

During our week in Hawaii, we chartered boats, went snorkeling, attended luaus—her family and my family, all of us together. On the day of our wedding, it rained. Some interpreted it as a sign; we did. Rain in the Hawaiian culture is a blessing.

I was determined to make our marriage that way. When I thought about being a husband, when we first got married, all I could think of was the people I've known who have been through divorces. I didn't want to have that happen to me. I considered divorce a failure, and I didn't want to fail at marriage. So I read all the relationship books I could, trying to be a better man, a better communicator, a better lover, trying to understand everything it took to become a Pro Bowl husband. Even today, I still work so hard at it, wanting to do better and better. Julie could see my passion for our relationship—and for my job.

Almost immediately, she got an idea of what her new life would be like. As she stood on the grass of the beautiful resort

ROMO

where we were staying, I asked her to pretend she was a tight end while I practiced my reads and drops. "Are you crazy?" she asked.

"No. This is what you need to do. Line up, step to the left, step to the right . . ." This was what I needed to do—constantly work on my game, striving for improvements.

Though Julie could have fought my antics and requests, she didn't. She went along. While most couples watch movies together, Julie and I would watch game films. Heck, she watched so many she could recognize offensive formations! She did everything for me. She made me whole. She was my blessing.

But then, an even larger one visited our lives in July. After craving lima beans and sweet potatoes throughout our visit to my childhood friend John Steed's relative's house in Virginia, Julie found out something that stole our breath. She was pregnant. How about that for a perfect trifecta? In five months, we had gotten engaged, married, and pregnant. Talk about a whirlwind.

If my head weren't already spinning, it was by the start of training camp. On one of the first days, I absorbed a hit that left me with another concussion and another entry into my medical records with the 49ers.

July 27, 1993

William Romanowski was evaluated on 7/23/93. As you are aware, he is a 27 year old man with a history of a period of loss of consciousness for approximately 10 seconds occurring 7/22/93. This happened as he was struck in the helmet on the right frontal region. The patient's helmet slid into the right eye area. The patient awoke and has complained of headaches since.

The patient also this morning had nausea and vomiting. He has some minimal blurred vision with up or down gaze with binocular vision. The patient for the last several hours has felt better and no nausea or vomiting has recurred.

IMPRESSION: It appears this individual has had a mild to moderate concussion. The patient's resulting post traumatic headaches may have had a vascular component and this may be related to the previous nausea, vomiting, and brief period of epistaxis. It would be recommended that the patient have a day off practice and resume activities as tolerated. If the vision symptoms should persist, re-evaluation by myself or ophthalmology may be indicated. However, if the patient continues to feel well I would think in the next few days he could resume normal activities and continue on the Naprosyn 500 mg b.i.d.

Dr. Richard N. Sauer
Roseville, Calif.

Meanwhile, my frustration and anger rose. It began to match the mood of the organization, which had not sniffed a Super Bowl in three long seasons, since my second season in the league. At a time that I should have been relaxed—I was a married, soon-to-be father—I was anything but. Anything could set me off. A few things did. One day at our training facility, I went after our running back Dexter Carter, all 160 pounds of him, like he was on another team. Boy, did he piss me off that day.

Back then, the team kitchen had one microwave that worked in slow motion. This thing was a piece of junk. If you stuck one item in it took five long minutes to cook. If you stuck another item in, it took quadruple the time—seemingly forever. Well, I put my meatball sandwich in there and then, moments later, Dexter walked in and put his sandwich in too. Without saying a word, I opened the door, removed his sandwich, and began to reheat mine. He proceeded to open the door, again, and try to put in his sandwich, again.

At which point, I grabbed him by the neck, ripped off his necklace, pinned him up against the Coke machine, and threatened to kill him. Over a heated meatball sandwich.

But really, it was more than that. We didn't have much time to eat at lunch, and I always wanted to get a lift in at that time. Dexter was messing with my schedule. In my anger, I trashed the microwave, so neither he nor anybody else could use it. I had to buy Dexter a new necklace, which he didn't need, and a new microwave for the team, which we did need.

Coach Seifert tried to use it as a motivational tool. Before the next game against New Orleans, Coach said he wanted everyone to play with the same intensity as Romo throwing that microwave. I'm not sure it worked, though—we lost the game.

So I did some things that, even I would admit, really were personally embarrassing. To the surprise of nobody on my team, sometimes I even would become a multiple offender in the same game. Most notably in our divisional game in January 1994, against the New York Giants.

After one play, when then-Giants' wide receiver Ed McCaffrey was lying on the ground, I walked over and cleated his nuts. Stepped on them pretty hard. And he didn't stay on the ground too long after that. Ed jumped up and shouted, "Screw you!"—a real surprise coming from such a usually polite guy.

"You little wussy," I told him as I walked away, knowing I got him good.

When I was at the bottom of the pile after another play in the same game, and I reached to rip the football out of the hand of Giants running back Dave Meggett, all I could get a good grip on was his finger. So I just grabbed it and *crrraaaccckkk*. Broke it like a chicken bone. I could hear him scream in agony. Oblivious, I got up and headed back to our huddle as if nothing happened. My thinking was, *Dave Meggett's finger is broken, and now he is going to have a little trouble catching the ball out of the backfield. Good. Better for our team. Helps our chances of winning*—which we did, 44–3.

My aggressiveness had reached new heights. It wasn't about me trying to get better any longer; now it was about me being scared of getting worse. The behaviors that I relied on to get better now were turned toward not allowing me to fail. Now it no longer was about a dream to be the best. It was about holding off the dragons as long as I could.

In San Francisco, I'd always take one Phentermine before the game and then, on the days I felt dead, listless, I'd come in at halftime and feel like I would need a little more. I'd take another half and tell myself, "Man, pick up your game." Sometimes, on the worst days, I'd even take an additional whole Phentermine at halftime, for that extra little boost I needed. I didn't yet realize that there are days when you can take whatever you want, but if you're not on, you're not going to be, no matter what you try.

There were also days when I took too much Phentermine. It happened during the January 1994 NFC Championship game against Dallas, our rematch against the Cowboys. Before the game, I took two Phentermine, more than I had for any one game. Julie noticed it when I got home that night, wired beyond words. "I don't like it, Billy. Whatever you're doing, you better stop it. Now! It's not my value system."

When I first told her about my game-day preparations, the name I used was Adipex, not Phentermine. Same thing, really. Right away, she went to her Physicians' Desk Reference that she had from Fresno State. Thousands of pages of descriptions of prescription drugs. She flipped open to the A's. She looked up Adipex. She read about it and learned the NFL was a different

R
O
M
O

world than she or most fans knew. She always wanted me to get off it.

After a while, I had to admit, she had a point. Anyone who looked at the tape of that NFC Championship game versus Dallas could tell I couldn't handle my Phentermine any longer. My play did not resemble that of the linebacker that led the 49ers in tackles in 1990, 1992, and 1993, as I did. My play resembled that of the linebacker who could not crack the starting lineup in 1989.

The team asked me to match up on Cowboys running back Emmitt Smith out of the backfield, and it didn't work. He was running routes that were difficult for me to defend. All game long, there were missed assignments, missed tackles. A missed chance. Awful, that's how I would describe my game, just awful. Instead of putting me in this intense zone, the Phentermine actually took me out of it. I had trouble remembering what defenses were called. I had difficulty reacting to plays. I didn't know where I was supposed to be. That game proved that Phentermine wasn't for me, not any longer.

Now, it also didn't help that two days before that game, Coach Seifert changed our entire defensive game plan. For reasons I still don't understand, he came to our unit the Friday before kickoff and told our defense that we would be playing a zone-man concept, which we hadn't all season. Guys were like, *What? What are we doing? Zone-man?*

After we lost our second consecutive NFC Championship game to Dallas, 38–21, it was clear we had lost our way. But after spending six seasons in San Francisco, I had a clue about what was next: get out. If they had gotten rid of Ronnie Lott, Roger Craig, Charles Haley, and Joe Montana, then I knew enough about our business to know the truth. They would be fixing to get rid of me.

After the season, they even got rid of Coach Zeman. He was

fired, as if he were the reason we lost the NFC Championship. When he came down into the training room to tell me the news, I remember being part angry, part disillusioned, thinking: *Anyone can be made into a scapegoat.* This time he was. But when you're in the NFL long enough, you realize it's just a matter of time before you're the next casualty.

Fortunately, Julie's pregnancy provided something important for me to focus on, so not all my worries were funneled into football. Each night I would read different children's books to her belly, play classical music, and do what Udo had taught me. I would softly rub her midsection, massaging it in the most gentle way possible. I would talk to her belly so much, I expected our child to know me when he came into this world.

I loved the idea of becoming a father, just like I loved the way Julie looked. To me, pregnant women are the most beautiful women on the face of the planet. They give off such a vibrant energy that it's hard not to smile around them.

On March 15, I rushed Julie to Stanford Hospital. Our boy Dalton entered the world at nine pounds eleven ounces. It was such a miracle, I started to cry. Just lost it. How could you not? There is nothing like witnessing the birth of a child, nothing. In between sobs, I looked over at my wife and asked, "How are you feeling, Jules?"

But the strangest thing happened when I asked the question. As soon as my voice sounded, Dalton's eyes darted over to me, to the sound he had heard in Julie's belly for months. My son and I locked eyes for the first time—my first mental snapshot of him. There were plenty more to come, such as when we brought Dalton home.

It was such a beautiful time in my life—but it also marked the start of a month unlike any other I've experienced. Soon, I heard the 49ers were shopping me around the league, trying to rid themselves of the $1.5 million salary they owed me when

ROMO

they were only $100,000 under the NFL's $34.6 million salary cap. I remember at one point running into Dwight Clark, who at the time was assistant to our GM, John McVay. He told me if only I'd take a million-dollar pay cut, we could work things out. Then, on the morning of the 1994 draft, McVay called me as I was driving to an autograph session for the team. "Bill, I want to thank you for the last six years," McVay told me. "But you have just been traded to the Eagles." My head was spinning as I went ahead with the signing, putting my name and number on all that 49er merchandise. It was a mind-bender. All I could think was, *I'll get them. I'll make them realize this was the worst decision they'd ever made.* I had a new baby at home and a wife who was nursing him. It was a time for stability, not this. But that was life in the NFL and the pressures players live with daily— you never know what's coming next.

(To his credit, I saw Dwight recently at a golf tour and he told me I was right and he was wrong, which was probably why he wasn't in the NFL anymore. I'm not sure about that, but I appreciated the gesture.)

Just like that, for third- and sixth-round draft choices, my time in San Francisco expired. Admittedly, it was the greatest time any young player could want. For my indoctrination into the NFL, I got to be around one of the best owners, some of the best coaches, some of the all-time greatest players, in a championship organization. I walked away with two Super Bowl rings, and the knowledge of what it took to win more. I was exposed to so much in my six years in San Francisco and my dreams got full rock-star treatment. They were serviced completely and entirely. But now it was time to assemble new dreams in a new city for a new organization. I treated the trade as if it were expected, as if this were just another wave to ride. "They don't want me here. I'll go make a name for myself there," I told Julie. "I'll make the best of it. This will be a good thing, you'll see."

I blew off any grief I was feeling; Julie couldn't. She reacted angrily, practically wanting to break the fingers of any 49ers front office executive. But this wasn't unusual. In time, she grieved enough for both of us whenever something went wrong. When you think about it, that's not surprising. If we don't deal with certain feelings, we tend to get them out of somebody else. I got mine out of Julie. She took all our 49ers sweatpants and hats and vowed that we never would wear them again. She purged our closets of all 49ers paraphernalia.

It was, understandably, tough on her. We had to pack our young family, leave her family, and move three thousand miles across the country to a city where we would be starting fresh. To top it off, the day we were traded to Philadelphia was April 24, one year to the day we exchanged wedding vows. Happy first anniversary.

Before we left, I said my good-byes to the coaches, to my teammates, to the first team that allowed me to enjoy the moments I did. One of the hardest good-byes was to Coach McPherson. I walked into his office and dropped a gift-wrapped box on his desk. "I want you to have this," I told him.

"What's this?"

"Please open it."

Coach McPherson looked at me, then the box. As he opened it, he looked like he was about to faint. Inside was a money clip with a football made of diamonds on the front of it. "Nobody's ever done anything like this for me," Coach said.

It was the least I could do for someone who had taught me so much. Now it was time to pack up what I'd learned and go to the City of Brotherly Love, which was in a time zone so different it may as well have been on another planet.

ROMO

7 PHILADELPHIA: JUST DO IT ON SUNDAY, BABE

When I watched the tape of my performance during my last season in San Francisco, I didn't like what I saw. I looked slow, felt slow, played slow. I wondered throughout the whole season, *Why am I so flat?* Thinking back now, I know. I didn't train the right way. I trained hard, but not right. For example, we were not a big lifting team in San Francisco. The 49ers' strength coach Jerry Attaway adopted the approach, "Do what you like to do because if you like it, you'll be more apt to do it. If you don't like it, you won't do it." It made sense, but Coach Attaway's real strengths dealt with nutrition and on-field football workouts, not weight-room ones.

Six to eight guys would lift regularly during the off-season, but that was it, no more. We weren't a big lifting team, we just had a lot of talented players. San Francisco's off-season program lacked the participation and intensity of others I've now seen around the NFL. My workout regimen—extensive running, light lifting, karate training—basically evolved on its own.

Before my last season in San Francisco, when I went on my free-agent visit to Washington, I spent most of the day in the weight room, listening to their strength and conditioning coach, Dan Riley, who now works with the Houston Texans. Dan taught me different things than Jerry. He preached to me the value of doing one set of ten reps for each exercise—two for the arms, and one for the chest, back, shoulders, neck, quads, hamstrings, calves, and core. The idea was to pick a weight that would be tough to lift ten times. Then once you could do it ten times, increase the weight by five pounds. But the goal was the same: Lift the weight until failure, until it could not be lifted anymore.

I liked the technique so much, I incorporated it into my weight training, but it was just one element of a program that I felt needed a complete overhaul. And now, with the change of scenery, I needed to push myself even harder. When someone tells you that you're not good enough, you're determined to prove them wrong. You're determined to show them you are.

After I hung up with McVay and Julie, my next telephone call went to my agent, Tom Condon. "Tommy, I need an edge. I really need something to make a difference. I want to go to camp in Philadelphia in great shape."

Pausing, thinking, Tom then said he knew of a man in San Diego named Benny Poda, nicknamed The Beast of the East, a former nationally ranked bodybuilder. Tom had gotten to know him after his former client, Raiders quarterback Todd Marinovich, hired him. Todd raved about Benny, and once Tom watched what Benny did with his clients, he did, too.

Once, Tom sent his client Joe Montana to Benny when Joe was nursing a hamstring injury. After only one session with Benny, Joe played golf in the afternoon and football on Sunday. Another time, Tom sent wide receiver Curtis Conway to Benny with a knee injury that prevented Curtis from running. After a

R
O
M
O

few sessions with Benny, Curtis was back on the track, running and screaming, "Oh my God!"

But the best of all might have come with Bill Maas, a former Chiefs' defensive tackle. Near the end of his career, Bill called Tom and said he wanted to play one more highly productive season and, with that goal in mind, wanted to hire a topflight training coach for the off-season. Tom sent Bill to Benny, and after a bunch of training sessions, Bill called Tom to report back on what he had encountered. "Hey, Condo," Bill said, using the nickname that Condon's clients do. "This guy Benny Poda? I think he's . . . Jesus Christ."

Once I heard these stories, I had to visit Benny. His background was equally mysterious and intriguing. When Benny became a competitive bodybuilder, he locked himself in a one-room apartment with no furniture and spent the next two full years studying health, eating right, and lifting weights, all day long. Every day. In the same apartment. For two years straight.

Benny sounded unusual enough to be made up. Only he wasn't. He was as real as the two days I spent with him in San Diego, training. What a mind-blowing experience. Benny tore apart my already healthy diet and acted like I had been consuming nothing but fast food. He wrote me up a new diet, which I took to Philadelphia with me.

From now on, Benny wanted me to eat steak three times a day and fertile eggs. Only fertile eggs. Lots of fertile eggs. His contention was that they contained energy, life, little dots of blood—the dots that eventually turned into little chickens. Eating little chickens, in his mind, was especially beneficial. Benny also handed me some little black pellets that he called Minh Mang. Now, I'm aware that Minh Mang was some king in Vietnam who ruled in the 1800s for twenty years. But Benny's Minh Mang were herb mixes designed to make you stronger. Don't even ask me what was in them, I have next to no idea. They had some ginseng, along with some substances that would pass any NFL drug test—or so I was told.

Benny also told me some incredible stories. In some Eastern land far away from civilization, Benny said he would fight his master until Benny was on the brink of death and seeing white flashes. Then he would have forty-five minutes to use Minh Mang and acupuncture to bring himself back to life. Otherwise, he was gone. Dead.

Benny did some really amazing things. He actually told me about hanging hundred-pound dumbbells from his scrotal sack. I never saw him do it, but I don't have any doubts he did. Just think—aren't there karate masters who chop thick blocks of wood in half with their bare hands? Aren't there other trained experts who can kick in cement blocks with their bare feet? Odd as it sounds, why can't Benny hold up one hundred-pound dumbbells with his scrotal sack? The mind is a powerful thing.

Listening to him, you would think he could do anything. Benny spoke with passion, conviction, preaching the value of dedication and motivation. When he sensed some of those traits already were instilled in me, he told me, "The sky is the limit for you, brother."

And that was it; I was off. After two days holed up in San Diego, I returned home feeling like a different person. As soon as I got home, I opened our refrigerator and with Julie looking on, began yanking items out of it. "Can't have this," I said, pulling out the non-fertile eggs and tossing them in the garbage. "Can't have that," I said, pulling out the bread and tossing that in the garbage, too.

"What are you doing?" Julie asked.

"Exactly what Benny Poda told me to do."

R
O
M
O

I filled our refrigerator with steak and fertile eggs. Our cabinets got stocked with Minh Mang. Julie did not like any of this. This didn't bode well.

Over time, I couldn't strictly adhere to Benny's program—there were too many struggles between Benny's ways and Julie's. Day to day it got hard, to the point where there were some practices I could follow, others not so much.

Since then, I don't know too many other athletes who have visited with Benny. Tom Condon told me the last time he saw Benny was late one night when he was watching a Chuck Norris movie and Benny was standing next to Chuck. When Tom asked around to see where he might be able to find him, he was told that Benny is now living in a cave, presumably in some faraway Eastern land.

Sometimes a simple drive leads us to unintended, fateful places. When I pulled into a truck stop along I-95 after arriving in Philadelphia, I thought my only purchases would be gas and water. But when I went inside to pay and looked down at the displays set up in front of the cashier, I noticed little round white pills I didn't recognize.

"What's that?" I asked the cashier.

"Mini-thins," he told me, matter of fact. "Ephedrin." What truck drivers used to stay awake at night. It got them going, like a strong coffee. As it turns out, it also got a lot of other people going.

Before the Food and Drug Administration banned the sale of it in December 2003, Ephedra, the herbal form of Ephedrin, became a fixture in the diet pill craze of the 1990s, when people took it for losing weight, building muscle, and boosting energy. The main ingredient is the product of a million-year-old species of plant, and it was probably taken by warriors and athletes from every civilization that ever existed and fought against one another. The men of the NFL and I were certainly no exceptions to that. We would keep that going as long as we could.

Ephedrin, just like its critics say, speeds you up and makes you feel different. It works just like Phentermine, by increasing adrenaline in your brain. Some people say Phentermine gives them more energy than Ephedrin, and some say the opposite. They both gave me a feeling of having more energy. But, like I said, it was probably more the feeling of having an edge that made it seem like a worthwhile thing to do.

Upon arriving in Philadelphia, I heard about it and thought it sounded good. Ephedrin was not banned in the NFL (not until before the start of the 2001 season), so I bought some. Before my first Eagles' spring minicamp practice, I took some.

Looking back on it, I wish I'd been more confident and believed just a little more in my training, skills, and preparation so I wouldn't have taken it. It may have made me better in some games and worse in others.

What was clearly better were the aftereffects. Coming down off it wasn't nearly as harsh. It lifted me up but, once it wore off, I didn't crash quite as hard. I wouldn't be wired straight through Tuesday night. I wouldn't go sleepless for two straight nights. I liked the Ephedrin enough that I kept buying it during my two seasons in Philadelphia and on into my days in Denver, up until the league banned it.

The league got rid of it after former Minnesota Vikings offensive tackle Korey Stringer tragically suffered heat stroke in the summer 2001 training camp and died. People blamed his death on Ephedrin, but from what I heard, Korey was trying to lose weight and became dehydrated when he took Ephedrin. For me, Ephedrin had its benefits, especially when used properly. It worked for me.

But in Philadelphia, I fortunately got turned on to more

ROMO

than Ephedrin. Unable to move Udo to Philadelphia, I found a new massage therapist, a man named Craig who provided his own benefits. Like Udo, I arranged for Craig to come to our training facility, to work on me and some of the guys. He brought his own strengths to the massage table, maybe the biggest being his awareness of nutrition.

As I lay on my stomach, Craig handed me a book to read. To this day, I still remember the book because it blew me away. *Optimum Sports Nutrition: Your Competitive Edge,* by Dr. Michael Colgan. It explained every vitamin, mineral, amino acid, fad health food, and sports supplement. It overwhelmed me. Everything in this book—Zinc, Vitamin C, vitamins I hadn't heard of—seemed like something I needed to take. Everything in the book introduced me to a world that, up until then, I had no idea existed.

How little I knew embarrassed me and motivated me. During every massage, I pored over the book's pages. When I was not getting a massage, I was reading Colgan's monthly column in the magazine *Muscular Development.* In addition, other strength magazines—*Testosterone, Intensity Magazine,* and *Muscle & Fitness*—riveted me and replaced any other reading I might have been doing. I subscribed to Mauro Di Pasquale's monthly *Think Muscle* newsletter, a wealth of information from the man who had created the renowned high-protein, high-fat, low-carbohydrate "Anabolic Diet." For me, a light went on. It enabled me to explore nutrition at a much higher and detailed level. In other areas, my knowledge also was multiplying.

Inside the locker room, players' lockers were filled with Met Rx protein powders, the first time I had ever seen anything like it. These were meal replacement protein drinks, used to build muscle, reduce fat, and maintain your fitness level—a delicious combination. All you had to do was pour the protein powder into water, shake everything together, and then you had an instant ready-made lunch. "Help yourself, any time," our kicker, Eddie Murray, told me when he saw me eyeing the protein packets. So I did, taking some chocolate, some vanilla, and getting my next few meals ready. Those packets instantly worked their way into my regimen.

More came from the Eagles themselves. At the same time they brought me to Philadelphia, they also brought over Baron Baptiste, the yoga trainer to Hollywood's stars. After working with clients such as Elisabeth Shue, Helen Hunt, Raquel Welch, and Eagles owner Jeffrey Lurie's wife Christina, Philadelphia named him the team's peak performance specialist. Baron has his own line of Power Yoga Videos, is a columnist for *Yoga Magazine,* and is the author of *Journey Into Power: How to Sculpt Your Ideal Body, Free Your True Self, and Transform Your Life with Yoga.*

His ideas were available to any of us, free of charge, but few players took advantage of his services. Throughout training camp, it seemed like I was one of the only players taking his classes. But that was the hang-up, right there. Even as good as Baron was, it was difficult to participate in yoga on a daily basis. I call it your Bang for the Buck: You had to pick and choose what would provide the most benefit. Yoga provided some, but not as much as other facets of my training.

There was one great thing about taking the Yoga class: Usually the only player there with me was none other than Herschel Walker. By then, he had bounced around the league and was now starting at running back for the Eagles. "Herschel," I told him the first time I met him in Philadelphia, "you will never know the impact you had on me."

"What do you mean?"

"That article in *Sports Illustrated* about the push-ups and sit-ups you did changed me forever. And I want you to know how much I appreciate you for it." I really did and I was glad to

R
O
M
O

be able to tell him. But apparently, not much had changed with Herschel. Our quarterback Bubby Brister was his roommate, and Bubby always reported to me how Herschel would stay up until two in the morning doing push-ups and sit-ups, then get up at five in the morning for more push-ups and sit-ups, as well as a prepractice five-mile jog. That just inspired me more.

My expanding fanaticism for taking care of my body was matched only by my intensity to hurt others. On Sundays, I would empty my bucket. It got to the point where I wanted to knock the crap out of people. I wanted to take them out of the game. I needed a psychological incentive, a psychological supplement. My new favorite supplement was hatred for the opposition.

Beginning on Monday, little by little, I would build up a hatred for the opposing team, the opposing coaches, the opposing players, and especially the specific player I would be matched against. I had to. The sport I played, the position I played, required me to be violent, which was not always easy for somebody who was entirely different off the field. It was a different me out there on Sunday, somebody my family and friends didn't recognize.

On Monday, I would start thinking about who I was going to play. Maybe it was going to be Giants tight end Howard Cross or, later in my career, Chiefs tight end Tony Gonzalez. Or Cowboys runningback Emmitt Smith or offensive tackle Eric Williams. Whoever it was, I just started focusing on them. And I would build up a hatred not only for them, but for everybody on the other team. I would hate their coaches, hate their fans, and hate their players to the point where I wanted to make them pay for my decreasing self-confidence. My rage was the orgasm of my fear.

By Wednesday, when I got to practice against the scout team

and a player wearing the number of the opponent I would be facing, my rage was building. I told myself, *Nobody is catching a ball on me in practice today,* and I approached every one of those practices like a real game. To me, I never practiced once; I always performed, playing the game every day in practice.

By Thursday and Friday, I could barely have conversations with people, and would answer with "yes" or "no." I was reserving all my energy in the tank for Sunday. On Saturday I'd take a three-hour nap, study, and watch more game films. I'd also eat the same meals before a game—spaghetti, salad, and chicken. This was all so ritualistic, as if I were preparing for a kill.

By Sunday, forget about it. My mouth was nearly frothing. I'd be standing there in pregame warm-ups, staring across at the players I would be going against, and I would be in a complete zone, not of this world. I would be so geeked up, nobody could talk to me. But I could talk to myself.

Under my breath, I would be muttering, "I hate you. I will knock you out. I will try to kill you. You can't block me." Again and again. As if I were some robot that could be programmed and I was commanding myself.

Bubby Brister remembers how he once approached me before our first preseason game together with the Eagles. We had become close friends, and our families had socialized. But right before that first preseason game, Bubby walked over to me and slapped my pads. And I just lifted my head real slow and looked up at him with my eye black on, like the lunatic I always turned in to on game day.

I was shaking, sweating, breathing hard, working up the fury. Bubby went, "Oh, shit! What in the hell is this?" like he had seen a werewolf. He got away from me as fast as he could, before he could get his answer. The answer was, it was me. Getting my game face on. Getting ready to go to battle.

More often than not, I had on my headphones, for that extra

bit of motivation. People would ask me all the time, What kind of music do you listen to to get into the zone to rip someone's head off? It's definitely different than people think. What gets me fired up before the game is listening to soft music, love songs. My taste ranges from Bread to Paul Anka to Elton John to Paul McCartney singing "The Long and Winding Road." Later in Denver, there was nothing I loved more than listening to John Denver's "Rocky Mountain High." In a sense, these songs represented the calm before the storm. I've actually read scientific studies stating that heavy metal is disruptive to your mindset, while the softer music is more conducive to healing and aligning. And I didn't need any more disruption. When I was wrapped tight, the music put me in a peaceful place right before I would try to decapitate the enemy.

Those battles were my version of the Crusades, with me playing to the echo of every whistle. My teammates in Philadelphia realized it right away. When we were playing Arizona, I roughed up Cardinals fullback Larry Centers at the bottom of the pile. He didn't appreciate it very much and when he had an unobstructed path to me, he threw the ball directly into my face mask. Well I didn't appreciate that.

So in return, using what George Chung had taught me in San Francisco, I kicked him five times in the head. Just went *whack, whack, whack, whack, whack!* Out on the street, I'd be charged for something like that, arrested for assault. But inside the football stadium, my punishment was being ejected (for the first and last time I might add) and fined $4,500 by the NFL—basically $900 per kick. That actually turned out to be the first time the league fined me. If I had known all the fines I would start accumulating from the NFL, I would have just set up an automatic monthly withdrawal.

As intense as I was, though, the mood surrounding the Eagles was a lot less so.

. . .

You don't know how rejuvenating it was to go from a team as tight as the IRS to a team that was practically a comedy club. In San Francisco, Coach Seifert and the rest of his assistants had turned the training complex into a giant pressure cooker. In Philadelphia, the pressure was relieved. For the first time since my first few years in San Francisco, football was fun again.

Unlike my time in San Francisco, Eagles' head coach Rich Kotite never summoned his players to his office to demand more of them. If anything, he would have told us he needed less. He was a players' coach, best suited for veterans. I loved playing for the guy. Because if you took care of your responsibilities and showed up to play Sunday, he left you alone. Every veteran wants a coach like that.

When I called Coach Kotite to see if it might be possible to miss the Eagles' May minicamp to attend my son Dalton's christening, his answer was not what I was expecting. "There is nothing more important than family," Coach said. "I want you to stay and enjoy your boy's baptism."

So my initial outlook on the Eagles was a positive one. But my next glimpse at them, not so much. From the moment we stepped into an oversized meeting to listen to Coach Kotite, my heart sank. San Francisco felt a lot farther than 3,000 miles away then.

"Our goal," Coach Kotite told us at our first team meeting, "is to hopefully make the playoffs."

I sat in that room shell-shocked, thinking: *What am I doing here? I've been with an organization that set a standard. Their goal every year is to win a championship. Now I'm playing with an organization whose goal is to make it to the playoffs— hopefully?*

To this day I'm pissed at myself that I didn't stand up right

R
O
M
O

there and shout, "That's the problem with the Philadelphia Eagles, that right there. Our goal ought to be to win a world championship, period. There is no other goal, okay? There is no rebuilding. There is no such thing."

With lower expectations came lower stress levels. Coach Kotite used to walk around at practice with a big fat cigar hanging out of his mouth, puffing away while players were huffing away. In San Francisco, if a receiver dropped a pass during practice, coaches would rip off his head and demand that the play be run again. In Philly, Coach Kotite would say, "Ah, just do it Sunday, babe." That was what he said to everybody. "Just get it on Sunday, babe."

Practice was loose, to say the least. Back when Jim McMahon played quarterback in Philadelphia from 1990–1992, players remembered how he showed up to practice wearing nothing more than cleats, a 1950's leather helmet, and a jock strap. However it happened, his attitude passed straight on down to our team. During practice, linebacker Byron Evans would drive the carts used to transport the blocking dummies and chase players around the field. Corner back Eric Allen and linebacker William Thomas would throw footballs at the defensive players, like they were back in high school.

My buddy, safety Michael Zordich and I watched and shook our heads and laughed at what was going on, every day. We couldn't believe the environment. Every day in the locker room, before we headed out to practice, I'd lean over to him and ask, "You ready to go out and watch the circus?"

It would get even crazier on gameday. At halftime of every game, I'd see defensive end Greg Townsend—who was a great guy—sitting in front of his locker, smoking cigarettes. He'd be sitting there like an NFL Puff Daddy, the whole locker room filling up with cigarette smoke and everybody coughing. Didn't matter. Greg was enjoying a good halftime smoke. When our starting quarterback, Randall Cunningham, struggled a bit early in the season, his backup Bubby offered to watch film with him and help him with his reads. Randall said no thanks, adding, "The Lord will help me with my reads."

He would say similar things to Coach Kotite during games. After one series where our offense got stopped, Coach Kotite walked up to Randall for an explanation. "They were in a cover two zone, and you threw the seven route," Kotite pointed out. "What did you see there?"

"Coach, can't you see I'm praying?" Randall responded.

Now, I have nothing against people's beliefs and religions. It's wonderful for people to have them. But there are times when your head coach is trying to talk to you and you don't sit there and tell him, "Can't you see I'm praying?"

Game plans were completely different from what I'd experienced as well. Our defensive coordinator, Bud Carson had an aggressive style to his play calling and would call blitzes on every other play. More often than not, they involved me. I rushed the quarterback more in one season in Philadelphia than I did in six in San Francisco. I really enjoyed playing for him.

The whole season was one big rush. We jumped out to a 7–2 start that included a 40–8 win at San Francisco, when we piled up a 23–0 lead the 49ers could not overcome. What stands out to me about that game is that it represented the first time in my career that I was playing against a former team. My intensity level and hatred for the 49ers was overwhelming. So overwhelming, in fact, that before the game I snuck into their locker room and took the offensive lineman's best friend—a bottle of silicone. Well, when my former teammates found out about it, they weren't too happy. "Romo, give us back the bottle!" they'd keep yelling and coming after me during the game. Sorry, fellas, you are now the enemy.

Early in the game, I slammed into tight end Brent Jones

ROMO

after he caught about a five-yard pass. As he fell to the ground, I gave him an extra shove, along with some choice words. Then I held him down so he couldn't get up. I was in my element, and I was all game.

Afterward, Coach Kotite gave me the game ball. That made my year, crushing San Francisco. But we also had other goals. We thought we were playoff bound and the media fed into it. I remember *Sports Illustrated* doing a piece on how we were Super Bowl–bound. But I guess we couldn't stand the leeway we were granted. We lost our final seven games that season and missed the playoffs.

Even though we did, and even though my former team went on to annihilate the San Diego Chargers 49–26 in Super Bowl XXIX, I wouldn't have traded places for anything. I wanted to win, of course, but it was good to have fun again and be around a good, if crazy group of guys. And with Coach Kotite on his way out, things could only get better with a new coach.

People have their drinks of choice, and teams have their performance enhancers of choice. The Eagles', clearly, were what they called Trauma I.V.s. They are supposed to be reserved for life-threatening situations such as serious car accidents. They hook you up to these Trauma I.V.s and—voilà! They bring you back from death's doorstep. You hope you never need even one in your lifetime. In Philadelphia, we got as many as we wanted. If you had an injury—a pulled hamstring, a sprained ankle, a bruised shoulder, anything—you could drive to the local hospital and get a Trauma I.V.

They would slide what they call an "8 French catheter"— not much different in size from a garden hose—into your arm and infuse you with a large amount of fluid in a short amount of time. The fluids would rush through this IV and reach you in about fifteen seconds. I don't care what the injury was, you would get up feeling fresh, feeling new. You were good to go.

Most mainstream doctors haven't even heard of Trauma I.V.s, and they couldn't venture a guess as to what they might include. I'm guessing Trauma I.V.s had butazolidan or some potent form of intravenous anti-inflammatory in them. It is an anti-inflammatory used in racehorses. A powerful prostaglandin inhibitor, it reduces a forest fire of inflammation down to ashes in a few minutes. The problem, as the FDA and the medical community found out, is butazolidan also suppresses white blood cell production in your bone marrow and can do so completely enough to cause immunodeficiency and even death.

Butazolidan was banned by the FDA in the early 70s and withdrawn from human use. It continued to be available, however, for use in horses. It's pure speculation on my part, but I think a few Eagles got some doses of that as well. But I do know those Trauma I.V.s were not glutathione, or glutathione alone, because I've had those types of I.V.s since and they didn't help me get over the soreness and pain like the Trauma I.V.s. All I know for sure is they were more powerful than any punch. Just ask one of my buddies from that Eagles team. That season, he had six of them.

Our legendary trainer, Otho Davis—who passed away in May 2000 after serving twenty-three years as the Eagles' trainer—used to push Trauma I.V.s on us all the time. And it's not like he was just some hyper-aggressive, diabolical trainer, either. He was named the Professional Trainer of the Year five times: 1977, 1978, 1980, 1981, and 1987. From 1971–1989, he served as the executive director of the National Athletic Trainers Association, and the organization's national office in Dallas is named in his honor. Otho knew what he was doing.

While I was leery, I was also intrigued. At first, I resisted them, as my 1994 medical report indicates.

R
O
M
O

10/9 Player had a rt distal lateral quad contusion, struck on the thigh by a helmet. Treated conservatively and denied a Trauma I.V. and took a dose pack anti-inflammatory.

10/24 Game against Houston. Player had a blow to the rt thigh lateral mid contusion. Like the injury two weeks ago. Player was stretched for this and received massage therapy. In the end of the third quarter the player took a severe blow to the head while attempting to make a tackle. Concussion was noted. Player failed conversion test on the field. Did see Dr. Torg and was then eliminated from play. Given oral Decadron. Denied Trauma I.V. for thigh. Was fine after the game he reported and went home.

11/20 First quarter. Hit directly in the left thigh. This was a very distal and lateral leg contusion. It was reported post game. Trauma I.V. was ordered but player did not go for it.

Like I said, I tried resisting them. But after I strained my hamstring in a 31–19 loss at Dallas on December 4 and could barely move out of bed the next morning, I acquiesced. I headed down to the hospital where my other teammates had been on a more regular basis.

12/4 Pre game warm-ups. Player felt a twinge in his left hamstring. This was upper and lateral. Able to finish the game but did need stretching and massage on the sidelines . . . Did take Trauma I.V. on 12/5 after seeing Dr. Sennet.

Let me tell you, I literally limped into the hospital on Monday. And walked out of there with no pain, feeling like it was the first day of training camp. I was so stunned with the treatment, loved it so much, that I tried another.

My Eagles' medical reports never documented it, but after I took a major hit to my thigh during a 16–13 loss to the New York Giants on December 18, 1994, I took myself straight back to the hospital for another Trauma I.V. They stuck the 8 French catheter into my arm and I watched the clear fluid stream into my body, healing my thigh. By the time I walked out of the hospital, I didn't feel it. I never felt it again.

Meeting one person often leads to the introduction of another, and another, and another, until a whole new circle of acquaintances is created from your initial introduction. Back in San Jose before I moved to Philadelphia, I met Steve Millard, who later became the strength and conditioning specialist for the NHL's San Jose Sharks. Steve would tell me about various supplements, give me certain vitamins to try, offer training tips. But his best one came after I returned to Milpitas in the 1995 off-season, when he arranged for me to train with his mentor, speed coach Remy Korchemny.

Remy was a fascinating guy who knew his craft. At the age of sixty, he was running the 40-yard dash in under 5 seconds flat. He had trained five Olympic medalists, including Valery Borzov of Ukraine, who ran for the Soviet Union in 1972 and 1976, and brought home double gold in the 1972 100-meter and 200-meter races, as well as a silver in the 4 × 400-meter relay. Remy had a twinkle in his eye that made you want to perform for him. You could tell that track was his life, not unlike football was mine. He'd rather be out on the track helping athletes than anything else. And every day when he went to the track, he was living his dream, which I loved.

The summer I met Remy, his prized pupil was sprinter Christie Gaines, who went on to win the gold in the 4 X 100-meter relay in the 1996 Olympics and bronze in 2000. To start with, Remy had me race Christie. For 40 yards, I had her . . . before she put on her jets and blazed past me. She blew me away, as did Remy with his coaching methods.

Everything I had done, everything I had learned, was squashed. My preexisting theories were obliterated. New regimens were introduced.

"What are you doing for your leg workouts?" Remy asked.

"Leg presses," I told him.

"You don't squat?"

"No, I hurt my back when I was in college."

"There's not a sprinter in the world who doesn't squat."

Hmmm, I hadn't known that. So I started squatting again, more and more weight. Finally, on the day I squatted 400 pounds, I reported back to Remy, all excited.

"Good," he said upon hearing what I thought was big news. "Now you can squat as much as my women sprinters."

That told me I had to get stronger and that I still had plenty to learn about training. Remy started teaching me. No more conditioning work, no more distance running, he insisted. From now on, it was all speed work, three days a week, two hours a day. One day it would be work on acceleration, the next work on speed endurance. Acceleration and speed endurance, that was all I worked on that off-season.

Remy had me pull a running sled for short distances, building up my burst, working on my running technique, coaching up my speed. Even during the times I could not work with Remy because I was with Julie's family in Fresno, he still had more tips. "Make sure that when you're in Fresno, you look up my friend and you can train with him while you're there," Remy said.

His Fresno friend was Randy Huntington, coach of the world's long jump record holder, Mike Powell. Randy lived in Fresno, I spent blocks of time in Fresno, and it made sense for us to work together. Where Randy really helped me was with recovery.

When I finished my workouts, he ordered me to put on a flotation device and get in the pool for thirty minutes. Floating in the deep end helped flush the lactic acid from my body. For range of motion, I also would do leg kicks like a Rockette. All the leg movements got rid of the lactic acid and prepared me to go through workouts at full strength the next day.

And when I started those workouts, Randy put me through a forty-five minute warm-up stretching routine. Forty-five minutes just for stretching! I never knew that was possible. We stretched my calves, my quads, my hamstrings, my abductors, my trunk, every muscle I used to run. Once I did it, I instantly saw and felt the value in it. From then on, I started approaching warm-ups and recovery with the intensity I had for my workouts.

Then at night, after we were done with a full day of running, it was—guess what? More stretching. Sitting with your legs straight out and reaching out to stretch your hamstrings. Lying on your back with your legs bent to do hip extensions. Doing whatever it took to make your body as limber as possible for the next day of work.

Randy even offered up his nutritional advice—take certain supplements in relation to your workouts. He had a working knowledge of nutrition, but he knew people who knew far more. He was only too happy to turn me on to them. Just as Steve introduced me to Remy . . . and Remy introduced me to Randy . . . Randy introduced me to Victor Conte Jr., the owner of Bay Area Laboratory Co-Operative, better known as BALCO Laboratories. And Victor introduced me to science.

Though Victor did not have a PhD or even a college degree, it was almost like he was a savant. Back in 1988, he provided free

ROMO

testing and supplements for a group he called "BALCO Olympians," then joined them at the Summer Games in Seoul. Minerals, that's where we started. A mineral testing kit from BALCO arrived in the mail to our new home in San Martin—about twenty miles south of San Jose—and I had to return it to him with my blood, urine, and pubic hair samples.

A local phlebotomist—a medical technician who draws blood for analysis—took care of that aspect of the test. The urine was easy enough to provide. But as I stood in the bathroom with scissors to my groin, retrieving a pubic hair sample, Julie walked in. "What the hell are you doing?" she asked. I told her.

"That's disgusting," Julie said, turning away.

Maybe so, but the process also was enlightening. After receiving and analyzing my results, Victor called me and told me more about myself than even I knew.

"I'll bet you have trouble sleeping at night; you're tossing and turning a lot," Victor said to me.

Yeah, I told him, mildly surprised. And without sleep, you can't dream.

A magnesium deficiency, he explained.

"You get light-headed sometimes in workouts, don't you?" he asked.

Yeah, I told him, even more surprised.

A chromium deficiency, he explained. Low blood sugar.

"Do your knees and shoulders and joints hurt as much as I think?" he asked.

Yeah, I told him, shaking my head.

Not enough copper in my system, he explained.

"Trouble keeping your testosterone levels up?"

Trouble? Big trouble.

Zinc, he explained. Zinc is one of the most anabolic minerals available. Without it, your body cannot produce the maximum amount of testosterone. Victor explained it all to me. He said, "You're deficient in all these minerals, and you are depriving yourself of reaching peak performance."

What he said was an extension of what Remy would tell me during our training sessions. "You don't get better on the track," Remy constantly would say. "You get better at night, after you go to bed. You get better when you are resting and recovering for the next workout. That's when you get better."

Victor had the formula to make me better. Listening to him, my eyes opened wide, eager to improve. All along, I had been concentrating on my macronutrients—proteins, carbohydrates, big-picture material. I had neglected the micronutrients—minerals that could help minimize, or completely neutralize, so many of the problems I was having.

The more Victor talked, the more I learned, the more I realized I had entered another new frontier. But I was about to explore the world even further. We scheduled a time for me to visit his Burlingame, California, BALCO offices for me to pick up those minerals from him.

On my first visit to BALCO in June 1995, I pulled up to a nondescript commercial office building in Burlingame, right along Highway 101, almost directly across the street from the hotel where the 49ers stayed the night before every home game. When I walked in, autographed pictures of Olympic athletes and body builders decorated the walls. Sprinters, long jumpers, hammer throwers. Each photo was inscribed with a thank-you note to Victor for his hard work.

I sat with Victor and Jim Valente, BALCO's vice president, who were both dressed in their white lab coats. Surrounding them were books, articles, charts, bottles, computers. Next door to their office was an oversized lab, packed with medical testing

ROMO

equipment, where mineral testing for companies around the country was conducted. I looked around and had one thought. *This,* I told myself, *is where science happens.*

For three hours, I listened to Victor spell out all the ways he could enhance my performance and my career. It had nothing to do with anything illegal, anything banned. This was all legal. This was all safe. This was all helpful, a way for me to prolong my career in a nutritionally sound way.

Before I left BALCO, Victor handed me bottles of magnesium, chromium, copper, zinc—every mineral I had been lacking. What it was, really, was the next stage in my evolution.

That night, for the first time in as long as I could remember, I slept through the night without waking, without even moving. From then on, my dreams were so real and so vivid that the only way I can describe it is this: It was as if the rare dreams I had were being broadcast in black and white. The new ones were being transmitted in high-definition TV. After an off-season with Remy, Randy, and Victor, I was opened up to a world of detail that only track athletes knew. I had turned their training methods into mine, and it was so evident what it had done for me. The leg workouts and all-natural minerals changed my career. It was enlightening, a reawakening that powered my surge into the season ahead.

When my Eagles teammates and I stepped into the auditorium for a team meeting to start the 1996 season, our new head coach was one of my old coaches from San Francisco, Ray Rhodes. Eagles owner Jeffrey Lurie had selected Rhodes over the then Minnesota Vikings defensive coordinator, Tony Dungy.

One thing about Coach Rhodes: His language lacked any taste. He loved fighting references, talking about fist fights, bloody fights, even a Super Bowl being decided by two coaches punching each other. And every other word he used was the F-word. Don't let any F-ing body come into our F-ing house and start F-ing with our livelihood. We'll F-ing fight 'em. There were enough F-bombs going off to declare our training complex a battle zone. We're not F-ing around this season, we're not F-ing rebuilding anymore, nobody should even think about F-ing us this year.

Other players had to be thinking what I was: How does he even think of stuff so crude, never mind say it? But I'll say this about Coach Rhodes. He knew how to win. Along with George Seifert, Bobb McKittrick, and Bill McPherson, Coach Rhodes was one of only four men to serve on the coaching staff of all five of the San Francisco 49ers' Super Bowl winning teams. "We have one goal and that's to win a world championship," Coach Rhodes told our team in minicamp.

Listening to his newest rant, I nodded my head and said to myself, *This is why I got traded, to be a part of this.* Joking was out, goal setting in. And punches were flying. Just twelve days into training camp, I traded insults and punches with rookie fullback Fred McCrary. He did some things to piss me off, and my fists started flying, just as Coach Rhodes liked to see with his players. All coaches liked to see their players practice and play with passion, something I was never short on. Couple this with the fact that we're all sore, tired, hot and cranky, and you'll always find fights breaking out in camp.

Meanwhile, our new defensive coordinator Emmitt Thomas, our new linebackers coach Joe Vitt, and our new defensive line coach Mike Trgovac—now the defensive coordinator for the 2003 NFC Champion Carolina Panthers—established a style the players really liked. Even better, they devised some new wrinkles that I hadn't seen used anywhere else. Before every game, they would set a series of eight to ten realistic goals for

R
O
M
O

our defense, something I later started to do in Denver, when I kept them in my playbook. They would say, "Okay, we've got to force three turnovers this week." The next week, it would be, "We've got to hold them to under 90 yards rushing." Then it would be, "We've got to limit them to a 30 percent third-down conversion percentage." Something different every game.

And you know what? Every week that we met our goals, we won. From that point on, I'd compile a list for myself to accomplish my own personal goals during a game—eight to twelve tackles, three big plays, one sack, one interception, one cause fumble, one fumble recovery, one big hit. I would also aim to dominate the tight end and not allow him to catch one ball while also not allowing myself to make any mental errors. It was about doing everything possible to help our defense dominate their offense. We reached our defensive goals in ten games, and won them all, no game being any bigger than our December 10, home match-up versus the defending world-champion Cowboys, when we double-teamed tight end Jay Novacek and wide receiver Michael Irvin.

Late in the game, with the Cowboys trailing 20–17 and facing a third-and-1, they handed off to Emmitt Smith. There was no surprise there. Emmitt was the top back in football, and he was running behind Daryl "Moose" Johnston, a fullback that I respected tremendously and the Cowboys unsung hero. He wasn't going to get the football but one or two times per game; what he was going to do was block linebackers for Emmitt so he could be the hero. On the third down, the Cowboys tried it again.

But the moment Emmitt reached the line of scrimmage, I smacked into him. Down he went—no gain. On fourth and 1, the Cowboys again tried Emmitt, who players typically don't get good shots at. I did. Nailed him at the line of scrimmage for no gain and the win. Another fight we had won. That was our Super Bowl that year, beating the Cowboys.

What I liked as much as the success we experienced were the relationships I formed. Coach Vitt was the first coach I ever had who told his players, "I love you." The first time he said it to me was when we were on the phone, talking about an upcoming game, and he ended the conversation by saying, "I love you, Romo." After telling him I loved him, too, I hung up the phone and realized how much that meant to me, hearing a coach verbalize his feelings. In a sport where showing your feelings is considered a weakness, I learned it could be a strength. This is the biggest lesson Coach Vitt taught me. It was the way he was, always. Before the game, he would bring together all the linebackers and say, "I love you guys. Kick butt today!"

After the game, win or lose, he would thank his players and say, "I appreciate what you guys did for me out there." It just made you want to fight that much harder for him, play that much better. I wish we could have drawn out the season, made it last even longer. But we lost our NFC Divisional Playoff at Dallas, 30–11.

At the time, my impression was that Coach Rhodes had the organization moving in the right direction. He wanted the best and was willing to do what it took to be the best. His problem was, at that time, Mr. Lurie didn't.

When my contract expired, I wanted to stay in Philadelphia. I thought they wanted me, too. Coach Vitt had told each of the three starting linebackers—me, Kurt Gouveia, and William Thomas—that he believed each of us played well enough in 1995 to deserve a trip to the Pro Bowl. After the season ended, though, I quickly realized the Eagles' front office thought differently than their linebackers coach.

"Go out and get an offer from somebody and bring it back

R
O
M
O

to us," the general manager at the time, Dick Daniels, told Tom Condon. "See what you're worth on the open market."

It was a slap at me, almost as if they doubted I was worth very much. What they hadn't realized—and what I hadn't told anybody but Julie—was that after we beat the Broncos at Veterans Stadium 31–13, Denver head coach Mike Shanahan made a point of seeking me out after the game.

Coach Shanahan and I had worked together in San Francisco, where he was the 49ers offensive coordinator from 1992–1994. We would always be in the weight room at the same time, talking football, talking life. When he saw me again that November 12 Sunday night in Philadelphia, he momentarily put aside his team's defeat and planted the seed for a future win.

"You're playing great, Romo," Coach Shanahan said to me near midfield, where players were shaking hands. "Let's talk after the season."

Our brief conversation told me plenty about what my off-season plans would hold. Coach Shanahan never said anything without thinking; he was too calculating for that. Three months before free agency, he already knew my contract was up. A man who learned about winning in San Francisco and who was determined to transport those ways to Denver was ready to discuss a deal as soon as NFL rules would allow it.

Until they did, Julie surprised me for Christmas with a gift that would help me prep for free agency. She handed me a stack of photos of this drop-dead, decked-out, state-of-the-art gym. Three rows of nine brand-new Hammer Strength machines. Mirrored walls. Cathedral ceilings. A stretching room. A changing room. A bathroom. Anything any fitness freak could have wanted.

"Yours," Julie told me. "My gift to you. Merry Christmas, Billy."

Turns out, while we were back in Philadelphia, Julie had the

3,000-square-foot gym built in a detached barn in the backyard of our San Martin home. Over the next two months, I rarely left it. And I had company.

My track coach, Randy Huntington, practically lived in my backyard. Our workouts were as tiring as they looked: all day affairs that were every bit as brutal as training camp. Stretching warm-ups, joint mobility exercises, skipping, jumping, lunging, running, sprinting, pool exercises, more stretching. Included in my new equipment was a high-tech treadmill that went as fast as 15 miles per hour. But I wasn't happy with it. I had to get some specialist to develop a computer chip to make it go faster. I wanted it to go 18 miles per hour. My training crossed a new frontier, all to get ready for the next season.

And sure enough, when the free-agent signing period opened in late February 1996, the first call was from Mike Shanahan.

What was interesting was that he was not alone. Calls started pouring in to Tom. Offers were floated, itineraries scheduled. My free-agent visits took me from Denver to Minnesota to Atlanta to San Diego. Fairly quickly, it became apparent that the decision would boil down to Denver and San Diego.

While Julie and I weighed our offers, Tom did his job. He called the Eagles one last time to see if they were willing to jump in to the bidding. When Dick Daniels heard the money on the table for me—five years, $9 million, including a $3 million signing bonus—he laughed. Actually laughed out loud to my agent. No way were they interested at that price, Mr. Daniels informed Tom. All I could think when Tom relayed the conversation to me was, "We'll see who laughs last." But at that time, that was the least of my worries. Finding a new employer was.

So Julie and I did the simplest and most logical thing. We made a list of pros and cons for each city. Denver had coaches I knew, players I respected, and skiing. As a high school senior,

R O M O

my two brothers had taken me skiing to Colorado and I never had forgotten it. To have the mountains in my backyard posed an enormous advantage. That was Denver.

San Diego had coaches I liked, players I respected, and surfing. On my free-agent visit there, Chargers general manager Bobby Beathard even showed me pictures of where he surfed each morning, and it looked like paradise. To have waves in my backyard posed an enormous advantage. That was San Diego.

Skiing or surfing. Mountains or water. Mike Shanahan or Chargers head coach Bobby Ross. Blue and orange; blue and yellow. As we weighed the pros and cons of each prospective place, Julie voiced one objection to San Diego, even though it was in her home state. "I don't think I want you playing with Junior Seau," she said. "Mark my words, Billy. Junior owns that defense and he owns that city. You need to make your name somewhere else."

Julie's was the voice of wisdom, once again. San Diego was in her home state, and she would have loved to have been closer to her family, but she was thinking about what was best for me. She knew. And her simple statement swung the vote. I was on my way to Denver. To make my name, and my mark, there.

8 DENVER: ROMANOWSKI, I'M GONNA OWN YOU

Most people starting a new job usually tread carefully and lay back, until they feel comfortable enough to step out front. As you might guess by now, "most people" would not include me. During my first minicamp with the Broncos, in my first full practice with my new team in May 1996, I made a statement.

It was on a simple drill. I was running stride for stride downfield with Broncos tight end Shannon Sharpe. When the football was thrown to Shannon and was just about to arrive, none of my teammates yelled, "Ball!" It's customary in football, when the ball is in the air and you can't see it coming, for your teammates to let you know. They have to shout out "Ball" so you can turn around and defend it.

After the play, I turned around, faced the whole defense, and screamed: "Where the hell is the ball call here!?! What the hell is going on!?!"

It shocked some players, but it pleased others whose opinions counted more. After the practice, our defensive coordinator, Greg Robinson, walked over to me and said: "That's the kind of attitude we need here, Romo. We needed that. We didn't have that last year. That's why you're here." His passion matched mine, and my career took off playing for such an energetic, bright mind. Coach Robinson became another of my mentors and I came to trust him, and he trusted me to run his defense. We grew so close that our family used to go to his house on Christmas. And you know what I really liked and respected about Coach Robinson? He was a family man, honest, ethical, and morally honorable. I would have done anything to help him and the team, and I mean anything.

When I toured the Broncos weight room for the first time, I noticed they were missing some of the Hammer Strength equipment that Julie had purchased for my home gym. So I asked our strength and conditioning coach Rich Tuten to order some of the missing parts. Then I went upstairs to the Broncos general manager John Beake and asked him to please deduct $10,000 out of my paychecks to pay for it.

I also arranged to have some of the equipment from my home gym transported into the Broncos complex, being that was where it would serve everybody. Soon enough, my calf-raise machine, my Kaiser squat, and my Kaiser multi-hip machine were in the Broncos weight room. My thinking was always *the team*. How can we make the team better?

Another way was through the meals we ate. I noticed that on their way into the training facility, 75 percent of the players were stopping for breakfast at McDonald's. And to me, if you eat crap, you're going to get crap on the field. Coach Shanahan was already providing the players lunch as a way to prevent them from going to McDonald's, but my idea was to provide breakfast, too. Eggs, oatmeal, fresh fruit. Healthy food. This way we would be controlling two of the players' meals—something the Broncos do to this day. One idea of mine they chose not to adopt was serving dinner to guys who were single or wanted to stay late at the facility.

So that explained why Coach Shanahan was so baffled when I showed up late for the start of the summer training camp in Greeley. Me, the man who prided himself on work and discipline, did not make it there when the rest of our team did. I was hours late. When I finally arrived, Coach Shanahan pulled me aside.

"Everything okay, Romo?"

"Oh yeah, Coach. Sorry about being late. It's just that Julie's . . . umm . . . ovulating."

Momentarily stunned, Coach Shanahan fumbled for his answer. "I've heard a lot of excuses and a lot of stories, Romo. But that is the absolute best."

Spared a fine, my training camp was underway. Julie was pregnant, I was ready for football, and I found myself in a playful championship atmosphere. During training camp, every player and coach had received a notice on official NFL stationery, along with two small plastic cups, requesting a urine and stool sample for a mandated drug test. Some of the guys were trying to figure out how in the world they were going to fit their stool samples into such a tiny cup. Guys were upset. But they shouldn't have been.

There in the corner of the locker room was our backup quarterback, Bill Musgrave, cracking up. Somehow, Bill had gotten hold of NFL stationery, typed up an official-looking letter, and secretly delivered it to every coach and player in our organization. The Broncos didn't have to worry about that test. They had at least sixteen other ones in the season ahead, each game day.

So by and large, why was my first season in Denver such a painful one? For one thing, I found myself going against

Broncos Pro-Bowl offensive tackle Gary Zimmerman in practice every now and then. Outside of former Buffalo guard Jim Richter, Gary was the toughest offensive lineman I had gone against. Strong, smart, workmanlike. Every time I would face him, I'd think to myself, *Oh no, I've got Gary.*

It wasn't like I hadn't heard about him either. My friend and San Francisco teammate Kevin Fagan would tell me how miserable it was to face Gary. Kevin told me he had more respect for Gary than any offensive tackle he lined up against. After facing Gary in practice, I could see why.

Another and more significant cause for my misery was an injury I'd suffered in the off-season, after the minicamp. It should have been a routine running drill with Remy. Bounding over the last hurdle on my last sprint on one of my last off-season workouts, I accidentally kicked the top of it. My right knee caught, and suddenly I was in extreme pain.

No MRIs were needed, but a little rest was. For the next few days, there was no running work with Remy, only some concerns about any damage I might have done. Something wasn't completely right. A person in touch with his body, a person who never missed a game in his life knew that.

My knee bothered me every day throughout the season. But I never thought of taking time off, not after Denver believed in me and invested in me. There was no way I was going to start my career in a new city with an injury I did not incur on the football field. I just popped one Naprosyn a day and went on.

I pushed through the pain and the season, hoping it would heal on its own. But even with all the strengthening and stretching exercises that Broncos trainer Steve Antonopulos put me through, nothing really helped.

As if that weren't enough, there were other injuries I had to play through. On September 29, at Cincinnati, I suffered at least my fourth NFL concussion and the first of too many to count in

Denver. My medical reports spell it out in a harmless-enough sounding way.

9/29/96
Body part injured: Head-Cerebellum
Injury condition: Concussion
Etiology: 13:45 first quarter; Running play; Came up to make tackle and was hit in the head with opponent's helmet.

It seemed, to me, like just part of the game. A ding, doctors called it. A ding, I repeated to Julie, as if it were nothing to worry about.

What helped propel me through the brain and knee injuries, aside from my desire to prove that Denver made the right decision in signing me, was my determination to be selected to my first Pro Bowl. Up until then, I never had been selected to one, though coaches had told me I deserved to go.

In the off-season before my first one in Denver, I read Jonathan P. Niednagel's motivational book, *Your Key to Sports Success.* It taught me about maximizing potential and setting goals. At which point it occurred to me: How could I make the Pro Bowl if I didn't establish it as one of my goals? Those things don't just happen unless your sights are focused on them.

For the 1996 season, for the first time, my goal was to make it to the Pro Bowl. It was on my mind for most of the team-high 128 tackles I made that season. It stuck with me for most of my 3 sacks, 3 interceptions, 3 fumble recoveries, and 12 pass defenses when my guys obviously were yelling, "Ball!"

But in many ways, it was not an easy season. When I got to Denver, Coach Robinson assigned me to play man-to-man strongside linebacker, meaning I had to line up over the tight end and cover him one-on-one. It was something I hadn't done

ROMO

in San Francisco, Philadelphia, or anywhere else I had been. Every day I turned up my intensity. I had no choice. It was either you covered the tight end or you didn't; you either kept him from making the catch or you didn't. There were not any in betweens. I loved the challenge.

But the tight end who provided me with the biggest challenge was not perennial Pro Bowl selection Shannon Sharpe, but the less heralded Byron Chamberlain. Shannon was more of a gamer, turning up his performance on gameday. Byron was tougher to cover every day. He made me a better coverage linebacker, prepping me for weekly divisional battles against tight ends such as Tony Gonzalez, Freddie Jones, Christian Fauria and Rickey Dudley.

Learning my position managed to distract me from the bad knee a little bit. Our team's success also did its part. We were rolling, and I didn't want to miss any part of it. We stormed out to a 12–1 start, stood atop our division and conference, and had home field advantage though the playoffs wrapped up on the ridiculously early date of December 1.

We had more than a month to tune up for our first postseason game, a home AFC Divisional Playoff. We had momentum. We had it all, including an incredibly favorable postseason match-up with the Jacksonville Jaguars, an expansion franchise that played its first games only one year earlier. The question wasn't whether we would win, but how much we would win by. The fans in Denver already were thinking about hosting the AFC Championship game eight days later. I think maybe our team was, too. And no one played any worse that day than me.

Twice against Jacksonville, I had wide open shots at its quarterback, Mark Brunell. And I flat whiffed. It felt like every move I made that day was the wrong one. Every spot I ran to that day was the wrong one. The weird part was, I had just had one of the best practice weeks of my life. I was so ready to play. But then, in the game, every time I went right, Brunell went left. Every time I went left, Brunell went right. And on the rare occasion when we did meet up, when he was right there in front of me, it was like trying to tackle a ghost. I couldn't bring him down, couldn't do anything. Worst game I've played in my career—even worse than my no big-play 1992 NFC Championship game versus Dallas. Our stunning 30–27 loss to Jacksonville—which most experts consider to be one of the biggest upsets in NFL playoff history—was the ultimate pain in a season full of them.

I felt largely responsible for it. But during my end-of-the-season meeting with Coach Shanahan, I explained how happy I was in Denver but how I felt like he had played an inadvertent role in the loss. Before the season, Coach told our team the goal was "to win our division, get home field advantage in the play-offs, and the rest would take care of itself."

"Mike, do you realize we met our goals this year?" I said to him.

"What do you mean, Bill?"

"You mentioned that our goals were to win the division and get homefield advantage in the playoffs. Were you afraid to talk Super Bowl? Because there was a natural letdown when we met our goal. The goal has to be to win a World Championship." And the next year, guess what our goals were? Just what they should have been the year before.

The season's only consolation came about two weeks later, while Julie and I were on a Caribbean cruise. When I returned to our room after a morning workout of lifting and running, Julie was excited. "Coach Coughlin just called," she said.

Coach Coughlin had taken over for Coach Bicknell at Boston College in 1991. When I would go back to Boston College in the early 90s, Coach Coughlin would hold me up as an example to his players, tell them: "Do you know what he's accomplished? Do you know how hard he's worked? You ought to follow this guy around."

From Boston College, Coach Coughlin went on to Jacksonville and was the Jaguars' head coach when they upset us. When the Jaguars lost the January 1997 AFC Championship game at New England, Coach Coughlin and his staff were appointed coaches of the AFC Pro Bowl team. Each head coach was permitted to select one "need" player to fill out his team.

"Coach Coughlin wants you to be his 'need' player for the Pro Bowl," Julie informed me. "Congratulations, Billy."

Tears filled my eyes. Almost every time I had set my mind to accomplishing something—the scholarship, the starting job, the Cotton Bowl, the Super Bowl—it happened. My celebrations always were marked with Kleenex.

The week of the Pro Bowl—what is normally a lax game in which players take the week to kick back in Hawaii—I was running around the way I did during summer drills my freshman year at Boston College. Shannon Sharpe and Ben Coates, the AFC's Pro Bowl tight ends, were telling me, "Slow down, Romo. Take it easy."

Coach Coughlin brought up the team after our first sloppy practice and told us, "You have pride, I have pride. How we practiced today is not going to get it done." Personally, even though some Pro Bowl players didn't like hearing that little speech, I loved it. I can just remember gaining that much more respect for Coach Coughlin. His standard was my standard.

When any uniform is on, so is my intensity. And that intensity carried straight through to the off-season. When I returned home to San Martin and resumed my workouts in the new gym that Julie had built for me, I added my own little decorative touch.

On the gym's front door, I hung an 8 x 11 color picture of

Mark Brunell. Each day on the way into my gym each morning, the first thing I would see was the most lasting picture in my mind. An image of Brunell, making a play, another play, just like the ones he made against me. "You're going down next time," I would growl at the picture whenever I passed it. "You're mine."

Nobody was going to make me feel that way again, I vowed. Nobody.

O nly there was a problem. From February into March, my knee pain persisted. Worsened, even. Forget about running; walking was becoming increasingly difficult. This could not just be patellar tendonitis, no way. Like the discomfort, my fears increased.

Julie often found me staring out windows, with tears in my eyes.

"I am in so much pain," I would tell her.

"This is ridiculous," she would say. "Let's figure out what is going on with you right now."

At the same hospital where Julie was getting regular check-ups for her pregnancy, Dr. Michael F. Dillingham, the same doctor who apprised us of Jeff Fuller's condition in 1989, reexamined the MRI performed on my knee a month earlier in Fresno. Those doctors told me I had patellar tendonitis. Dr. Dillingham viewed the MRI differently.

On April 1, 1997, he performed surgery and filed this report for my Broncos medical records shortly thereafter:

At the time of open procedure, there was found to be a cavitation of the tendon with serous fluid under tension, which squired out when a 15 blade was put into this cavity. The area involved was about half a centimeter wide and almost a centimeter long. The surrounding abnormal scar-

R
O
M
O

ified and gelatinous soft tissue doubled this area in width and went distally about 3 to 4 cm. There was significant thickening of the prepatellar tendon retinaculum and bursa, and this was not normal.

In other words, I played the 1996 season and trained well into the 1997 off-season with a partially torn patellar tendon. Definitely not smart, but it never has been a question of smarts when my obsession takes over.

Julie and I practically could have gotten adjoining hospital rooms. Three days after my surgery, she gave birth to our angel, Alexandra. Having a baby girl thrilled me beyond words. Having a knee injury filled me with fear. Surgery wiped out the results of March's training, minimized the results of April's and prevented me from being able to peak just before training camp. These were, in my world, huge setbacks. A panic unlike any previous anxiety was kicking in. My body was how I made my living. Having it taken away from me, however briefly, I feared I would be reduced to just another pedestrian player.

Needing a way to heal faster, I did one of the only things I thought I could. Four hours after the surgery, even though I was still groggy from the anesthesia and one of my trainers, Danny Carvalho, had to hold me upright, I was back in my San Martin weight room, lifting weights with my good left knee. Randy Huntington had told me that with bilateral transformation, the brain can't tell if you're working on your right leg or your left. It's the phantom leg theory, which came from war victims who lost a limb but still felt pain in that spot. So I just kept working the left leg, from four hours after the surgery through the off-season. I also willed myself into the swimming pool to walk and run. But in my mind, gripped by the fear that I might not be good enough to start anymore, of not being able to continue my consecutive game streak, of not coming back at all, of not being able to support my family with Alexandra having just been born, I couldn't help but think back to my parents sitting at the kitchen table, talking and worrying about how they were going to get by. Now I was the adult at my own kitchen table.

Anyway, with all the hard work I recovered precisely when the doctors said I would. When the 1997 season kicked off five months later, my consecutive game streak would be intact. That season, I started every one of our games.

Meanwhile, I continued with my supplementation. On game day, I would mix up Creatine and Vitamin B-12 and doctors would inject it in the usual spot in my glute, high and outside. The idea of injecting it was to get it directly into the bloodstream rather than having it pass through the gut. I took my injections with Ephedra. Then at halftime, I'd head to the training room and have one of our team doctors give me an extra boost with another Creatine injection.

Injectable Creatine, which was produced in Italy with the name Neotone, was supposed to help generate adenosine triphosphate, or ATP, the main source of energy used by our bodies' cells. Injectable B-12, which I used extensively during my years in San Francisco, is used to promote new cell development as it aids your nervous system. Did they work? I think so. But I was taking so many supplements, and training so hard, I'll be honest: It's hard to tell what gave me the biggest boost.

There was some good that came out of my knee injury. While visiting one of my former 49ers doctors, Jeryl J. Wiens, in Fresno before the tear was detected, he referred me to a biomechanic specialist, Greg Roskopf.

Greg allowed me to realize that my knee injury probably did not come from kicking that last hurdle, but rather from tightness in my hips, soreness in my foot, other biomechanical prob-

R
O
M
O

lems I had been experiencing for years. He explained that just because a training program was right for one person didn't mean it was right for another. Each person's muscles were different, no body the same. Each person had to tailor training practices to his body. Against the prevailing conventional wisdom, Greg believed protocol training might contribute to injury rather than prevent it.

Then he put me through a set of drills, testing my body. When he watched me move my big right toe, he instantly detected that I lacked normal range of motion. As he pointed out, my seemingly minor podiatric problem was forcing me to favor the inside of my right foot, thus straining the outside of the knee. Up until then I had no idea. Five minutes into Greg's explanations, I interrupted him. "You belong in the NFL," I told him.

He continued telling me about his systematic approach for identifying and treating muscular imbalances through noninvasive manual therapy. MAT, he called it. Muscle Activation Therapy. It points to muscle tightness as the body's way of trying to protect itself and stabilize the joints. His key point was that the body is an amazing compensator. Athletes run out of compensations, and that's when you get hurt. When you tackle those issues, you don't get hurt. That's what helped me. MAT addresses the muscle weakness rather than tightness, trying to restore body alignment, decreasing pain and reducing the risk of injury.

Today MAT is spreading across the sports, health, and fitness industries. Back when I first met him, Greg was revolutionizing it. He was so far ahead of his time, I had to have all my teammates exposed to him and his ideas. "Would you be interested in working for the Denver Broncos during the upcoming season?" I asked him.

Out of my own pocket, I paid Greg $50,000 to work with me

and the rest of my teammates during training camp. I flew him in to Colorado that summer and asked the Broncos to assign him the dormitory training camp room next to mine. The Broncos went one better, giving me the entire top floor of the players' dorm, Lawrenson Hall, where I set up a portable hot tub, chiropractic tables, massage tables, masseuses, and Greg.

And sure enough, it wasn't long before his work was needed. The first week of August, when we were playing the Miami Dolphins in a Monday night preseason game at Estadio Guillermo Canedo in Mexico City, our quarterback John Elway blew out the biceps tendon in his right arm. This wasn't just any injury: this was a potentially career-ending injury. Nobody knew if John ever would be able to throw again. Back in Greeley, I told John, "I've got someone for you to see."

Now, I don't know what Greg did to him, other than tirelessly work on his injured arm. But whatever it was, John was back at practice that week, throwing bee-bees. A strong argument could be made that, without Greg, John's career is not prolonged and Denver does not win back-to-back Super Bowls. An overstatement? Probably. Out of the question? Probably not.

After John saw Greg, he told me, "We need to get the Broncos to hire this dude full-time." To this day, Greg still works for the Broncos, as well as the NBA's Denver Nuggets and Utah Jazz.

R O M O

For everything I did on the field in San Francisco and Philadelphia, I didn't start being known as the most controversial player in the league until 1996, when I arrived in Denver. There, my stature grew, my salary increased, my game elevated, and my antics acquired a following they never before had. I fed off it.

For my whole career, before every game, I had always taken a stick of eye black and rubbed a band-aid-sized stripe of it below each of my eyes. But in Denver, I began thinking of my eye black as war paint. It became my pregame ritual. Whether I needed it or not, it was time to put on the war paint. Time to go to battle.

Once I arrived in Denver, there were enough of them. One of the biggest came the week after our trip to Mexico City and the scary injury to John, in a 1997 preseason game against the Carolina Panthers. It was a supposed exhibition. On one play, I came off the edge and went to hit Carolina's quarterback, Kerry Collins, with my shoulder. But he turned into me as he was throwing the ball, and it was the perfect hit, just picture perfect. Collins crumpled to the ground and lay motionless, his jaw broken in two places.

I still remember our veteran defensive line coach John Teerlinck telling me, as I walked to our sidelines, that it was one of the best hits he'd ever seen. He said he knew as soon as I hit him that Collins was done. The hit stirred a huge debate, though, from Carolina to Denver. Carolina's head coach, Dom Capers, called it "a textbook case of an illegal hit." Green Bay's defensive end, Reggie White, defended the hit saying, "I will be very upset and disappointed, even though the guy's not on my team, if the NFL fines Bill Romanowski."

The league took its own hard-line stance. It fined me again, this time $20,000 more for "ramming Kerry in the neck, chin and face." If you ask me, the league was just trying to make an example of the hit. I told reporters then, and I feel the same way now, it was not going to change the way I would play. Next time I played Collins, I would try to hit him harder.

After that hit, I don't think Kerry was the same quarterback again, at least not in Carolina. He would go on to resurrect his career in New York and lead the Giants to a Super Bowl.

If you ask me, he held me responsible for it. He says he didn't, but he did. We were supposed to appear at the same charity function in the 2003 off-season, but as soon as he found out I was going to be there, he cancelled. Didn't show. Maybe Kerry didn't understand, but these were the hits that set the tone in a game. They meant more than you know. Basically, you're trying to knock crap out of people on every single play. There's nothing in this game that can fire someone up like a good hit. Interceptions are nice, touchdowns nicer. But when you knock the you-know-what out of someone, the rush cannot be duplicated. And I'm not talking about just me hitting somebody. When Steve Atwater or any of my defensive teammates blew up somebody, it fired us all up.

As time went on, I realized I sometimes could do as much damage with my mouth as my fists. Some players, like former Miami first-round draft pick John Avery, were really easy to get. When we would play the Dolphins, Avery would scare me with his speed. But when I hit him, I would scream in his face, call him a wus, a wimp, every name in the book. I would shout it with all the anger I could, and you could see the fear in his eyes.

Then there was veteran NFL running back Ricky Watters. Talk about easy. Ricky wasn't somebody who got scared. Ricky got pissed off. After each play, I'd push his buttons with nothing more than a simple question. "Hey, Ricky, how come they're not giving you the football today?" I'd ask. And Ricky would go back to the huddle, screaming at the quarterback for the football.

"Hey, Ricky, how come your offensive line isn't blocking for you today?" I'd ask. Next thing you know, Ricky would be back in the huddle, yelling at his offensive linemen to block.

One way or another, I wanted to get inside my enemy's head. Usually I did. I remember telling tight end Christian Fau-

ROMO

ria when he was a rookie, "You couldn't block my grandmother." I would tell other tight ends, "If you catch one pass today, I'll retire." My favorite line was, "I'll rip your heart out and feed it to my dog." Coach Robinson once said that I was "like the catcher who's asking about your girlfriend as soon as you step into the batter's box."

But for all the talking, there still was no substitute for hard hitting. One big hit would fire up your whole team, something I learned in San Francisco from Ronnie Lott. When he put bone-shattering hits on receivers coming across the middle, our defense felt like it had scored a touchdown.

During my second season in Denver, I had another idea for how to bring the team together. Outside our locker room at Mile High Stadium, one of our security guards, Rick Anderson, worked for EAS—the Golden, Colorado-based private nutritional supplements company, which stood for Experimental and Applied Sciences. Bill Phillips, author of the bestselling book *Body for Life,* started the company in 1995. It didn't take long for word about the company to spread.

My first year in Denver, Rick and I discussed EAS, its mission, its products. EAS' goal, as Rick told me, was to inspire its consumers "to live a healthier, more fulfilling lifestyle through science-based nutrition and exercise." It interested me in the way MAT did. Shannon Sharpe was already endorsing the company, and I was hoping to force my way into the company's rotation during my second season in Denver, for my benefit as well as the team's.

Before our August 23 preseason game against the San Francisco 49ers, I pitched my proposal to Anderson: "Pay me half of what you're paying Shannon," which at that time was $120,000, "and I'll give you twice as much in return."

After Rick consulted with EAS' founder Bill Phillips, a marriage was arranged. For the $60,000 they agreed to pay, they got millions of dollars' worth of exposure. For starters, I had EAS drop ship boxes of protein powders, energy bars, and supplements, and I stashed them in the two empty lockers next to mine. Soon enough, most of the players on the team were passing by and taking what they wanted. It was as if our locker room had been transformed to a GNC store that didn't charge anything.

I then convinced EAS to send one of their employees to the Broncos' training facility every morning to whip up some breakfast protein shakes for the players. Eventually, players were drinking them at their lockers, in meetings, all around the training facility. When that worked, I asked Rick if he could arrange for EAS to individually design supplement programs for any player who wanted one. No problem. By the end of the season, 75 percent of the players in our locker room were carrying around compartmentalized custom-made tackle boxes stocked with pills for bone strength, pills for muscle recovery. All legal stuff, all healthy stuff.

Players committed to the supplement culture in which I was thought to be the high priest. My personal tackle box, split into two levels containing well over 500 pills on any given day, was the size of a welcome mat. There were so many pills in it that, one time, when I inadvertently knocked it over, it took me three hours to pick them all up and put them back into their compartments. Then I knew just where to look for them. Like a game plan, my daily intakes were spelled out for me in the form of five meals per day.

BREAKFAST
- 50 mg coenzyme Q10: Helps the body produce energy.
- 2,000 mg vitamin C: A powerful antioxidant.

- 400 IUs vitamin E: For maintaining a stronger immune system.
- 5 g creatine-monohydrate: Increases the body's energy.
- 1,800 mg essential fatty acids (EFA): Fats not produced by the body; helps prevent inflammation.
- 1,000 mg beta-hydroxy-beta-methylbutyrate (HMB): An amino acid metabolite that increases the body's ability to build muscle and burn fat.
- A protein powder shake with 40 g whey protein powder. And boy, did I love those vanilla shakes.
- 800 mg chondroitin sulfate with 1,000 mg glucosamine: Taken together, this dietary supplement combination may strengthen connective tissue and lube the joints, keeping them feeling good.

MIDMORNING

- 8 g glutamine supplement: An energy producer that helps the immune system.
- 200 mg chromium polynicotinate: Helps regulate blood sugar.
- 2 mg copper sebacate: May strengthen connective tissue, ligaments, and tendons.

LUNCH

- 2,000 mg Vitamin C
- 1,800 mg EFA.
- 1,000 mg HMB.
- 800 mg chondroitin sulfate with 1,000 mg glucosamine.
- A protein powder shake with 40 g whey protein powder.

DINNER

- Same as breakfast.

ONE HOUR BEFORE BED

- 30 mg zinc monomethionine/aspartate: Always thinking of my testosterone.
- 450 mg magnesium aspartate: Helps me relax.

RIGHT BEFORE BED

- One more whey powder protein shake.

Nothing I took was just for the hell of it. Everything had a purpose. Julie liked to joke that I had the most expensive urine in the world, that I would make a great old guy one day—she never would have to remind me how to separate my medications.

Today my intake is a bit different, a bit more complex. But the list of my daily consumption is an illustration of the path I was traveling. But EAS didn't stop there. It helped the Broncos even more. It delivered pallets of protein powders and power bars to my Littleton, Colorado, house. It was like the ice cream man had come to our house. "Can you believe all this?" I would say to Julie, and she couldn't, especially when it found its way into our garage and kitchen cabinets.

"Hey, buddy," Julie told me, more than a bit annoyed. "You can't just take over our kitchen like that. You get one cabinet and one cabinet only—that's it." The more EAS did for me and the team, the more I wanted to help it. Eventually, I helped convince Terrell Davis and John Elway to sign on, so that now EAS had the biggest Broncos' names endorsing its products. A marketing machine was just beginning to rev its engine when I floated another idea to Rick.

"You know what, Rick?" I said. "Why don't you send some EAS hats down to our training facility?" Two days later, there were sixty EAS hats, in Broncos blue and white, in our locker

R
O
M
O

room. I passed them out to all the players, who wore them after practices, after games, always during television interviews.

When it started getting chilly out, I had another idea.

"You know what, Rick? Why don't you send some EAS mock turtlenecks down to the facility? With our numbers embroidered on the neck."

Two days later, there they were. Around the training facility, players were wearing EAS hats, EAS turtlenecks, carrying EAS tackle boxes filled with EAS products. EAS emblazoned everywhere. Eventually and not surprisingly, the initials made their way to national television on November 24, when we played the Raiders on Monday Night Football. After we put away the Raiders and the game 31–3, players wore their EAS hats on the sideline and in live postgame interviews.

Now the rest of the country had the same curiosity as Colorado. What is EAS? This was advertising no company could buy. Suddenly, the media craze was on.

It paled in comparison to the one I was about to endure.

If I weren't geeked up enough already, this one game had all the ingredients to do it even more: a Monday night December 15 game, in San Francisco, against the team that traded me away, after a week in which the Broncos were blown out 35–24 in Pittsburgh, virtually guaranteeing that we were not going to win our division and would have to go into the playoffs as a wild card.

Even worse, we were getting demolished again in San Francisco, down 17. Let's just say, I had better days. I was in my zone—panting, shaking, freaking—and others knew it. During the third quarter, officials flagged me for unnecessary roughness after I flattened 49ers quarterback Steve Young. Then three plays later, I did the unconscionable. At the bottom of the pile, I tried to rip the ball out of wide receiver J. J. Stokes's hands. I didn't get the ball, but I got his testicles in my hand, and I became a human nutcracker. I squeezed them and twisted them with all my anger. He jumped up, woofing: "That's bullshit, Romanowski! That's dirty!" And for some reason, I was like, "Who the hell are you?" And, without thinking, just spit in his face. *Splat!*

Didn't think anything of it, either. Guys had been spit on in the NFL for fifty years. I had been spit at myself. Former Raiders Center Barret Robbins tried it with me, as did others whose faces I never even saw. But as I was walking off the field after the 49ers beat us 34–17, a TV reporter from Denver stuck a microphone in my face and asked, "Did you spit in J. J. Stokes's face?" I couldn't believe it. I was caught totally off guard. I was like, "Damn, how'd they know that?"

What I hadn't known was that, unlike all the other spit that had flown around football fields in the past, one of Monday Night Football's cameras caught me and the loogie seen around the world. Replays were all over the local news and *SportsCenter*. The tables were turned. I was nailed.

"I might have," I told the TV reporter. But by then, nobody needed any confession from me. It was right there, on tape, clear as saliva. Then the hits starting pouring in. The NFL fined me another $7,500, which was the least of my problems. A Denver newspaper columnist wondered what kind of example I was setting for my children. Broncos wide receiver Willie Green recalled that his forebears had marched with Martin Luther King Jr. and had been spat on. A spokeswoman for the Denver branch of the NAACP described the act as "the ultimate form of degradation, fairly close to cross burning."

And that hurt more than anything, that someone would think my actions were racially motivated. Classless, yes. Racist, no. I don't discriminate against color—not white, black, green, or yellow. I discriminate equally against all opponents. That's all I see—the enemy. But I was being tried in the court of public opinion as a racist, and that really bothered me.

Some of my friends called to offer their support. Claude Lemieux, the most hated player in the NHL at that time and a friend who I met in the Denver area, telephoned with a message that, to this day, I still remember. "Answer the questions and say you're sorry, and that's all you can do," Lemieux told me.

And that's what I did. I apologized to everybody I could. I tried to explain my side, how when emotion runs high, logic runs low. I called my agent, Tom Condon, who also represented Stokes, to pass along an apology. Our team even met for forty-five minutes two days after the incident for me to try to reinforce to them how badly I felt about my actions.

Finally, our leader John Elway stood up, addressed the room, and, once and for all, tried to put the matter to rest. "This guy's done everything but get down on his knees," Elway told our team. "Let's put this behind us and go out and play some great football."

Which is exactly what happened. Even though we had lost two straight games at that point, the press ripped me instead of our team. And while the media was all over me, it allowed everybody else on our team to relax and to focus on football.

Three years later, in December 2000, when we played Stokes and the 49ers again I used the incident to play some mind games with Stokes and his teammates.

"Hopefully this time he'll fight back," I told *The Denver Post* that week. "To me, he's got no fight in him. If someone did that to me, they'd have to throw me out of the game. Because I'd go after him. What I did was wrong. But if somebody did that to me? . . ."

I didn't have to finish my thought. Anyone who knew me knew the answer. My ploy worked, because that game was the dirtiest one I ever played. 49ers offensive linemen were coming at me all game long, and Stokes was jawing at me. They were distracted and we beat them up 38–9.

After the game, Jerry Rice walked off the field for what everybody knew would be his last game as a Niner. His great run in San Francisco—and nobody in the NFL ever produced more than Jerry—was coming to a close. Our fans knew it. They were chanting, "Jer-ry! Jer-ry! Jer-ry!" And I wanted to congratulate him in my own way. I spotted him across the field, ran over to him, and hugged him, my acknowledgment of his greatness. Some might have thought this gesture was strange, but for me it was par for the course. Even when I had to spend most of the day being nasty, when that final whistle blew I was still a human being.

My goal to make EAS the most renowned nutritional supplements company was now in full swing. After we locked up a wild-card spot with a 12–4 regular-season record, I issued my newest request to Rick. "You really want to maximize this thing, take it to another level?" I said to him. He nodded. "Bring me $60,000," I told him. "In cash."

Trusting me, Rick did just what was asked of him. Before the playoffs kicked off, he showed up at our training facility and handed me a sack—with $60,000 in fresh, beautiful bills. Restoring some of my standing with the team, I went on a friendly recruiting trip around our locker room, signing up anyone who was willing. Upon hearing the deal, almost everyone was.

One of the first players I approached was our wide receiver Ed McCaffrey. By now he had overlooked the fact that I treated him like the enemy he was in our postseason meeting back in San Francisco, at a time when he played for the Giants and I

R

O

M

O

played for the 49ers. "If you wear your EAS hat or mock turtle-neck on the field and in postgame interviews, I'll give you $5,000 in cash," I told Ed. Done. One player signed on.

On to defensive end Neil Smith, who was offered a similar deal. Done. Two players signed on. Around the locker room, players couldn't consent fast enough. Wide receiver Rod Smith, fullback Howard Griffith, defensive end Alfred Williams— players were lining up to endorse EAS. The funny thing is, you've got players making hundreds of thousands of dollars per year, but $5,000 in $100 bills seemed like a bigger deal to them than their first contracts. They would stick the bills in their pocket, happy as larks, and wander off with some newfound spending money.

By the time the postseason kicked off, the Broncos and EAS were teaming up to make an extended historic run. Some people in our organization had fun with my cheerleading for EAS. Before one of our practices, Broncos owner Pat Bowlen volunteered to lead the players' stretching drills. Our team was thinking, "Wow, here is the owner of our team, breaking us down, stretching us out." Mr. Bowlen was getting into it, waving his arms, moving his hips, jumping around. And then, all of a sudden, our owner turned around, pulled down his pants, and shouted, at the precise moment he mooned me, "This one's for you, Romo!"

And painted on Mr. Bowlen's left butt cheek was a big E. Painted on his right butt cheek was a big S. The body part between them represented the A, which he didn't even bother writing in. Our whole team lost it—the last time we would lose that postseason.

It was a storybook-type postseason, the playoffs going just the way we would have wanted. We opened in Denver, at Mile High Stadium, against Jacksonville. A revenge game everyone in Denver thirsted for. For one year, I had looked at the same picture of Jaguars quarterback Mark Brunell. Now I was going to get a different look at him.

On one play, I remember hitting him out of bounds, grabbing his throat and squeezing it like it was Silly Putty. "You cheap shot artist!" Brunell screamed at me.

"You're going down, Brunell! I looked at your friggin' face every day for a friggin' year! I've waited all year for this!"

As did everyone on our team. In our December 27, AFC wild card playoff rematch versus the Jaguars, there would be no more upsets. If anything, we were upset we only won by 25 points, 42–17.

As we marched through the playoffs during the 1997 season, my verbal taunts got louder and bolder. After Pittsburgh's quarterback, Kordell Stewart, had three interceptions against us in the January 1998 AFC Championship game, I mocked him by whacking my head again and again while I shouted to him: "You dumb shit. You're one of the dumbest guys I've ever played against. Duh!"

All these years later, I can't even say that he was dumb. I don't know Kordell Stewart as a person. He's probably a pretty good guy. But it didn't matter. I was playing against him. That's what mattered.

Next up was Super Bowl XXXII against Green Bay. I'll admit that when our team was going through its daily workout at the San Diego Chargers' training facility, I was a little nervous. Our backup quarterback, my former teammate in Philadelphia, Bubby Brister, put on an exhibition. After watching our defense get shredded yet again, I turned to Coach Robinson and said, "I only hope Brett Favre doesn't play as good as Bubby did this week. If he does, we're in trouble."

Other than our defense looking miserable during practice, the rest of the two weeks leading up to Super Bowl XXXII had gone exactly as planned. Before we left, Coach Shanahan pro-

ROMO

vided every player with specific instructions: boost up the Packers as much as possible.

For two straight weeks, all we talked about was how good
the Packers offense was, how tough their defense was, how out-
standing their coaching was. Every cliché in the book, we used.
Every time I uttered another compliment about the Packers to
the press, I wanted to puke. By the time the game kicked off, we
wanted them to be full of themselves.

But when we got on the field I showed my true colors. I lined
up across from Packers tight end and fellow Boston College
alumnus Mark Chmura, and had some choice words for him.
"You're the biggest idiot that ever came out of Boston College,"
I yelled at him. "I'm insulted that we could have gone to the
same school."

"Romanowski," Chmura answered, "I'm gonna own you."

I was pumped and we were hungrier. If you looked at the
way they played, they were soft. We were anything but. We beat
them not only with a great game plan, not only with the great
coaching we had, but with our force of will.

A couple months after the game I watched a video of the
television broadcast of our 31–24 win over the Packers. I was
shocked not by what I saw, but by what I heard. I rewound the
tape just to make sure I wasn't imagining it. I closed my eyes
and listened—and you know what I heard? I heard the biggest
difference in the game. I heard the hitting on our side compared
to theirs. Our defense crushed their offense.

People remember John Elway's whirly-bird helicopter dive
and Terrell Davis's three touchdown runs as the biggest reasons
Denver finally won a Super Bowl. But the biggest difference in
that game was the way our defense hit. It told the full story. We
wanted the game more than they did.

On the final play, when our linebacker John Mobley batted

down a pass from Favre—a Hall-of-Fame quarterback who fortunately did not play the way Bubby did in practice—the feeling I had was unlike any other I've experienced in my life. I had won Super Bowls and been selected to Pro Bowls, but nothing compared to this. This was sheer exhilaration that could come only through painful defeats and sweat equity.

As a player who had won Super Bowls in each of his first two seasons, I hadn't fully grasped how hard it was to reach the final Sunday of the season and emerge a winner—not until I got back eight years after I first was there. Not only did I appreciate it more, but I was also in a different place. Back with the Niners, Joe, Jerry, and Ronnie were the stars. They were given their own floats on the victory parade through the streets of San Francisco. I was just along for the ride, on the back of somebody else's float. In Denver, I had my own fire truck, waving to our fans as we snaked through the jam-packed downtown streets. Our fans were chanting my name, wearing my Number 53 jersey. It represented the arc of change from one Super Bowl victory to another, as well as the change in my confidence level. I went from struggling to be a starter in San Francisco to dominating in Denver.

When I returned home to San Martin in the off-season, I took down the picture of Brunell and replaced it with one of me, my arms raised, howling after the Super Bowl. It was a reminder of how awesome it was to win. Every day when I went out to the weight room, I would look at that picture and say, "I want to feel that again."

It was why, even though Randy Huntington told me to take off training during the next month, I broke down after two days. I couldn't take resting and relaxing anymore. There was more work to do, for me and my team.

Here was my mind set: while we went to the Super Bowl, the

ROMO

other players in the league had an extra month off to train. While I was playing football, they were lifting, running, improving. I wasn't able to get my month off, or even a couple of weeks off. So I already was behind, and it was time to punch the clock. Time to get back to work.

The Romanowski clan, circa 1969. Clockwise from left, my dad, Bill; my big brother Mike; mom Donna; brother Joe; Suzie; and my baby sister, Tricia. I'm on my dad's lap. *(Courtesy of the author)*

Don't I look like I'm already feeling It? Age eleven, flashing my football pride, accompanied by my favorite teammate, Charlie (wearing the all-black jersey). *(Courtesy of the author)*

I played 'em all in high school: football in the fall, basketball in winter, and baseball in the spring. Baseball was something I got from my dad. We both played catcher. I hate to admit it, but I never played as well as my pops. *(Courtesy of the author)*

At Boston College, there wasn't a party, class, or girlfriend that was going to interfere with my dream. The guys I played with were great people and great athletes. We treated our sport with the utmost respect. Clockwise from top left: Jim Bell, me, Mike Power, Darren Flutie, and Jim Dienes. *(Courtesy of the author)*

My family always supported me and would come out to watch as many games as possible. Here I am with my siblings, who came up for a weekend at BC. *(Courtesy of the author)*

BOSTON COLLEGE FOOTBALL

My parents were thrilled when they received this Boston College–issued postcard with me on the front. On the back it read "#53 All-American LB Bill Romanowski." *(Courtesy of the author)*

At our first team meeting, SF head coach Bill Walsh said, "We have one goal and one goal only . . . and that goal is to win a world championship." I never imagined I'd win one my first year in the NFL. Here we are on the big day, Super Bowl XXIII, January 22, 1989. I'm on the far right. With me are (from left): Riki Ellison, Jim Fahnhorst, Michael Walter, Keena Turner, Coach Bill McPherson, Charles Haley, Ron Hadley, and Sam Kennedy. Kneeling are Head Coach Bill Walsh and team owner Eddie DeBartolo. (© by Michael Zagaris)

After our second Super Bowl win, I got to meet the then-president, George Bush. Here I am checking to see if he was doing his job as well as we did ours. (© by Michael Zagaris)

Family was—and still is—the most important thing to me. I always made it back to Connecticut for the big events. Here mom and I are dancing at my friend's wedding. *(Courtesy of the author)*

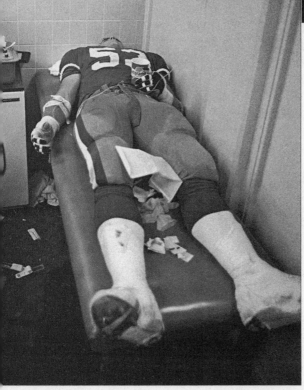

September 13, 1992. My eyes had been opened to the worlds of Eastern and alternative medicines, but I still occasionally needed a bit of Western help. Here I got IV fluids at halftime. *(© by Michael Zagaris)*

It took two years to reel in this beautiful woman! Here's Julie and me in Hawaii, April 1993, the day before we made it official—the first day of the rest of my life. (*Courtesy of the author*)

Traded to Philly from San Francisco in 1994, my initial disappointment turned to excitement because I became team-mates with my childhood idol, Herschel Walker. (*Hunter Martin/Philadelphia Eagles*)

Meeting up with Kerry Collins for the first time after I had broken his jaw in two places. Carolina's coach had called it "a textbook case of an illegal hit," for which I was fined $20,000. Here, Kerry is telling me, "No hard feelings." I'm thinking to myself, *He's a better man than me!* *(Ryan McKee/Rich Clarkson & Associates)*

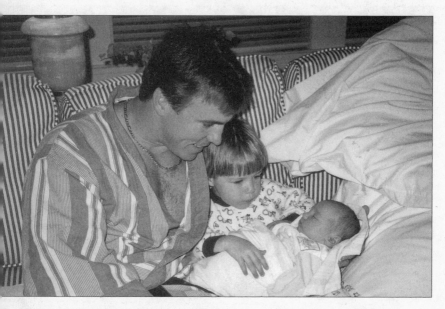

Our angel Alexandra was born in 1997. Here I am with my kids—a rare, tender moment to savor. *(Courtesy of the author)*

There's something about getting to the quarterback that cannot be duplicated, emotionally. For me, it's that instant of domination. Football is ultimately about who imposes his will upon whom. When you subdue the enemy's QB, you take something out of their will. Here's Drew Bledsoe giving up more than a few yards. *(David Gonzales/Rich Clarkson & Assoc.)*

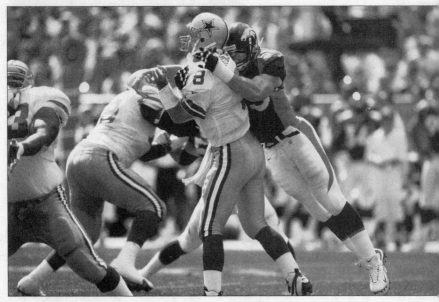

Cowboy Troy Aikman had already gotten rid of the ball, but damned if I was going to stop having my fun! *(Eric Lars Bakke/Rich Clarkson & Assoc.)*

It took me a full year to get even with Jaguar QB Mark Brunell. It was worth the wait. It always was. *(David Gonzales/Rich Clarkson & Assoc.)*

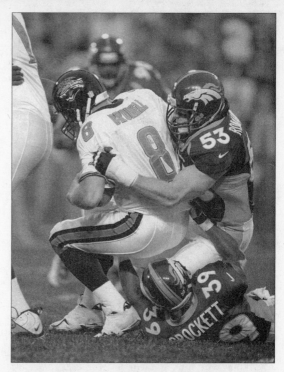

Nice to meet you, Mr. Marino. Hey, I'm not through yet! I'll let you up when I'm good and ready. *(Ryan McKee/Rich Clarkson & Assoc.)*

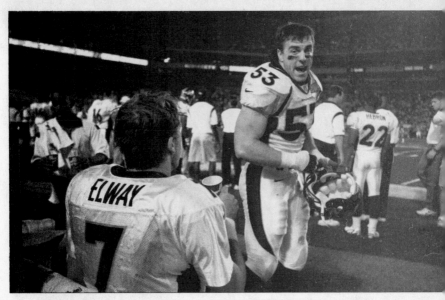

Gotta keep each other fired up for the full sixty minutes. Breaks are never mental; there's always something to review or anticipate. Here I am jawing with John Elway on the sidelines at Super Bowl XXXIII, January 1999. What a special player he was! This was his last performance. I was lucky to be able to play with him, and win. *(Eric Lars Bakke/Rich Clarkson & Associates)*

Julie always made sure to integrate our family with Daddy's job. Here, she and the kids are picking me up at my "office" after a hard day's work. *(Eric Lars Bakke/Rich Clarkson & Assoc.)*

The intensity of pro football and the daily price we pay to be our best brings us closer because of mutual respect and the common cause. Here's one of my best buds, Bubby Brister, and I "sacking" us some local trout. *(Courtesy of the author)*

Julie and I posing for the *Sports Illustrated* swimsuit issue in 2000—a moment to enjoy all of the body-punishing hard work.
*(© Mark Abrahams/*Sports Illustrated*)*

My own personal "meet and greet" with one of the all-time best running backs, Emmit Smith (#22). A perfect wrap-up to Thanksgiving Day Classics, 2001. *(Eric Lars Bakke/Rich Clarkson & Assoc.)*

When I hit someone this well, it's not just the sack, it's the feeling that I've taken a piece of his heart. Check out the pain on Raider QB Rich Gannon's face. *(Eric Lars Bakke/Rich Clarkson & Assoc.)*

We spent Christmas 2001 at home with my in-laws and "extended family" Tim Adams *(left)* and Riki Ellison. *(Courtesy of the author)*

There's nothing more painful than knowing your dreams are going to end sooner or later. So when you get a chance to extend the life of your career, it rejuvenates you. I was grateful for Bruce Allen and the Raiders' believing that I could still bring them something I needed. And I was going to prove to the Broncos what I already knew—that #53 was far from washed up. *(Courtesy of the Oakland Raiders)*

Raiders versus Kansas City. Chiefs All-Pro tight end Tony Gonzales (#88) is on the left. In 1999, the league slapped me with a $5,000 fine for belting him. Tony and I were always going at it, pounding each other, trying to psych each other out. Competing against Tony twice every year was one of the highlights of my career. This action was at Kansas City—a fabulous interception on my part—do I look like I'm over the hill?! *(Courtesy of the Oakland Raiders)*

The evolution of a celebration: Through the years, I was always transported by a win. Getting started at Boston College . . . *(Courtesy of Boston College)*

. . . winning SB XXXII with Denver . . . *(John Iacono/*Sports Illustrated*)*

. . . and at my peak with the Raiders. *(Paul Chinn/* San Francisco Chronicle*)*

Surfing—one of my favorite pastimes—with my new pal Adam Sandler (he's back there, somewhere) on break from filming *The Longest Yard*. *(© Tracy Bennett)*

Now that I'm retired, this older family shot reminds me how easy it is for our most important priorities to be overlooked. *(Ryan McKee/Rich Clarkson & Assoc.)*

9 EAS & ZMA

Super Bowl victories propel players to such heights. The inevitable perks that follow those super wins do the same. After the Broncos and EAS came out on top of the 1997 NFL season, I stepped right into the high life. Rewarding me for past contributions as well as the ones he knew I was bound to make, EAS founder Bill Phillips handed me two pieces of paper.

The first was a $100,000 bonus for work previously rendered. The second was a $120,000 contract for work that would be rendered in the coming season—exactly what EAS had paid Shannon Sharpe during our Super Bowl year. As if those gestures weren't enough, as if the past season hadn't been enough of a wild ride, Bill provided one more.

Bill invited Shannon and I to Columbus, Ohio, to attend the March 7 Arnold Schwarzenegger Classic—professional body-building competitions as well as an expo with hundreds of booths featuring the latest fitness equipment, clothing, and nutritional supplements. To fly twelve of us from Denver to Columbus for the weekend, Bill chartered a luxurious Gulfstream G4 with wood paneling, large-screen TVs, and leather seats that folded down to become beds. Once aboard, it was easy to see why Gulfstreams are so popular in corporate America.

Inside an EAS booth set up to display its numerous products at Veterans Memorial Auditorium, I noticed Dr. Mauro DiPasquale, milling around inside it. Right away, I recognized him as the author of the monthly newsletter *Think Muscle*. An EAS advisory board member, Dr. DiPasquale was an internationally renowned hormone therapy expert. He was also a former world champion power lifter who, as I mentioned earlier, went on to develop the Anabolic Diet and the Metabolic Diet.

Dr. DiPasquale had a medical degree in nutrition and sports medicine, with honors in biological science. Among his written works were the groundbreaking books *Beyond Anabolic Steroids* and *Anabolic Steroid Side Effects: Fact, Fiction and Treatment*.

Some people get a huge rush out of meeting athletes; I get a rush out of meeting experts in the field of health and nutrition. I'd much rather spend a day with Linus Pauling—the only person to win two unshared Nobel prizes for Chemistry and Peace, as well as a researcher of Vitamin C—than Walter Payton, who ran himself into the Pro Football Hall of Fame with 16,726 rushing yards.

As I expected, Dr. DiPasquale's knowledge completely floored me. I told him about how, during intense training, my testosterone was dropping to almost nonexistent levels. He wound up prescribing Arimidex for me, an aromatase inhibitor that keeps testosterone levels up. The Arimidex worked, preventing my testosterone from breaking down into estrogen.

We spent hours together and hit it off. But best of all, when we ran out of time, he pulled out his business card and handed it to me. "Call any time you need any advice," he said.

Are you kidding? Dr. DiPasquale as one of my personal

brain trusts? No athlete's autograph could have made any fan any happier. Even better, Dr. DiPasquale became one of my most trusted doctors. Our team came to trust other medical advisors.

After seeing what Victor's mineral recommendations helped me accomplish during the 1997 season—sixteen regular-season starts and four more in the postseason, second on the team with 117 tackles, 2 sacks, 1 interception, 2 pass defenses, 2 forced fumbles—I wanted everyone else on our team to have those same benefits.

In April, I sought permission from our trainer Steve "Greek" Antonopulos to have Victor examine the blood work of any willing player on our team. When I explained to Greek how it worked, he received clearance from up above, so I arranged for Victor and BALCO vice president James Valente to arrive in Denver the day before our May minicamp. Like the Broncos team of doctors, they set up shop at an adjoining table where each player underwent his pre minicamp physical at the Steadman Hawkins Clinic in Greenwood Village, Colorado, a few miles due northwest of the Broncos training complex.

Victor and James had their medical kits, ready to siphon off some of the blood and urine samples the Broncos were giving to their doctors. After each player's physical, they could listen to Victor and James's presentation on minerals and how BALCO might be able to help. If they agreed, BALCO would test their blood and then could inform players of which minerals they were deficient.

How many players went for it? I'm not sure of any who didn't. To my knowledge, just about everybody agreed to send vials of their blood and urine back to BALCO, where Victor analyzed it the way he had mine. What he found was, to say the least, surprising: 70 percent of my Broncos teammates were depleted in zinc, magnesium chromium, and copper. NFL players, some of the world's best athletes, were not performing to their optimum levels.

So what did Victor do? He shipped cases of mineral supplements to the Broncos training complex in Englewood, Colorado, to be distributed to my teammates. For free, just like EAS did.

And what did we do that year? We kicked ass. For the 1998 season that we started 13–0 before having an undefeated season and our unbeaten streak snapped during a 20–16 loss to the Giants at Giants Stadium on December 13, Victor ensured our zinc, magnesium, chromium, and copper were at the proper levels. Word of Victor's work spread around the NFL so that, the very next season, the Miami Dolphins adopted the same practices. Victor tested their blood and urine and prescribed every mineral the Dolphins were deficient in for free. Eventually, Victor was treating NFL players across the league.

Victor did the Broncos a huge favor. Now it was time for me to do him one. Victor was searching for funding for a study that would validate his recently developed product, ZMA—a zinc-magnesium supplement designed to increase anabolic hormone levels and muscle strength while a person slept. I had been taking it throughout the 1997 season and could swear by its effectiveness; it changed my life.

At the time, there already had been individual studies on zinc and magnesium, but not together as Victor's ZMA product. Playing matchmaker, I called Bill Phillips and arranged a meeting at his Golden offices, sort of an impromptu health summit between EAS and Victor.

With me sitting in as the facilitator, Victor and James detailed their product to Bill. As Victor talked, Bill sat behind his desk, scribbling notes on a yellow legal pad. After Victor's lengthy and detailed presentation, Bill admitted his desire to become the exclusive supplier of ZMA. Problem was, Bill was locked into the start of negotiations to sell EAS to North Castle Partners.

So instead of partnering with BALCO, Bill did the next best thing. He wrote out a check for $10,000 and handed it to Victor. Just as he had backed the Broncos, Bill backed Victor by helping to pay for the ZMA study. EAS had the deep pockets to write such a check. After founding the company in 1995 and the sudden thrust of exposure during our Super Bowl run, EAS' sales skyrocketed to $150 million in one year.

Nobody capitalized on a relationship with the Broncos like EAS. On its website, EAS touted itself as the "official sports supplements providers of the Super Bowl Champion Denver Broncos." More and more, people began noticing EAS, including, unfortunately, the NFL.

In August 1998, the NFL summoned all our players into the team auditorium at the Broncos training facility and warned us about wearing clothes and endorsing a company that wasn't a league licensee. Other league licensees such as Nike had been paying the NFL millions of dollars to have its brand endorsed. Yet EAS got all the exposure that companies like Nike did—and maybe even more—without paying the NFL a single dime. Let's just say this did not go over well in the NFL's offices on Park Avenue.

League officials warned us, in no uncertain language, that we better not be caught wearing EAS hats or turtlenecks on the sidelines or in postgame interviews anymore—or we would be subject to fines starting at $10,000. The NFL delivered its message to EAS as well. Almost immediately, EAS changed the wording on its website from the "official" supplier of the Broncos to the "exclusive" supplier of the Broncos. My thought was

R
O
M
O

that the NFL was trying to do its job, and I had to keep trying to do mine.

I wouldn't wear an EAS hat or mock turtleneck in the postgame locker room anymore, just as the NFL ordered. But I would wear EAS clothing in the locker room at the Broncos training facility. I would wear it whenever I was doing local television interviews. Outside of gameday and the Mile High Stadium locker room, I would wear whatever I wanted. I wasn't going to turn my back on EAS.

I've always enjoyed helping my friends. Case in point: When Bubby Brister was out of football during the 1996 season after a poor 1995 season, I was busy making telephone calls, doing what I could to try to help him get a job. I even spoke to Bill McPherson about him, but couldn't convince the 49ers to take a look at Bubby. I had more success with the Broncos.

When Denver's backup quarterback, Bill Musgrave—now the NFL's youngest offensive coordinator in Jacksonville—underwent career-threatening shoulder surgery in the winter of 1997, I thought it'd be great to get Bubby back to the NFL and to reunite him with me in Denver.

Before I did, I had to track him down at his house on the bayou, in Monroe, Louisiana. When he came to the phone, I asked him, "Hey, Bub, how big is your lot down there?"

In his thick Louisiana accent, Bubby answered, "Well, Romo, if I went outside and I was standing at the boat dock, and I threw the football out to the street, it's about 50 yards. And if I went to the other side of the property and threw a football over the house, it would be 75 yards. So that's how big my lot is— 50 yards by 75 yards."

However big it was, Bubby was ready to come back. I pitched the idea to Coach Shanahan, telling him about my experiences of playing with Bubby in Philadelphia. "When Bubby played, everybody responded," I told Coach Shanahan. "But it was a situation where Randall Cunningham was making a few million bucks a year and he was the guy. But personally, I could clearly see that Bubby was the better quarterback. You could sense around the locker room that everybody had more faith in Bubby. I promise you, you'll love this guy. John Elway will love this guy. He's awesome in the locker room."

Sure enough, the Broncos signed him. And even came to rely on him. During our historic 1998 season, John Elway pulled his right hamstring near the end of the second game against Dallas, then aggravated the injury the next week during our 34–17 win at Oakland. He could not play the next four games. Bubby relieved John, and Shannon Sharpe said it best: It was as if Bubby were handed the keys to the Ferrari—with instructions not to wreck it—and he did as he was instructed.

Bubby led our team to victories in the four games he started, including a 41–16 blowout of Philadelphia when he completed 16-of-29 passes for 203 yards and 4 touchdowns. Bubby continued our unbeaten streak that lasted into December.

Almost every day at practice, Bubby's message to me would be the same. "Thanks for giving me a shot, Romo."

"You're the one who did it, Bubby. All I did was talk to somebody. But your ability took over after that."

Bubby was a tough leader at a time when we really needed him. Toughness was a trademark we shared, and it was constantly being tested, particularly by pain. It's a constant companion and one that needs to be treated by whatever medicine works. There is no debate over how many football players are quietly treated: virtually everyone but the kicker and punter.

There is no other way to make it to and through Sunday. In our opening 1998 game, a Monday nighter against the New England Patriots, I aggravated a shoulder injury. The day before our game against the Dallas Cowboys, I visited our training room, from where this report was filed:

DATE SEEN BRONCOS TRAINING FACILITY: 9/12/98
  9/12/98: Bill sustained a right latissimus or serratus strain last week. He is improving but is still quite sore. He is wondering about a Toradol injection. After reviewing the risks of a Toradol injection, 60mg is administered under sterile technique into his right buttock.
  Martin Boublik, MD
  MB/NLH T: 9/16/98

  Cc: Steve Antonopulos, ATC
  Richard J. Hawkins, MD

Toradol is a pain killer as tough as muscle. But it also can cause gastric and intestinal ulcers, as well as decreased blood flow to the kidneys. Ongoing use of it for chronic problems, as I began experiencing later in my career, is considered dangerous, if not life-threatening. Back then, Toradol was new to me. Once you're exposed to it, it can be hard to get by without it.

The day before our September 13 game versus Dallas, I took my first—but far from my last—Toradol injection. It wiped away the pain that day, but could do nothing to withstand the inevitable effects of the rest of the season.

Two weeks later at Washington, I felt a shooting sensation through my groin. Right away, pain and fear simultaneously set in. It felt as if playing the following Sunday's game against Philadelphia would be an impossibility. Somehow, I made it halfway through before realizing I had a problem for next week's game against Seattle. My consecutive game playing streak was in jeopardy, and when it was, I turned to those I trusted most.

From his work with the Utah Jazz, Greg Roskopf knew Craig Buhler, a clinical kinesiologist who also worked for the team. But the NBA was on strike in 1998 and Craig had no commitments. So at my expense, I flew him to Denver and underwent muscle testing that fascinated me.

Using acupuncture points and stimulating my muscles, Craig worked on me for ten straight hours. He taught me about the nervous system and how it controls muscle function. He explained that when a muscle is overloaded beyond its ability to handle stress, one of two things happen. Either the muscle fibers tear or the brain neurologically deactivates the muscle through the nerve centers in the muscle itself. Once that occurs, the muscles don't fire under workload situations.

To combat it, Craig activated my eight reflex systems—three vertebra in the spine that count as one, an acupuncture point, a vascular reflex point, a lymphatic reflex point, the origin and insertion of the muscle, the spindle cells of the muscle itself, and then two organ reflex points—causing my muscles to fire once again. Maybe the simplest way to describe the work Craig did on me is like this: I was blown away. By the time we were finished, I was ready to hire him right then. Pay him whatever he wanted.

He could help me, he could help my teammates, he could help anyone. I wanted access to Craig every day, but he lived in Utah. For the next year, I kept asking around to see if anyone knew anybody like Craig.

In the interim, I had what I needed: a healthy enough groin to play the following Sunday against Seattle. I would be out there, my consecutive game streak intact. I couldn't imagine not playing a divisional game, especially during a season in which so much went right for me and our team.

We had the confidence from the season before, and I had more confidence than ever before. Let me give you a perfect

R
O
M
O

example. Earlier in my career, former Penn State and then Raiders guard Steve Wisniewski would hit me and growl, "I'm going to dominate you like I did at BC." That would bother me.

That was the type of approach I used, and he deployed it on me, the game within the game. But after Denver won its first Super Bowl, there was no way Wisniewski nor any other player was going to piss me off. I didn't have a fear of anybody because I was playing at a higher level than ever. My training was more advanced than before, my supplementation, too. And our team was performing at the same high level.

In 1998, we finished 14–2, winning our division and clinching homefield advantage throughout the playoffs. And I racked up 95 tackles, a career-best 7.5 sacks, 2 interceptions, 9 pass defenses, 3 forced fumbles, 3 fumble recoveries, and one other honor that meant more than any of those statistics: The players, despite how controversial I'd become, voted me to my second Pro Bowl. This time, unlike the last time, there were no tears shed. Maybe because my fourth Super Bowl victory was within view. There was a postseason to get ready for.

After clobbering the Miami Dolphins 38–3 in our January 9, 1999, Divisional Playoff in a game not as close as the score would indicate, I clobbered my own brain against the New York Jets in the AFC Championship game.

A little more than a minute into the third quarter, I collided with Jets' running back, Curtis Martin: two battering rams hitting each other with full force. Usually when I would get up after a big hit, it would be slowly. This time when I got up I looked like a drunk, staggering around, struggling to stay upright. Up in the stands, Julie turned to her mother and said, "This is not good." She could tell what was happening at a time I couldn't. I just wanted to play. This was for a trip to the Super

Bowl, every players' dream. This was for a repeat. Nothing was going to keep me off the field, not even another brain bruise.

And so a short time later—I can't remember exactly when, I was so disoriented I sat on Elway's lap instead of the bench—I returned to the game and hit Martin again, this time head on. My brain, as my medical report touched on, was being pummeled.

Jan. 17, 1999

13:56 of third quarter; Run play; Direct impact making tackle, hit head to running back's body; Was dazed and ran off field on own power; Saw Dr. Schlegel/Hawkins/ Ziporin; Refer to their notes; Returned to the game and hit running back head on again; Removed from the game for 3 series; Came back and played with no problems; Was OK post game.

Was I really okay? At that moment, it sure seemed like it. Despite how woozy I felt, we had beaten the Jets 23–10 to earn our second straight trip to the Super Bowl. These were the moments you trained for, sweated for—a chance to play on the season's final Sunday. For me it represented a chance to become one of only three players in NFL history—along with former Green Bay Packer and Miami Dolphin Marv Fleming, and my old friend former San Francisco 49er and Dallas Cowboy Charles Haley—to win back-to-back Super Bowls with two different organizations.

It also represented one last chance to maximize EAS' exposure before Bill sold 65 percent of the company to North Castle Partners for $245 million. The week before Super Bowl XXXIII, in Miami on January 31, I worked with EAS to publicize the company without breaking the NFL's rules.

Just before our team flew to Miami, I handed out black

R
O
M
O

EAS leather bags with the players' names and numbers embroidered on them. Each bag was stuffed with EAS shirts and CD players—an advance thank you to my teammates. To every press conference, to every practice, players carried their black EAS leather bags. Cameras captured it all. At our team hotel in Fort Lauderdale, it was arranged for EAS' executives to have a block of rooms. They were there with all the supplements we needed.

We also had something else motivating us: This would be John Elway's final game, and there was no way our team was going to allow him to lose it. That was obvious from the start.

On the Atlanta Falcons' first series of the game, after they already had driven to our 8-yard line, I came in unblocked and sacked Chris Chandler on a third-down blitz. Just nailed him. It was one of those hits where you could hear him moaning at the bottom of the pile. To me, those moans sound as sweet as ocean waves. There's nothing better to hear. There's nothing better than knocking somebody out, seeing them struggle to get up, and watching a stretcher brought out to carry them off.

It's the way they used to play in the NFL, back in the day. In the days of NFL Hall of Famers Ray Nitschke and Dick Butkus, everything went. They didn't get fined $20,000 for hitting a quarterback hard. They got a pat on the back.

Over the years, you don't know how many former NFL players have come up to me and said, "You play the game the way it's supposed to be played, Romo. You're a throwback. You belong playing with us back in the 60s or 70s." Sometimes I wish I was able to play back when the rest of those players did, back when being nasty and dirty or whatever people call me was praised rather than criticized. But the older players, the veterans I respected, still would come up to me all the time and tell me: "Keep playing just the way you are, Romo. We love it." I would tell them: "Great, as long as you pay my fines. I keep playing like this, I'm going to end up in the poorhouse."

But after our 34–19 win over the Falcons, the poorhouse would wait. It was my fourth Super Bowl win.

I was on top of the world the week we returned to Colorado. Bill Phillips called and asked Julie and I to stop by the local Mercedes dealership. When we arrived, he told us to pick a car, any car we wanted.

Now, I've never been much of a car guy myself. Give me a pickup truck, and I'm fine. You're dealing with a guy who drove a multicolored '68 International pickup in high school, with rust being the main color. From there I graduated to a '71 Ford F 100, and then the mud-brown 1977 Toyota Sport Coup at Boston College. Cars never were my thing. But Julie fell for a fully loaded black Mercedes SL600 convertible with a V12 engine, one of the rarest models in the country.

"Is this the one?" I asked.

"This is the one," Julie answered.

After Bill spoke with the dealer, Julie and I drove off the lot in the $138,000 car—a very nice farewell gift.

In 1999, the Broncos hired a new linebackers coach, a white-haired, pipe-smoking gentleman named Larry Coyer who had more than thirty years of coaching experience. He took over for Frank Bush—another coach I loved—who had moved over to special teams. When I met Coach Coyer I instantly liked him. He talked to me about my role and the way he wanted to use me. Aside from him sending the defensive play calls into me in the huddle, Coach Coyer also wanted me to play closer to the tight end, what he called "heavier, more physical," where I used my hands more.

ROMO

To help do it, Coach Coyer wanted me working against a blocking sled. So his first week on the job, I showed up on Friday morning at 9 A.M. and spent the next two hours honing my linebacking technique and the manner in which I used my hands.

Soon enough, one of our other young linebackers, Steve Russ, joined us. Then veteran linebacker John Mobley did the same. Pretty soon, we had all the linebackers working on this blocking sled, me offering them tips the way Riki Ellison and Jim Burt once had done for me. For the remainder of the off-season, we beat that sled to death.

I felt like I was helping myself, as well as the rest of our linebackers. But to my surprise, Coach Coyer thought I was helping him. Later, Coach Coyer thanked me for bringing him instant credibility amongst our linebackers. Everyone accepted him from day one. It's no surprise that today he is one of the best assistant coaches in the NFL.

While working with Coach Coyer, I also helped convince Coach Shanahan to hire Randy Huntington as the Broncos' speed coach.

Bubby Brister and Ed McCaffrey started using him, but the problem they faced was similar to the one everyone did. Our strength coach Rich Tuten's workouts were designed to last 30–45 intense minutes. Randy's stretching warmups were 30–45 minutes. How many guys do you think wanted to go through Randy's workouts and then Rich's? Not too many.

Hiring Randy wound up adding more tension than benefits. His methods didn't blend with the rest of the training staff's. Our strength coaches were teaching one thing, Randy another. After one year, the experiment ended and Denver let him go. I think all my ideas were well intentioned, but not necessarily well executed.

• • •

On June 2, 1999, a story moved across health news service wires. ZMA was about to go big.

SEATTLE (BW HealthWire)—Lorrie Brilla, PhD, a sports performance researcher at Western Washington University, announced today that a novel zinc-magnesium supplement called "ZMA" significantly increased muscle strength in NCAA football players.

The ZMA study results are being presented today by Dr. Brilla at the 46th Annual Meeting of the American College of Sports Medicine in Seattle, Washington. These findings were recently published in the official ACSM journal, <u>Medicine & Science in Sports & Exercise</u>, Vol. 31, No. 5.

According to Dr. Brilla, "A group of competitive NCAA football players who took ZMA nightly during an 8 week spring training program had 2.5 times greater muscle strength gains than a placebo group. Pre and post leg strength measurements were made using a Biodex isokinetic dynamometer." The strength of the ZMA group increased by 11.6% compared to only a 4.6% increase in the placebo group.

"The muscle strength increases may have been mediated by the anabolic hormone increases in the ZMA group. The ZMA group had 30% increases in free and total testosterone levels compared to 10% decreases in the placebo group. The ZMA group also had a slight increase in insulin-like growth factor-1 (IGF-1) levels compared to a 20% decrease in the

R
O
M
O

placebo group. This study shows that anabolic hormone and muscle strength increases can be induced in already strength-trained athletes by using a novel zinc-magnesium preparation," said Brilla.

According to co-investigator Victor Conte, Director of BALCO Laboratories in Burlingame, California, "ZMA is the only all natural product that has been clinically proven to increase anabolic hormone levels and muscle strength in trained athletes." The dosage of ZMA used in the study contains 30 mg of zinc and 450 mg of magnesium. "There has never been a study reporting adverse health effects at these moderate dosages," said Conte.

John Gamble, strength and conditioning coach for the Miami Dolphins, reports that "players using ZMA are cramping much less and seem to be getting a more deep and restful sleep which enhances their recovery."

A story that stemmed from a meeting in Bill Phillips' Golden offices now was going nationwide. It was just what Victor needed. All along, ZMA was his primary product, his money-maker. Now that he had a study to validate the product, he could get athletes like me and Barry Bonds to endorse it. Which is exactly what happened. Athletes started showing up in *Muscle & Fitness* magazine, promoting the benefits of ZMA.

Former Buffalo Bills and Jacksonville Jaguars defensive end Bryce Paup was quoted as saying: "When I take ZMA, I sleep better and more soundly, and I feel more rested when I wake up. The more I rest and the better I sleep, the better I perform on the field."

ZMA's benefits went beyond sleep. I wound up giving it to our star running back, Terrell Davis, to cure his migraines. People who get headaches are usually deficient in magnesium, and once Terrell started taking the ZMA that I gave him, he told me his migraines disappeared. It worked so well with him, I tried it on other people. One of Julie's girlfriends used to get six to eight raging migraines a year, to where she would be knocked out for a week. Once I put her on ZMA, the headaches went away and, to this day, she still hasn't had another migraine.

It was easy to see why ZMA's popularity was spreading. Eventually Victor told me that 250 NFL players and more than 25 IFBB pro bodybuilders were using ZMA, and those were just some of the people he knew. Who knows how many more were out there? But every time I saw another story about another athlete using ZMA, it reminded me of how high life can lift you.

But then, as Julie and I were about to find out, there also was a flip side. The higher you are, the harder you fall. And we were about to pay a huge price for my impulsive need to push the limits.

ROMO

10

IF HE PLEADS GUILTY TO SPITTING ON THE SIDEWALK, HE'S GOING TO BE SUSPENDED

August 21, 1999, is a date I'll never forget. One of my child-hood buddies living in the basement of our Littleton house went to pick up a Phentermine prescription at the local Safe-way. Instead of bringing home the Phentermine, though, he brought home unwelcome intruders.

Julie and I were sharing a quiet moment with our children when three U.S. Drug Enforcement Administration agents and three police officers from the Douglas County Sheriff's Department charged into the foyer, right behind my friend. They started screaming. Our children started crying. I started trembling. Before my eyes, our world was crumbling.

In the midst of the chaos, the cops separated us, pulling me into the living room, our friend into my office, and Julie into the kitchen. Worse, they rounded up our five-year-old son and two-year-old daughter and put them in our basement so they could not see or hear what the rest of Colorado soon would find out.

For the past year, authorities had been conducting a secret investigation that focused on Julie and me but extended to one of our doctors and another family friend. Since September 1998, Douglas County authorities said, this physician had written several Phentermine prescriptions for Julie and her friend.

What their investigation and newspaper reporters failed to uncover was the story behind the story, the whole truth. Julie had developed a friendship with a woman who introduced us to a doctor who would become one of my medical confidants, helping me with my concussions. I told him I was worried about my brain malfunctioning. I'd experienced eight documented concussions, and what I would estimate was another half dozen or so that I never told team doctors about out of fear for my job. As I've mentioned, in my mind, sharing the truth about my brain with my team would be professional suicide.

At the same time, I was getting more and more scared. I found myself losing my keys, misplacing my wallet, rarely being able to remember where I put my personal belongings. My memory loss was becoming more noticeable, while the dings I was suffering in games were growing more severe.

As I learned to trust this doctor's sincere intentions and medical wisdom, I did something I would later regret. I took advantage of someone who was only trying to help me. I asked him to write me scrip for Phentermine.

By now, the Phentermine no longer was for me. I was on to other substances, and more advanced science, using Ephedrine, injectable Creatine and B-12, ZMA, supplements that most people never heard of. Phentermine was the last thing I needed or wanted; in the long run, it was too hard on my system. The crashing it caused wasn't worth it anymore.

But the Phentermine apparently didn't affect others as negatively. They wanted it. And they had asked me if I knew how to get it. I did, and in the course of another of my impetuous thoughtless acts, I rationalized it: Phentermine was not on the NFL's banned-substance list. To protect my anonymity, we prescribed it in Julie's and her friend's names. Anyone else's but mine. I won't ever let myself forget how I exposed my loving wife and other innocent people.

Julie agreed to help out of loyalty. Like me, she had no intention of using them. She couldn't. Aside from the fact that she is beautifully thin, she is a Medic Alert, allergic to any medication. Taking a Tylenol is an ordeal for her.

The authorities later alleged that I got the Phentermine through fraud and deceit, yet the doctor knew exactly who it was for. The people who picked it up knew exactly who it was for. Now, was I wrong to involve others? Absolutely. But what amazed me was that the U.S. Drug Enforcement Administration agents and Douglas County Sheriff's Department used an inordinate amount of taxpayer dollars investigating a case that involved nothing more than a simple diet drug. Yet the authorities treated the raid on our house like some spectacular bust.

The whole fight turned out to be a long one, longer than I think anybody would have expected. During the trial, I had plenty of time to think about the wrong I had done. The events were a wake-up call.

Here I am, a public figure with increasing popularity, feeling as if I could do anything I wanted, as if I were above the law. When you get so consumed with the end result, you engage in activities you shouldn't. When I didn't catch myself, someone needed to catch me. The authorities did, and for this, I'm thankful. They caught the warning signs that I ignored.

■　■　■

As soon as the headline "Romo Faces Drug Charges" was splashed across our city's tabloid newspaper, as soon as word of the case spread, Phentermine use dried up. Nobody wanted to go anywhere near it anymore.

Other challenges were already rocking our team as we attempted to become the first team in NFL history to three-peat; next to none of them were good. In June, a player was arrested on charges of reckless driving and driving while impaired. Then, a week before my house was raided, Coach Shanahan elected to yank Bubby Brister from the starting lineup and replace him with the untested and unproven quarterback Brian Griese, a move that invited controversy and criticism.

We lost our first three games, the last one of those coming in Tampa, a 13–10 defeat I don't remember much about without my medical reports.

HEAD CONCUSSION
9/26/99
Recorder: KELLER, JIM
Supervisor: ANTONOPULOS, STEVE
Progress Notes: 11:48 of the third quarter; Making tackle on run play and took direct hit to head; Removed from the field; Saw Dr. Boublik: Returned next series; OK; Post game; Negative neuro signs.

As my concussions continued piling up—were we now on eight? Ten? Twelve?—so did the misery of the season. The very next week, in our fourth straight defeat, we suffered our biggest loss yet.

Our Pro Bowl running back Terrell Davis, who the season before had become one of only four players in NFL history to rush for more than 2,000 yards, blew out his knee trying to

R
O
M
O

tackle Jets safety Victor Green after he had intercepted a Griese pass. Watching Terrell writhe around on the ground in pain made me sick. It almost felt as if the football gods were lashing out at us for all the fun we had the past two years.

Our success was definitely up. Instead, fines were in. It seemed like every time I hit somebody, the NFL noticed. I piled up a fortune's worth of fines in 1999. The league slapped me with a $5,000 fine for hitting Chiefs tight end Tony Gonzales . . . $10,000 for a helmet-to-helmet hit against Tampa Bay quarterback Trent Dilfer . . . $2,500 for throwing a football at Jets linebacker Bryan Cox . . . $15,000 for a helmet-to-helmet hit on Jaguars running back Fred Taylor . . . and $10,000 for illegally hitting Gonzalez in the head again on a play I didn't even remember until the NFL sent me a letter, notifying me of the fine.

Tony and I were always going at it, hitting each other, yelling at each other, challenging each other. Playing against him twice a year was one of the highlights of my career. Not only was he a phenomenal pass catcher, he was a great blocker. He would fight me. When we played, he brought it. After our second game that season against the Chiefs, Tony came over to me and said, "Hey, as dirty as you are, I still respect you." He might have respected me, but the league did not like me, not at all.

My total in fines that season grew to $42,500; my fines from the previous three seasons grew to $70,000—not the kind of write-off that anybody wants, and one that bothers me more today than it did then. Eventually Coach Shanahan had to warn me: The next time the league had to fine me that season, it was going to suspend me, too. A league built on violence—highlights of it, celebrations of it—seemed hypocritical at best. Either way, that was it for me with fines for the rest of the season. But my real troubles were just beginning.

On November 23, when our 4–7 record eliminated any hopes we had of making history or even the playoffs, the Douglas County Sheriff's Office piled on. It hit us with the hardest blow yet, charging Julie with conspiracy and obtaining a controlled substance by fraud and deceit.

Here's a situation where my wife was helping me, risking everything for me. I had totally underestimated the consequences of my and her actions, and the impact they would have. Aside from her legal troubles, some players' wives began ignoring her. Some charities she was affiliated with began dropping her. There are not very many women who could have handled that type of criticism.

Me, I've always had a unique ability to compartmentalize my emotions. I could block out what I couldn't control and focus on what I could. In this case, I could focus on football, which is one reason why I failed to show Julie anywhere near the compassion she deserved. I was too caught up in what Romo had to do to get ready for the next game, what Romo had to do to keep his consecutive game streak alive.

On the field, I could hear the cheers and know that Denver still believed in its gladiator. But Julie never heard any of those cheers, from the crowd or me. She was just trying to keep the family together, shielding our children from all the critics. She was amazingly tough, bravely facing down charges that carried the possibility of an $800,000 fine and five-and-a-half years in prison while trying to maintain a normal home life and keep me on the playing field. The scars, to this day, remain. My sanctuary, as usual, was doing what I had to do to get ready for the next game. But the case continued unfolding.

The doctor, meanwhile, pleaded guilty to a misdemeanor charge of unlawful dispensing of a controlled substance and got eighteen months probation. Julie's friend pleaded guilty to con-

ROMO

spiracy and was given community service and a one-year deferred sentence. And my childhood buddy plea bargained on a conspiracy charge.

Now that their cases were settled, authorities could focus on their prime suspects—Julie and me. They already had charged Julie; they were coming after me next. "Trying to land the Big Fish," Harvey Steinberg liked to say to us. "A big-time defendant on small-time allegation."

And still, my obsession continued. To counter the increasing stresses in my life, I found even more alternative medicines to distract me and neutralize them. For more than a year, I had been scouring the country for a Craig Buhler–type doctor, flying to a number of cities to visit different chiropractors, acupuncturists, and nutritionists. Finally, Bobby Hill, one of the massage therapists I helped bring to the Broncos, told me about a doctor in Boulder, Colorado, who packaged together all the skills I desired in one practice.

Dr. Dean Raffelock was a chiropractor who had earned diplomas in applied kinesiology, nutrition, and acupuncture, and also held a separate certification as a clinical nutritionist. Raffelock taught research-based clinical nutrition to a number of medical groups and knew things about nutrition that very few doctors with any type of degree did. This sounded like my type of doctor.

Problem was, when I called to see about his next available appointment, his wife, Stephanie, who runs his office, told me he could see me in about six months. But after momentarily mulling over the matter, she said, "You know, Mr. Romanowski, Dr. Raffelock is a big Broncos fan, so let me see if he'll come in earlier to see you."

Football continued opening doors for me. Raffelock made

the time and two days later, I drove to Boulder, about forty-five miles northwest of my Littleton house, to meet the next man to mold my career.

By this time, I already felt my knowledge of nutrition and natural health was very broad. It was now about to expand even more. For thirty minutes, I asked Raffelock questions about nutrition. In turn, he showed me charts of how the body made energy that was broken down into all the specific nutrients needed to help the various metabolic "pathways" do their jobs better.

After our initial Q-and-A session, Raffelock studied my posture and tested my muscles like Dr. Buehler had, tracing the possibility of a whole group of muscles not working properly due to one or two specific areas. For instance, he might find twelve different muscles in my hips, knees, shoulders, and head testing weak—and find one spot in my foot that was the reason for it. Once he would make those corrections, all my muscles would turn back on. I would be ready to go.

Not only would I be ready to go, but I could get into positions that I couldn't before. He also showed me how specific acupuncture points could strengthen muscles and relieve pain, lessons I would later use.

"Can I come in for a few hours a day after games so you can put me back together?" I asked him. Raffelock explained that his practice was really busy, but we came to an arrangement that included him helping me find good doctors in other cities when we were playing out of town.

Raffelock then took me into his nutrient room and natural pharmacy, a floor-to-ceiling area, fifteen feet long, filled with specific nutrients and herbs that he used to balance certain conditions. I was like a kid in a candy store, a new world appearing. Anyone who has his own store of supplements, like Raffelock does, is my kind of guy.

ROMO

I didn't know that so many different kinds of nutrients and herbs existed, but he assured me that each had a purpose and, most important, all were safe and legal. Some of the herbs were Western herbs, some were Chinese herbs. To understand which herbs and nutrients would help me most, Raffelock explained the many types of blood and urine testing available. Those tests, like others I had taken, would reveal which nutrients my body was deficient in, either because I was using them up at a very high rate or they just weren't getting into my diet.

"Let's test everything," I told him.

We wound up doing a lot of different kinds of testing, most of them measuring blood levels of the different vitamins and minerals, antioxidants, amino acids, and fatty acids—all the basic building blocks that make our bodies work. We also tested various hormones and other key substances that affect how well you feel and how healthy you are.

After testing my urine for free levels of twelve different hormones, Raffelock put me on a hormone called DHEA—dehydroepiandrosterone—which helps improve immunity, bone density, muscle density, heart health, memory, skin tone, and general well-being. Once most of us turn thirty, especially if we are stressed out, our blood DHEA level decreases dramatically, which I had not known. Raffelock solved that problem, and more.

On one of my first visits to him, Raffelock gave me a Chinese herb formula called "Dynamic Warrior." My questions then, as they were with any new substances I tried, were the same: Did the NFL ban it? How would it help me? No, it was not banned, and it could help me in more ways than I knew. Raffelock explained that everything in Chinese medicine is about balance—yin and yang. He knew I was taking Ephedra, injectable Creatine and B-12. But the Dynamic Warrior balanced out the Ephedrin and Creatine by nourishing my kidneys and heart and, consequently, strengthening the muscles that support my lower back. Any danger was neutralized.

Before every practice and game, I would swallow a tincture of Dynamic Warrior, a terrible tasting liquid. Then when the league banned Ephedrin before the start of the 2001 season, I became even more reliant on Dynamic Warrior, which provided a boost of its own, though not as strong. Raffelock also turned me on to other Chinese herbs.

One was a special "Yin Formula" he would make for me to take after games and practices so I could relax and sleep much better. He said that too much of the stimulating "Yang" substances like Ephedrin could create big-time health problems unless you used Yin formulas to help the body calm down and regain moisture in the organs that were stressed and overstimulated from the Ephedrin.

Some of the best overall herbal experiences with Raffelock would be when Julie, one of the children, or I would have colds or the flu. Whenever Raffelock gave us the Chinese herbs Yin Chiao, Gan Mao Ling, Zhong Gan Ling, Bi Yan Pian, San She Dan, or Osha Root Cough Syrup, our sicknesses vanished in days if not hours. Without fail.

Raffelock's knowledge went beyond herbs, chiropractic, and acupuncture. He also showed me devices I had not seen. He started with a hyperbaric chamber, not much bigger than a coffin but with just the opposite result. A hyperbaric chamber, as I discovered, brings you to life. Once you lie down inside it, your lungs and blood cells are flooded with oxygen, which stimulates the production of the healing-protein collagen, decreases tissue inflammation, and increases the development of new blood vessels and a healthier immune system.

"Go ahead and give it a try," Raffelock told me. After one session, I was hooked. I figured if I could increase recovery, I was going to play at higher levels even longer. I was going to be big-

R
O
M
O

ger, stronger, faster. Healthier. I had to have one. Raffelock arranged for me to buy my own portable hyperbaric chamber that I started taking with me to the Broncos training facility and to training camp. It cost me $6,000, which was a bargain compared to the top-of-the-line hyperbaric chambers that can cost anywhere from $50,000 to $200,000. He made sure that I always took enough antioxidant vitamins because they were even more important to have in my system when I was flooding my body with extra oxygen in the chamber.

The other advantage of the hyperbaric chamber was taking the time to lie there and relax. Maybe that was the real reason I would emerge feeling like I could whip the world. Relaxation is not noted anywhere in the NFL training manual. It is unfortunately frowned upon and often thought to be an expression of laziness. Fortunately it doesn't look like you're "only relaxing" when you're in the chamber.

As my visits to Boulder became more frequent—now I was going two, three times a week—Raffelock showed me other treatments. He performed a balance of the best chiropractic adjustments and muscle testing I'd ever had, with acupuncture and his precise nutritional workups. The most captivating and least scientific were the Bach Flower remedies, which a renowned physician from London named Edward Bach developed in the 1930s.

The way Raffelock explained it, Dr. Bach was one of the first doctors to realize the connection between emotional and physical health. He categorized thirty-eight negative states of mind and formulated a flower-based remedy to treat each emotional state. Dr. Raffelock told me that unresolved negative emotions could not only weaken the energy to our organs but also weaken our muscles. Initially, Dr. Raffelock thought the concept was a little bit too far out, so he first used the remedies on his dog, a big black lab, twenty-five years ago. And what happened? Amazing results. Gradually, once he realized they were safe with no negative side effects, he began to use them on people.

When a person lacked confidence, he would use the Larch flower. When a person felt gloom, he would treat them with the Mustard flower. When a person experienced anguish, he would administer the Sweet Chestnut. People swore by these treatments.

Heck, I was willing to try it. Why not? To determine my mental state and the proper remedy to treat it, Raffelock had me lie down while I held my arm straight up in the air, perpendicular to my body, tight as I could. One by one, he would hold each of the thirty-eight Bach Flowers up against my arm, making it go weak. When my arm stayed strong against one flower, the forces of energy enabling it to remain that way, Raffelock looked at the card to see which one it was. Neither of us was surprised.

Gentian. Discouragement after a setback. Like every Bach Flower treatment I've tried, it was, to a tee, exactly how I was feeling at that moment. Raffelock made up a little tincture of Gentian and I took a couple of drops under my tongue three times a day. Right away it felt like a cement block had dropped off my shoulders. Any sense of discouragement evaporated. I really appreciated Raffelock. I needed help on lots of levels given all the stress I had. No doctor helped me more, ever.

Within a two-week span, I had four other chiropractors I was working with call Dr. Raffelock to ask about some of the methods he tried on me. I wanted each of them to know as much as possible, to be as helpful as possible. I wanted everybody to be the best they could.

Coming off our 6–10 season in 1999, you won't be surprised to know that I had to do my part to make sure the Broncos got

R
O
M
O

back on track. Of course, after over a decade of playing in this league, I knew that no supplement, no device, no chiropractor, no massage therapist could replace hard work.

My passion for training continued. Part of it at this point was the pure escapism of it. When I was on the track, in the weight room, or in the cold and hot tubs, I was able to shut out everything else in my life. Every problem, every concern, everything from spitting in someone's face to my ongoing Phentermine trial, vanished.

As tired as I was at times, when I started training, that's when it was time for me to perform. That's when it was time to do what I did. I realized that my flying around during an off-season workout or in-season practice helped raise everybody's level of talent. Guys would see me working that hard and realize they should try to do the same.

By now I knew that to outwork everybody else took zero talent—zero. All it took was pure heart and pure determination, in equal supplies. Just like in college, every time I started another training session or practice, my thought was this: *Nobody is going to outwork me. Nobody.*

In the off-season, that meant starting in February, spending six hours a day working out, gradually building up to ten hours a day, all so I could report to training camp in top condition. Not many could handle this kind of regimen. Heck, not many wanted it.

Looking back, it's clear there was an evolution to my off-season training, starting with the push-ups, sit-ups, and sprints I did in high school; the hills I ran and karate classes I took at Boston College; the even steeper hills I ran even harder in San Francisco; and the high-intensity lifting I did in Philadelphia. In Denver, I improved on it all with Randy Huntington's method of stretching and running. When he left Denver, Broncos' strength and conditioning coach Rich Tuten's assistant,

Tim Adams, an Air Force Academy graduate with a master's degree in exercise physiology, became my own personal trainer.

Tim and I began working together six days a week, religiously. Typically, on Mondays we worked on acceleration. On Tuesdays we worked on speed. Wednesday, speed endurance. Thursday, an off day from running. Friday, more acceleration. Saturday, more speed endurance. Sunday, water recovery work in the pool, getting rid of the by-products that had built up in my body that week.

I became so addicted to Tim's workouts, so dependent on them, that I wouldn't think of going through the off-season without them. When Julie and I planned our seven-year anniversary trip—one night in Monterey, California, then four more in Napa—I filled her in on a little surprise right before we left. Tim would be coming along.

"You know that song, 'You and I'?" Julie said. "Well, I guess this is, 'You, you and I.' " I knew it wasn't easy for her, but I loved her for being so understanding. The mornings went more to Tim's liking than Julie's. She thought there was nothing romantic about them. Well, no, but they were effective. He would have me run eight 60-yard dashes, twenty-five 20-yard dashes, six 150-yard dashes, until we were done and it was time to relax and have a drink. When a waiter walked over to us, Julie would order a glass of Pinot Noir, and I would hand the waiter a packet of protein powder for him to make me a colostrum root beer shake.

The arrangement with Tim worked so well that when our family went away to Hawaii for the summer, as we usually did, I brought Tim along again. This was a lot to ask of him, and more to ask of my family. But there was no way I could have survived in the league as long as I did without them. Their support and love allowed me to follow my dedication.

And during the years, my philosophy evolved into one that

ROMO

I wish more athletes would follow. Nutrition fueled my training. Training fueled my confidence. And confidence fueled my game. By the time I reported to training camp in July, I knew there was nobody in the universe more prepared for the rigors of the sport and the physical and mental challenges it presented.

"Romo," Tim told me one day, after watching me go through another series of sprints, "I have never seen anybody work as hard as you. I guarantee you that if there were other guys that worked that hard, I'd be out of a job."

It never changed, either, my attitude. That summer during training camp, Coach Coyer tried to get me to take a few practices off. I refused, flat refused. The only time I ever took a practice off was when Coach Shanahan would allow the veterans to have a day off, which was a quarter of the team by that point. Otherwise I was out there every day, every single day, just like any other worker wearing a hard hat, punching the clock.

On Aug. 9, 2000, while I was going through another morning training camp practice, a Douglas County grand jury handed down a four-count felony indictment against me. They charged me with one count of unlawful possession of a controlled substance, two counts of conspiracy and one count of obtaining a controlled substance by fraud and deceit. If convicted, I was facing a $100,000 fine and up to nine years in prison.

Those charges were hardly the most severe levied against me. One week later, on the night we broke training camp in Greeley, *Sports Illustrated* reported that a white player had told the grand jury I had told him that substances such as Phentermine would allow us to compete on a level field with African-American players. "(Romanowski's) exact words were, 'We have to go up against the black guys . . . ' " the player told SI. "He said, 'They're faster and stronger, and we have to take advantage of this. It is the only way we can compete with the black guys.' He didn't say 'black guys,' he used the 'n' word."

Well. Let's not hide behind any cloaks of anonymity here, okay? The unnamed player was defensive end Martin Harrison, whom I played with in San Francisco, helped train for a job in Minnesota, and then helped bring to Denver in the winter of 1998.

I never used the "n" word. Julie and I prided ourselves on raising our children not to see color—it's a value system in our lives and our home. What I had said was that I'm not as gifted as most of the guys in the NFL, that I need to work harder in every aspect of my football improvement. But never did I use the "n" word. When Martin Harrison tries to ruin my name with false racial charges, that's enough. To prove I was telling the truth, I underwent a polygraph test the day the *Sports Illustrated* story broke. Passed it.

Then the next day, at a team meeting, I took another more public polygraph. I stood in front of our team meeting room, and with tears in my eyes, I told my teammates that what they were hearing and reading was an absolute lie. I never made the statement that Martin attributed to me. Never.

My guess is my teammates believed me. They supported me every bit as much as the great Denver fans. When the time came for the team to elect its captains before our September 13 regular-season opener against the Miami Dolphins, they picked me. I was so amazed and so proud.

Captain of our defense. What I couldn't achieve at Boston College, I scratched and battled and willed myself to achieve in the NFL. Captain. I liked the sound of that.

■   ■   ■

One of my favorite ways to heal during the 2000 season was with acupuncture, the technique of inserting fine, sterile needles into specific body points in order to regulate the body's energy. By restoring energetic balance to the body, the body is allowed to heal itself. The body's energy is called Qi (pronounced "chee") and is the vital life force; the acupuncture points are located on the pathways where the Qi flows, and these pathways are called Meridians.

Dr. Raffelock used to administer acupuncture to me in Boulder two, three times a week. But there were enough times when time-wise I struggled to get up there—the old bang for your buck theory—and I needed a different acupuncturist in Denver. Annabel Bowlen, the wife of the Broncos owner Pat Bowlen, came through for me. She recommended a local acupuncturist named Nandi, someone she raved about. Nandi would come to our house and give acupuncture to me and our kids. They loved it, and so did I.

During our sessions together, Nandi and Raffelock taught me a crash course on key points on the body: the Sea of Qi, the energy point below your belly button; the respiration point right in the middle of your solar plexus, called the Shanzhong; and the area on the top of your head that benefits the brain, calms the spirit, and raises your Yang, the Baihui.

Eventually, I learned enough so that I was comfortable sticking the needles into myself. My philosophy mirrored that of the Chinese—steep and deep. That's how I would take the needles and stick them right into my acupuncture points—the Sea of Qi, the Shanzhong, the Baihui. Steep and deep. I'd routinely do it at home, but sometimes I would do it at the Broncos' facilities, too.

We would come off the field after practice and get ready for linebacker meetings. I would take off my shirt and stick the needles into my abdomen, my chest, even the top of my head. Then I would go off to meetings, with needles sticking out of me like arrows.

"Romo, you're nuts!" Mobley would tell me.

"Wacked," our middle linebacker Al Wilson would say, shaking his head. But the guys were intrigued enough that some of them let me perform it on them. I acupunctured defensive end Trevor Pryce one day, then cornerback Jimmy Spencer another. Most of the guys resisted, but I wasn't going to force it on anyone.

They were more open to some of my other ideas, one of the best of which was not mine. One of my doctors had put me in touch with a doctor who lived in Canada. I've never known Gunnar's last name and tried to find it out but couldn't. Anyway, Gunnar would say to me, "Hell, the best thing you could do is go into the other teams' locker room and fill it up with Gatorade. By halftime, they will be ready to crash. Gatorade is the worst thing you could drink at halftime." It's loaded with sugar, so there will be an insulin crash and you'll be wiped out in the second half.

The best thing to eat was a concoction that Gunnar himself had come up with—Super Soup. It included a mixture of brown rice, potatoes, sirloin, onions, fresh peas, and carrots. Each of the foods had a different glycemic burn to it. When the brown rice would wear off, the potatoes would take over. When the potatoes wore off, the sirloin would take over. Then the vegetables would. You could really feel the difference in your energy levels during the second half.

Julie made me up a batch of it and I took it in some Tupperware to our November 5 game against the New York Jets. Well, some of the guys noticed me eating the Super Soup two hours before the game. After we won 30–23, they wanted to try it the

R

O

M

O

next week. So I brought a little more the next Sunday, and we beat the Oakland Raiders 27–24, though more because of them than me.

When we won seven of our last eight games to finish the season 11–5 and clinch a wild-card berth, Julie was making pots of Super Soup. It would practically take her all week to cook up eight bags of potatoes, four dozen ears of corn, and bags of onions, peas, carrots and pounds of sirloin and brown rice. But by the end of the season, almost all the guys were slurping it up before the game. It became our unofficial pregame meal.

By then, Gunnar also had modified my diet. He had me eating rice cakes with almond butter at halftime—the almond butter being a fatty protein substance that would slow down the burn of the other carbohydrates. If we were playing a cold-weather game, he insisted I eat only the meat of an animal that lived in cold weather; I had to have venison, elk, or moose because I was ingesting an animal that lived in and could handle the cold weather. Hey, it was worth a shot.

Gunnar had developed a live cell therapy program, which involved ingesting processed tissue from animal embryos, fetuses, or organs. The organs and glands used in cell treatment include the brain, pituitary, thyroid, adrenals, thymus, liver, kidney, pancreas, spleen, heart, ovary, testis, and parotid.

Live cell, which thrives in Europe and Mexico, has been around for decades. A Swiss physician, Paul Niehans, discovered it when he treated a woman whose parathyroid had been accidentally removed in a surgical procedure. Knowing the woman faced death, Dr. Niehans injected her with a whole diced parathyroid gland from a freshly slaughtered sheep. The woman not only survived, she lived into her nineties.

Later, Dr. Niehans became the founder of the oldest antiaging spa in the world, Clinic La Prairie in Switzerland, where he has been injecting and giving clients this tonic since the mid-

1930s. He demonstrated the ability of these sheep stem cells to influence growth and repair of human tissue, not in a Petri dish but in his many willing clients. In his time, he treated the kings, queens, and Hollywood royalty to elixirs and tonics.

Most people injected the stuff, but drinking it has similar advantages. The cells are then transported to the target organs, where they supposedly strengthen them and regenerate their structure. I heard of some who used it and never got sick—not even a cold. When I heard that, that told me I was missing out on something. I asked Gunnar to get me some, as soon as possible.

The first live cell therapy I tried was bovine liver cells. First you had to hold the frozen container, no bigger than a bottle of nail polish, in your hand until it was defrosted. Then I put the liver cells under my tongue, let them sit there for a few minutes, and swallowed. Sometimes when I drank the bovine live cell I thought I was going to heave. It wasn't the taste, in fact there was no taste; it was just the idea that I was downing, say, a sterilized vial of bovine stem cells.

It wasn't cheap, either. A monthly supply of bovine cells, with a box of eight vials, cost $1,000. But if they would help me heal up, repair my aging muscle and connective tissue, and help me be a better player, bring them on. I was ready to take some more and pay the price.

I began keeping vials of live cell therapy in the freezer at our house. Whenever I felt like I was getting sick, I'd drink a sterilized vial of it.

By this time, I had entered another new frontier. Dr. Raffelock was helping me with acupuncture, nutrition, supplements, and emotional well-being. Victor was working on my minerals, while Greg Roskopf was activating my dormant muscles. Dr. DiPasquale was on my speed-dial for any nutrition questions regarding optimal hormone levels. And Gunnar was helping

ROMO

me with Super Soup and live cell therapy. At one time, Gunnar actually suggested to me urine therapy, aka drinking your own urine. Don't laugh. More than three million Chinese drink their own urine in the belief that it is good for their health, according to the official Xinhua news agency. Some drink it straight, others steaming hot, and still others mix it with juice or serve it over fruit. Really.

And it's not just the Chinese. Holy men in India have been drinking urine for thousands of years, believing there's nothing it can't cure. It's said to be effective against the flu, the common cold, broken bones, toothaches, and skin problems. Gunnar's explanation was that a lot of your electrolytes, nutrients, and hormones pass through your urine, so why not retain them?

I figured if it was good enough for the Chinese and the holy men of India, it was good enough for me. So I researched the idea even more, brought it home, discussed it with Julie . . . and had it shot down.

This whole incident proves yet again how I'd be willing to try anything to improve—and how out there Gunnar was. Eventually he began to scare me, so after a year, I stopped using him. I felt like I needed a certified medical doctor with an even greater understanding of nutrition.

With my trusty staff behind me, I was the resident nutrition and training expert in the locker room. When a player had a problem, he might have gone to see the trainer. But he also came to see me. Our trainers didn't appreciate it all that much, and ditto for our strength and conditioning coaches. Here I was doing my linebacking job, then trying to do their jobs, too. They didn't see it the way I did, but I was just trying to help.

My only wish was that all the expertise I was using would have helped me more. It was not the best season for me, not close to it. In fact, I couldn't remember having a worse season than the one I had in 2000. Patriots running back J. R. Redmond had beaten me out of the backfield for one touchdown. Chargers tight end Freddie Jones had beaten me for another. There were at least two other touchdowns I had surrendered on plays I routinely had made in the past.

Those plays I failed to make told me I was losing some speed. And what set in with the loss of speed was the insecurity I started feeling back in San Francisco. All of a sudden, you start wondering: Are you going to lose your job? Are you going to be cut? Are you going to lose your salary? Are you going to lose your biggest passion in life—your livelihood?

The fear set in. My $2 million-a-year salary, my job—my job for the past thirteen years—all of it now was at stake. And I would have plenty of time to think about it when our season ended abruptly in the opening round of the playoffs, in a wild-card game, with a 21–3 loss to the eventual world-champion Baltimore Ravens. What stood out during the game were the battles I had with Baltimore's Sam Gash, the best fullback I played against during my career.

Sam was a player I had battled during the six seasons he played in New England, and he always had the capability of knocking the crap out of me. He could charge full speed, plant you on your chest, and put you on your back like you were an upside-down turtle. I had seen him do it to other linebackers but I was determined not to let him do it to me. He didn't. On this day, in that particular game, I felt like I got the better of him for once. But the Ravens got the better of us. It's not the game I remember so much as what happened directly after it.

Near midfield, I spotted the Ravens' Pro-Bowl middle linebacker Ray Lewis, who was charged in February 2000 with murder in the stabbing deaths of two men at an Atlanta nightclub following Super Bowl XXXIV; Ray pleaded guilty to a misde-

ROMO

meanor charge of obstruction of justice early in his trial, and he was sentenced to twelve months probation. His two codefendants were acquitted.

When I reached him, we hugged. No words were said, and none needed to be. This was a case of two linebackers who could identify with the other, each going through his own private hell.

Difference then was, his trial had been all wrapped up. Mine was on deck.

As the case progressed, prosecutors realized it was, fortunately, as weak as I had hoped. At a hearing in May, Douglas County District Court Judge Thomas Curry ruled that the statements we made to the agents that August 1999 day, when they barged into our house, were inadmissible during trials because agents entered our home illegally. They never even read us our Miranda rights. Judge Curry even called the lead special agent on the case "not credible."

But the District Attorney's office was desperate for some type of conviction. And who knows what the NFL had in mind.

Once the Douglas County District Attorney's office offered a plea, my lawyer Harvey Steinberg called NFL executive vice president Jeff Pash to see what would happen if I accepted the terms of the lesser crime.

"Harvey," Jeff Pash said, "if he pleads guilty to spitting on the sidewalk, he's going to be suspended."

So here was my choice: Take the misdemeanor that assured no jail time but would include an NFL suspension of at least one game and quite possibly plenty more. Or, ignore the offer for a misdemeanor, and risk it all. One by one, my advisers began to weigh in.

"Romo, the NFL understands that in terms of the case against you, it's very weak," Tom Condon told me before the trial kicked off. "So I truly believe we can get this down to a one-game suspension."

"I'm not going to do it, Tom."

"Romo, you'll lose one game check. You've made tons of money already."

"What does that have to do with it, the money? I'm not going to take a chance on ruining my consecutive game streak."

"Romo, you don't know what a jury will do. If you get convicted, you're going to jail. And the NFL will throw you out of the league for life."

"I'll take my chances." For my consecutive game streak, for the right to be there for my team when they needed me, I did.

We went to trial the last week in June. I wanted to testify. I thought I could have been pretty convincing. One day, Harvey wanted me to testify, but his partner Jeff Springer didn't want me to; the next their stances were reversed. But that's why they're so successful. They balance each other out, like Yin and Yang.

Just before we had to make the final decision, Jeff said, "Harvey, this guy's a star, let him do it." But Harvey cast the deciding vote. No. No taking the stand for me. His call was fine with me. This was Harvey and Jeff's case, their big game. That's what I was paying them for. And Harvey and Jeff did the incredible job I thought they would.

They pointed out how at an autograph signing show I did at the Park Meadows Mall near our house, one of the sheriff's investigators stood in line to get an autographed photo, then framed it and placed it on his desk with a label on it. "Proud to be drug free." It was a big joke to investigators, playing with somebody's life, trying to ruin it.

R
O
M
O

Harvey and Jeff also cited a phone conversation between the doctor and me that Drug Enforcement Administration agents taped.

"If you don't feel comfortable with it, that's okay," Julie told the doctor. "If you want to put it under his . . ."

He then told Julie he would use my friend's name, at which point I got on the telephone.

"Is that all right, doing that?" I asked him.

No problem, the doctor answered.

To which Harvey added: "What this case comes down to is much ado about nothing. He was trying to protect what he was concerned about, the high profile of Mr. Romanowski."

Even the prosecution's first witness did not work out the way they would have hoped. When it called our friend to the stand, she testified that she knew the Phentermine was for me and that Dr. Snook said it was all right to put the prescriptions in her name. "It was a diet pill," she testified. "I didn't think it was a big deal. Bill is known. To not have it in his name made sense to me."

On the final day of testimony, Harvey played a videotaped statement taken from me August 6, 2000, when I described the contents of more than a dozen bottles of supplements and a twenty-four-slot tackle box filled with more vitamins and supplements. "I don't go anywhere without this," I said in the video.

In the same video, I said I started using supplements during my days in San Francisco and learned enough that my teammates now leaned on me for advice. "If they're tired, they're weak, if they want to know something, a lot of guys will come talk to me," I said in the video.

Those were the only words the jury heard from me. The next day, they were expected to reach their verdict.

The interesting thing is, throughout the trial, I would always closely watch the jurors. There was one guy who always made eye contact, and when they came back in from reaching a verdict on Friday, June 29, he winked at me, as if to say everything was going to be all right. I leaned over to Harvey and whispered, "We're all set."

When the judge read the verdict, it was just what I pictured in my head, like I pictured so many events in my life. Innocent! Innocent! At which point I bowed my head and cried. It was nearly two full years of this protracted legal battle, my name and my wife's name being trashed in the newspapers, trashed on talk radio, trashed in the public.

But finally, we were innocent, free from the courts and the NFL's tentacles. Turning to each of the jurors, especially the one who winked at me, I mouthed the words, "Thank you, thank you, thank you." To every one of them.

Then I went outside and made an admission to reporters that some athletes wouldn't. "I care about what people think about me," I told them. "I take a lot of pride in being a good person, being a role model, and a lot of that was in question for sure during the last two years."

During the trial, Julie and our children were out of town. Harvey and Jeff recommended that they not return for it. They stayed in Hawaii and the morning the verdict was supposed to be read, Alexandra woke Julie.

"Mommy, I was having a dream."

"You were? What was your dream."

"I dreamed that it was you and me and Dalton and Daddy in this bed. You know Daddy is going to be okay, don't you?"

Her daddy was okay. By that night, I was in Hawaii, in bed with the three of them.

Things only got better when, almost three weeks later, on July 18, prosecutors dropped fraud and conspiracy charges against Julie. She prevailed, too, the woman who never should have been dragged into it.

ROMO

The case that started in 1998 when my friend went to pick up some Phentermine at the Safeway around the corner was over. A huge burden was lifted and we—me, Julie, and the kids—survived, a little battered but not beaten, and a lot wiser. Now it was time to get back to business and face a host of other challenges that awaited me on the playing field.

11 TRYING TO TAP THE FOUNTAIN OF YOUTH

Each profession puts a premium on certain traits. Hollywood loves looks, politics values diplomacy, and football craves speed. Without it, you'll be out of the league faster than you can run. The older I became, the harder it was to keep up.

To prepare for the 2001 season, I hired Dan Pfaff, the best speed coach on this planet. I worked with so many others during my NFL career, from Remi Korchemny to Randy Huntington to Tim Adams, but Dan had rare insight. He has coached twenty-seven Olympians, including Donovan Bailey who, under Dan's tutelage shattered the world-record time in the 100 meters at the 1996 Olympics in Atlanta.

Dan could see things other track coaches couldn't. During warm-ups for the World's Fastest Human competition at Toronto's SkyDome in June 1997, Dan looked at Michael Johnson's biomechanics and said, "Watch, he's going to pull up lame." Sure enough, after 70 meters, Johnson pulled up—with a lame right leg.

Dan did something similar with me. During my first running workout for him in Austin, Texas, as I was going through a series of 40-yard dashes, he stood behind me and shouted out, "Romo, you've got something going on with your left shoulder."

Dr. Mark Lindsay, one of the chiropractors I had been working closely with, pulled his massage table right out on the track and began performing Active Release Therapy on my left shoulder. Active Release Therapy is designed to restore proper muscle function to allow the body to perform at its most efficient level.

After Dr. Lindsay finished, I got up and sprinted another 40-yard dash before Dan cut me off and shouted: "No, you didn't get it, Mark. There's a rib out of balance right there."

Through my baggy shirt, Dan pointed to the area causing my running to be out of whack. Lindsay worked on it and I was off and running again. Dan showed me what Donovan Bailey did on the track every day to win his gold medal, and Lindsay supplied the stretching and chiropractic work I needed to keep running. None of the training sessions were easy, and some were especially challenging.

There was one day down in Austin that has permanently seared itself into my memory. After Dan and I finished lunch, we headed back to the track to resume our workout. Thing is, it was Texas-summer hot—105 degrees, with 90 percent humidity. The sun was so scorching, the groundskeepers quit mowing the lawn.

"You sure you want to do this?" Dan asked.

We had a big workout planned—six 200-meter sprints. Dan called them "up-backs," where you would sprint 100 meters up the field, then sprint 100 meters back. There would be a three-minute break, before starting up on your next 200-meter up-back. Dan wanted me to run these up-backs in twelve seconds.

"Let's do it," I told him.

Even with the heat suffocating me, even with the grounds-keepers watching, I took off and did six 200-meter up-backs. Did them in twelve seconds each.

I felt like I was about to die, but I wouldn't stop. I couldn't stop. I was afraid that, if I did, other players would catch me. And so I kept running, mornings, afternoons, all while Dan analyzed my motion and recommended ways I could improve my speed.

The one thing he found right away was that I had foot problems that were impeding my speed. My feet were not striking the ground properly, not like a normal person's would. Dan had a therapist work on my feet, and when the therapist took a first look at them, he grew wide-eyed and said to Dan, "How does this guy even run?" Dan compared my feet to *A Nightmare on Elm Street.*

As he explained, all the bones in your foot are held together by ligaments. But because of all the trauma of cutting and starting and planting and stopping that is required to play in the NFL, the ligaments in your foot develop small tears, and then heal with scar tissue. After a while, the scar tissue sticks together and pretty soon, it's nothing but one big tangled ball of yarn. My feet were the biggest tangled ball of yarn Dan had seen.

This led to regular massages, where the therapist would break up the scar tissue in my feet and try to get my feet back to functional levels. Once the scar tissue was reduced, one of my chiropractors would realign the bones, back to the positions they should be in. I then could go up to a week without any problems. But once training camp resumed, or a game was played, forget it. We were right back to where we started. More foot pain. More problems.

The interesting thing was, I was doing so much track work, I actually could feel myself getting faster, despite my foot problems. My trainers used to regularly time me in the 40-yard dash,

R
O
M
O

the best feedback mechanism there was for the work we were doing. In spikes, on a track, at 242 pounds (plus or minus a burrito), I routinely was running the 40-yard dash in 4.45 seconds—considerably faster than the 4.78 I ran in college.

After running that time again I called to check in with Bill McPherson, my former linebackers coach and defensive coordinator in San Francisco. I'd call my former coaches out of the blue—sometimes it would be Coach Dunn, other times Coach Bicknell, other times Coach Zeman, and this time, Coach McPherson. By now, he was the 49ers' pro personnel director.

"Hey, Coach Mac, do me a favor. Take out the sheets from this year's scouting combine, the sheets with the 40-yard dash times of every defensive back."

Coach rifled through his papers, dug out the 40-yard dash times of each defensive back prospect. He went down the line, reading the times. A 4.5, a 4.7, a 4.55, a 4.6.

"See," I interrupted. "I'm running faster than all those DBs coming out of college! How old am I, Mac?" I challenged. "How old am I?" more insistent. "Thirty-seven years old, that's how old!"

My 4.45 lifted my spirits, boosted my confidence. Every time I turned in one of those fast times, it inspired me to put in another day on the track, another day in the weight room. Everyone saw the results of my work on Sunday. But very few people saw all the work that went into it.

Even I had to admit, though, that the results were becoming increasingly difficult to maintain. The training I had depended on was not as easy to get through; the pressure of hanging was increasing. There were reminders of it constantly. Yes, I trained and ate and slept harder, better, and longer than ever before. But I seemed to need more. The backs never were slower, the tight ends never weaker, the coaches and owners never less determined to win. Nor was I.

With all this running through my mind, Victor Conte Jr. recommended something I was unfamiliar with: "The Clear," later determined to be THG, tetrayhdrogestrinone, which by now has become as much of a household name in the sporting world as BALCO.

Victor had tested the substance, sent it to laboratories, had it studied extensively and scientifically. And not only was it legal at that time, not only was it not on the NFL's banned list, but it had been shown not to have any adverse effects on a person's kidneys, cholesterol, or health. None. With all those matters squarely and soundly addressed, there was no reason in my mind not to experiment with it.

The first time I took THG was in the spring of 2001. By simply measuring and supplementing my minerals, Victor already had helped me reach a whole new level of natural ability. He had been a great source of nutritional insight, he had worked with doctors, and he knew science. Why not listen to him about THG? There was no reason then, or now, not to trust him like a mentor.

He handed me two bullet-sized, two-inch vials of golden-colored liquid of The Clear, and told me that at the recommended dosage, it would keep my strength up and help my recovery. Perfect.

But the toughest part about the THG was simply taking it. Over the years, I've taken a lot of things that taste like crap. But THG was foul. The night before my workouts, I would drop a tenth of a cc, almost half a teaspoon, under my tongue and swallow, quick and hard. It was plain nasty-tasting.

Victor had me follow this protocol on Monday, Wednesday, and Friday. Then for three weeks you would repeat the same cycle before taking a full week off. I felt the effects pretty quickly. During my workouts, I started to like how I was feeling, and it was a lot easier to get through them. I felt like I had an

ROMO

extra rep or two at the end of each bench press. On my squats, I felt like my legs could take more pounding and weight than they ever had. I could go through an intense workout one day and the very next day feel good enough to go through another.

That was, by far, the biggest effect of THG—enhanced recovery. It didn't make me bigger or faster or stronger, necessarily. It made me less stiff and sore after my strenuous workouts, helped me recover from workouts, and reduced soreness, enabling me to work at a higher level longer. There were even more frequent trips to the track and weight room, and that time equated to more strength, more endurance, and more power.

More important, THG would help me stay strong enough and quick enough to avoid serious injury. It gave me an edge that my diet, sleep, and endless training sessions could no longer provide. But don't get the wrong idea. THG was not some silver bullet, not even close. Without the proper nutrition, extensive training, and proper sleep, the effects of THG would have been greatly reduced, or quite possibly completely nullified.

When I first started taking THG, I asked two questions: Was it banned by the NFL, and would it hurt me now or later? I was assured the answer to each was no. But with me, assurances weren't enough. I need more detailed explanations. After checking it out with other widely respected, world-renowned doctors, I got confirmation. There was nothing wrong, and nothing illegal, about THG.

At the time, not only was THG off the radar, it was an unknown in the more mainstream world. Except for a handful of ingenious chemists and more than a few athletes, nobody knew about THG nor cared about it. It wasn't until after BALCO broke in the summer of 2003 that the Food and Drug Administration even learned what it was.

And it wasn't officially declared illegal until President

George W. Bush signed the Steroids Control Act on Oct. 22, 2004, more than thirteen months after I played my final NFL game.

O ver the past year, I began noticing that I was having less memory recall. There actually was one time when I could not remember that Van Morrison sang "Brown Eyed Girl," even though it was one of my favorites. I would have to ask Julie to help me remember dates, events, things I never had a problem with in the past. I'm not sure if I didn't know, or knew and simply ignored it, but somewhere within my brain I sensed the growing problem with concussive injury and sought ways to help it.

Ginkgo biloba helped. It's derived from the root of a tree believed to be a member of the world's oldest living species, about 200 million years old. The ginkgo tree has been used in traditional Chinese medicine for more than 4,000 years. In Germany, ginkgo is a top-selling prescription drug, touted to do everything from treating eye conditions to relieving leg pain in people with bad arteries. All I wanted it to do was improve circulation to my brain, and I was sure it did that.

Each time I took the ginkgo by itself—I was taking 240 milligrams each morning—I could feel myself brighten up, similar to the effect of a little coffee without the jittery part. I was taking it to offset the occasional bouts of dizziness, ringing in my ears, and headaches. They weren't happening often, but I didn't want them to happen at all.

I also read about this medication, selegeline, that people pursuing antiaging strategies use. It's usually prescribed for people with dementia from not getting enough blood to their brain. It's not known exactly how selegeline works, but some experts who studied the agent more recently suspect it helps

R
O
M
O

reduce oxidative stress in the neuron. Once I started taking 2 milligrams each morning, I can't say that I felt it. But I did feel better for having taken it.

I found I could get it mixed into the same capsule as my ginkgo and be guaranteed of pharmaceutical grade in both agents. Not long after, I learned about vinpocetine, an extract from the periwinkle plant used around the world. In Europe, vinpocetine is sold as a drug called Cavinton, the only "drug" known to improve cerebral metabolism (glucose and oxygen uptake), increase ATP concentration, and increase blood flow to the brain without lowering blood flow to other parts of the body. When I read about vinpocetine I used it—1 to 5 milligrams twice a day—to replace my ginkgo-selegeline combination. It was easier because I didn't need a prescription to get it and it didn't carry the stigma of a drug. Vinpocetine is available over the counter in supplement form here in the United States.

Paying attention to what natural agents are being studied for things like antioxidant ability and increasing circulation often led me to some excellent supplements. This was the case with CDP Choline.

CDP Choline—also called Citicholine—is being studied at Mount Sinai hospital as a potential agent to help stroke, brain cancer, and dementia patients. It is a precursor to the neurotransmitter acetylcholine that does a lot of jobs in the body including making muscles twitch and contract, but in this CDP form it seems to help the brain heal. It is the only substance in the natural world that can stimulate new brain cell growth. I may not have known to what extent I needed that, but I suspected it would be a good thing to take.

The other agent under study that I ran across was phosphatidyl serine—called PS for short. I took 100 milligrams of PS, two capsules twice a day, to help keep my brain hormone receptors alive and working well. The more sensitive these receptors, the better chance I had to recover from trauma and grow stronger. And that's what it is all about.

From the start of the off-season, the Broncos were so convinced I wouldn't get off in my Phentermine trial that they signed former Atlanta Falcons free-agent linebacker Henri Crockett.

When they signed him in April, just days before the NFL draft, one of the Broncos' officials told Crockett, "We don't think Bill is going to be with us this year." Once they found I was, that I had escaped the wrath of local authorities and the league, Coach Shanahan called me into his office for the talk that just about every NFL veteran eventually hears if he plays long enough.

"Bill, I watched all the film last year and you really had only one great game, and that was against San Francisco," Coach said, referring to the game in which I had a season-high 13 tackles, 1 sack, and a couple of real good confrontations with J. J. Stokes. When he got to the point, it was to ask me to take a pay cut. He wanted me to shave $500,000 off my base pay, bringing me down close to the veteran minimum salary.

What bothered me about that was he could have asked me to do the same thing in March, when teams hadn't spent their money in the free-agent market yet, when teams still had funds available. By now, mid-June, every team was financially tapped out.

Still, Tom Condon called Raiders coach Jon Gruden to see if he would be interested in his client—me. Coach Gruden told Tom, verbatim, "I will kiss your ass for Bill Romanowski." I wanted to go play for the Raiders right then so badly, but there was a part of me that didn't feel it was right. I was worried the Raiders would get hit with tampering charges.

R
O
M
O

Plus, as it was, I still had a contract. The Broncos, overall, had treated me fairly. I had become very close with their owner, Pat Bowlen, whom I still consider one of my best friends and one of the best owners in all of sports. And Julie told me: "You know what, Billy? Play out this year and go to Oakland next year."

I listened to Julie. I accepted the half-million-dollar pay cut and decided to play it out.

An invitation to a Denver-area hyperbaric center, the Cellular Medicine Institute, arrived for me shortly before the 2001 season began. Somehow, the doctors over there had heard I owned a portable version of a hyperbaric and they wanted to show off theirs to me. With good reason.

Theirs was ten times more powerful than mine. Theirs was the exact type of machine that Dan Pfaff told me Donovan Bailey used after he tore his Achilles tendon playing basketball, when he lay in it three hours a day, six days a week. Within three months—unheard of after an Achilles tear—Donovan was back to running on a treadmill.

As I inspected the biggest hyperbaric chamber I had seen, I kept wondering why these machines were not in every NFL training room. Here you have the number-one spectator sport in the world, the most violent, with injuries occurring every day, and teams are missing a critical device that could help rehab their $85-million payrolls. It made no sense to me not to have every player overdosing on Nature's Steroid—oxygen.

But hyperbaric chambers are a new frontier, machines that athletic trainers did not learn about in school. Me, I couldn't learn enough. Right before I stepped into this monster chamber for the first time, the doctors at the clinic offered to enhance the experience by giving me I.V. therapy. Taking vitamins or medication through your gut in capsule, powder, or tablet form results in a very small amount being absorbed. Taking it by I.V. means you get the entire dose. This sounded very appealing to me.

Up until then, the only I.V.s I'd had were the Trauma I.V.s in Philadelphia, but those were bad for you. These weren't. "Sure, why not," I told them. "Let's go."

We thought an I.V. Glutathione—what doctors and chemists call GSH—would be a nice one to start with. GSH is a powerful antioxidant capable of helping the body generate lots of energy and healing ability. The doctors slid the needle into my arm, set up the I.V., and stuck me in the chamber. This, to me, was pure heaven. Oxygen being pumped into my body, Glutathione being pumped into my bloodstream and, best of all, the doctors playing the movie *Caddyshack* on the overhead screen.

As soon as I stepped out of the chamber, I wanted to get right back in. I wanted to bring my teammates by to try it, too. I wanted to educate everybody on what I learned. Unfortunately I was one of the few who felt that way. Cellular Medicine closed a short time later, but not before it exposed me to all kinds of ways to help my performance.

I wanted to try all the other I.V. therapies, especially vitamin C, which really did wonders. Your gut has a limit for absorbing vitamin C. After 5 or 6 grams the average person develops a pretty bad case of diarrhea. Four to five grams is a good dose for the average guy, but it doesn't come near the dose you need to recover from one day in the NFL. That dose was more like the 50–60 grams you could only take through I.V. These I.V.s were like gifts from nature.

To have the vitamins and minerals shot right into your bloodstream rather than first passing through your gut, which sometimes struggled to break them down, was a big advantage. It was an advantage I wanted as often as possible.

Eventually, I started sampling the I.V. therapies at home,

ROMO

without any assistance from doctors. I would slide the needle right into my vein, tape it to my arm, and conduct my normal everyday business around the house. Other times I would go back to Cellular Medicine, get it done there, and lay around in its hyperbaric chamber. When I was playing against the likes of Shannon Sharpe in practice and Tony Gonzalez on Sunday, I knew I was going to take a beating and would need all the energy and healing power I could get. I took I.V. GSH the day before, of, and after each game that whole year.

One of the other doctors who delivered I.V.s to the clinic saw how much I valued and appreciated them and asked me one day, "Have you heard of ionized water?"

No, I hadn't. Well, he explained, the pH of tap water is somewhere between 6 and 7. Zero is considered totally acid, 14 totally alkaline, and 7 is neutral. The higher the alkaline, the better; the higher the acid, the worse. But our body has a tough time maintaining a slightly alkaline state as it is. When it metabolizes foods, acids are produced. The body's natural ways of eliminating excess acid are through its lungs, kidneys, and skin, but these systems can become overworked with too much acid. If the right amounts of alkaline do not neutralize the acids, the body begins to experience headache, illness, colds, allergy, virus, and disease. All this dysfunction is a sign that the body is trying to balance its sensitive pH level.

Well, a water ionizer increases the alkaline and fights the acid. A little story about how much I believe in it: One of the longest-living race of people in the world are called the Hunza, who live in mountain valleys in northern Pakistan. Many Hunza claim to be 150 years old; many others are documented centenarians, older than 100. For years, scientists wondered why they lived so long. Eventually the mystery was solved when they tested the water that flowed into the Hunza villages from the surrounding glaciers. Highly alkaline.

Still a doubter? I bought a water ionizer and hooked it up to my kitchen faucet. Our son, Dalton, had struggled for years with asthma. No doctor could help him. Once the water ionizer was installed and he started drinking from it, his asthma improved. Not bad, wouldn't you say?

Everything I learned became a part of my postgame routine, a method to extend my career. After every football game, I'd start an I.V. of 50 grams of vitamin C and 5 grams of glutathione to fight the massive amount of stress I had put on my body, and I'd lie in the hyperbaric chamber. Then I'd ride the stationary bike to work out the lactic acid, get a forty-five-minute soft-tissue massage, and, of course, make sure to drink as much ionized water as I could.

Julie and the kids would come to some of my games and bring themselves a sack lunch to eat while they waited for me to emerge from the locker room. Usually, they'd be locking up the stadium, turning off the lights.

But by then, I needed all the help I could find. My last season in Denver, every game I was getting dinged and woozy. Every game I would hide it from Broncos trainers out of fear for my job. After every game I would apprise Tom of my condition and then speak to an independent neurologist.

Maybe the worst it got was a Monday night game in Oakland, November 5, 2001. On one goal-line play, I ran full speed, head on, into Raiders fullback Jon Ritchie, and it hurt. When I wobbled to our sideline, there was an unusual lingering dizziness. Usually my dizziness would go away after about sixty seconds. But this time it lasted for the next twenty minutes. For the rest of the season, it didn't get any better. This was my most significant problem that season. But there was one other that should be mentioned in connection to what was clearly shaping up as my last season in Denver.

After the 2000 season, Denver fired its defensive coordina-

R O M O

tor, Greg Robinson, whom I liked and respected. His replacement? None other than Ray Rhodes, my former coach and friend from San Francisco and Philadelphia. Now you tell me whether or not this is coincidence: In 1993, Coach Rhodes left his job as Green Bay's defensive coordinator to take the same job in San Francisco; just weeks later, I was traded to Philadelphia. In 1995, Coach Rhodes left his job as San Francisco's defensive coordinator to become Philadelphia's head coach; I'm not resigned, and I'm allowed to go to Denver. When he arrived in Denver, it seemed like Coach Rhodes felt bad for the two prior instances in which our paths crossed and I wound up being kicked out the door. He told the media: "I need Romo. I've told all the coaches, I need his intensity." He was very polite about it, but Coach Rhodes went so overboard in his praise for me it almost sounded rehearsed, fake.

So after years of service, this was where I stood after fourteen seasons: My head coach didn't believe in me, my defensive coordinator didn't want me, and my brain didn't cooperate with me.

To help prolong the ride, I relied on the nice little herb formula of Dynamic Warrior that Dr. Raffelock prescribed and the THG I got from BALCO. At that point, my head had been hit so often, I was just trying to ensure I could get back out there. I always sought that edge. I viewed it as me doing what I had to do, within the letter of the law, to help me in my closing years.

It wasn't always easy. I played through my mental stress and extreme physical pain, just like Matt Millen once instructed me to do. During our second game of the season at Arizona, our safety Eric Brown inadvertently speared me while trying to make a tackle on one of the Cardinals running backs. This was the type of excruciating pain I had not felt, one of the worst hits I had taken in my career. I went in at halftime and had my hip injected in eight different areas with Xylocaine—a local anesthetic used topically on the skin and mucous membranes. It reminded me of when I was in San Francisco during my third year and I had to get my shoulder shot up six straight games just to make it through the season. But this time, the eight injections didn't work. During the second half, I couldn't run. I could barely move.

Most players, I'd think, would have missed at least the next week. Not me. The game meant too much to me, no matter how much pain I was in. The following Sunday when we hosted Baltimore in a game we lost 20–13, I played. Not real well, but I played.

That week I also had an unexpected reminder of my age, of how long I had stuck around the NFL. Before the game against the Ravens, some of our defensive players were discussing the great job that Baltimore executive and Hall-of-Fame tight end Ozzie Newsome had done building his team.

I told some of our linebackers—Al Wilson, Ian Gold and John Mobley—that I had played against Ozzie when I was a rookie and he was a veteran tight end for the Cleveland Browns. Well, when Al and Ian heard that they couldn't believe it.

"You played against Ozzie Newsome?" Al asked.

"I played against Ozzie Newsome."

This cracked up my teammates. But it hammered home another reminder of my age and my longevity. Here I am in my mid-thirties, and my teammates were players that probably were in diapers when I was lying in my first minicamp hotel room, staring at my San Francisco 49ers helmet. My drive was not to let the greatest experience I ever had come to an end.

R O M O

I n 2001, the Broncos closed down the great old Mile High Stadium and opened the more modern INVESCO Field at Mile High.

During our second home game on September 30 against the Ravens, our owner Pat Bowlen invited back as many of the former Broncos alumni as could make it. This is one of the great things about Mr. Bowlen; he treats those who work for him as a family, and he looks after them.

One of the players who returned was a former defensive back from 1962–63, Bob Zeman, who was also my former linebackers coach in San Francisco. Since the 49ers fired him during the off-season that they traded me, I had not gotten a chance to see him and never had the opportunity to give him the gift I'd gotten for him. Every now and then, I would call him out of the blue to check in and see how he was doing. But we hadn't had a chance to meet face to face since 1994.

So finally I brought with me to the game a nice pair of cowboy boots and a belt buckle with a Z on it. I'd had them for seven years and they'd traveled to Philly and Denver with me, so it was gratifying to see the look on Coach Zeman's face. He seemed surprised that anyone would go out of their way like that, and maybe even a bit proud that he meant enough to someone to have him do something like I did. These types of gestures, in which I showed my support and appreciation, always meant as much to me as them. I always wanted my former coaches to know how much they meant to me, how much they influenced me, how much they contributed to whatever success I was fortunate enough to achieve.

Now that I was near the end of my contract with Denver, I'd probably be handing out some more good-bye gifts. My last game in Denver came in Indianapolis, in the RCA Dome, a game that was supposed to have been played in September but was rescheduled for January 6, 2002, after our country was attacked on September 11.

By then, both teams had long been eliminated from the playoff race and we were playing for nothing more than pride. There were so few fans in the stands, and the RCA Dome was so quiet, it was like being at practice. You could hear players talking on the field.

Our defense fought its guts out that day, and our loss could have been 50–0, instead of the 29–10 outcome it was. Sometimes, just for the effort you give, you remember those games more than the ones you win. As we walked off the field, I thought that this could be my last game as a Bronco. The signs—the pay cut last year, a new contract to be negotiated, Denver wanting to give Ian Gold more playing time—were too obvious to miss. Before we got to the locker room, I took one long look around the field, then glanced over at Coach Coyer.

"I don't know what's going to happen, Larry, but I just want you to know, I love you." We hugged, a thanks for what each of us had done for the other. Of all the coaches I played for in the NFL, none were any better than Larry Coyer. He was so smart, it was almost as if he learned the game at the shoulder of Vince Lombardi. By the time Coach Coyer had given out each week's game plan to his linebackers, we knew exactly how the opposing offenses were going to attack us. Coach Coyer could break down the other team's offensive strengths, weaknesses, and tendencies and predict how they would correlate into Sunday's game.

Plus, he was loyal. He defended his players, even when the situation failed to work out. It would be too hard to remember all the times when one of my position coaches told me to do something, it didn't work out, and the head coach blasted the move. I've had defensive coaches who were afraid to stand up and say, "I told him to do that, Coach." Not Coach Coyer. He would stand up and say to the head coach, "That's on me."

It is the reason that, when I left Denver, I framed one of my

R
O
M
O

Broncos jerseys, autographed it, and wrote, "To Larry, the best football coach I've had in the NFL. Bill Romanowski."

And when Denver fired my friend and longtime defensive coordinator Greg Robinson after the 2000 season, I called Pat Bowlen with a long-distance endorsement: "Pat, if anybody other than Larry Coyer is hired as defensive coordinator, it'll be the biggest mistake you've ever made. He's the best coach in that building and probably the best in this country. I have that much respect for him."

By then I was long gone from Denver, as I knew I would be. After our 2001 season ended with a disappointing 8–8 finish, Pat and his wife Annabel invited Julie and I to stay with them at their house in Oahu. One night we went to dinner with the Bowlens, Mike and Peggy Shanahan, and former 49ers' and Browns' executive Carmen Policy and his wife Gail. Throughout the evening, I could just sense something was not right.

At the end of the night, Coach Shanahan's wife, Peggy, came up to us and thanked us for everything we had done. Past tense. Like there was no more future in Denver with the Broncos. Peggy knew what we were about to find out.

The next week, the Broncos left me exposed for the Houston Texans' February 18 expansion draft. No big surprise there, nor was it when the Texans passed on me because of my age and my medical background. But once they did, Coach Shanahan summoned me into his office for a talk I had been expecting for a year.

"Bill, I really believe that [linebacker] Ian Gold can be something special in this league and I can't justify paying you $2.5 million next season. So what I would like to do is cut you down, pay you veteran minimum. And what I'll do is build in incentives to where if you start, you'll still make a good salary.

"But what I'm also going to do is, I'm going to give Ian most of your reps in training camp. I'll give you enough reps just to keep you sharp, but I want to see if Ian can be the special player I think he can be."

I thanked Coach Shanahan for his time, walked out to my car in the players' parking lot, and made two phone calls. The first was to my agent Tom Condon, telling him to call the Broncos to inform them I wanted to be released. The second was to Raiders owner Al Davis. His secretary, Fudgie Otten, answered the telephone.

"Please tell Mr. Davis that this is Bill Romanowski. I want to help him win another Super Bowl."

Seconds later, Fudgie called back and said, "Mr. Davis thinks you would look good in silver and black."

The next night, Mr. Davis called me to convey a similar message himself. What stunned me was how a man much older than seventy had a better memory than mine. He started recalling plays from San Francisco's NFC Championship game against Dallas in 1992, when our safety Dana Hall took a terrible angle on Cowboys wide receiver Alvin Harper on a play that went to the 8-yard line. He recalled plays that you could not possibly know unless you studied a ton of football tape. And those plays didn't even involve his team.

Then he rolled out the list of players whose careers the Raiders had resurrected. Many of them were teammates in San Francisco: Ronnie Lott, Roger Craig, Riki Ellison, Jerry Rice. Each had been cut, each had signed with Oakland, and each had prospered in his own way.

"I think we can resurrect your career, too," Mr. Davis told me.

"I think you're right, Mr. Davis. I would look good in silver and black."

R
O
M
O

12 TWILIGHT IN SILVER AND BLACK

Work enough, produce enough, and stick around long enough and I guess eventually, you become a model for imitation and inspiration. After I signed with the Raiders, Greg Robinson, then the defensive coordinator in Kansas City, called while I was on vacation to inform me that he had put together a highlight tape of my plays to show one of his young linebackers, Scott Fujita.

Coach wanted Scott to see the way a linebacker with a similar build—Fujita is six foot five and 247 pounds; I'm six foot four, 242—a long-and-tall frame, could be a weapon. "Toughness is a term that's thrown around this game, only some guys aren't that tough," Coach Robinson told me. "Some guys don't look tough because they don't know how to utilize their body in the most effective ways. But you were very effective in the way you utilized your body. You got every ounce of your body into contact." I was flattered by his words, grateful that someone as respected as Coach had noticed.

It gave me a nice boost while I was in Hawaii, my usual off-season refuge. Most of my off-seasons were spent in Hawaii—sometimes at Annabel and Pat Bowlen's guest house in Oahu, other times at a nearby house we rented. One of the people I was inroduced to while we were in Hawaii was a close friend of Mr. Bowlen's, June Jones, the University of Hawaii football coach.

One day I was telling June about all the different ways I was taking care of my body: hyperbaric chambers, I.V. therapy, ionized water, acupuncture, Bach Flowers, my supplement briefcase. Then I told him all about my team—not the Oakland Raiders, but my chiropractors, acupuncturists, specialists, Reiki therapists.

"Hold on, Romo," he interrupted.

He told me about an oncologist named Samuel Grimes whom June had gotten to know when he played quarterback for the Atlanta Falcons from 1977–1979.

Dr. Grimes didn't treat all his patients with the standard chemo and radiation. He deployed some alternative treatment practices, some real potent I.V. therapies that included megadoses of vitamins and minerals, anti-oxidants to handle oxidative stress, along with DMSO, dimethyl sulfoxide.

Having first been exposed to it in San Francisco and having read books on it, I can vouch that DMSO absolutely gets rid of inflammation in the body. It also leaves you with the nastiest garlic breath you ever smelled. But it was worth it. What some people call "the king antioxidant," DMSO comes in a cream that seeps right through your skin and kills the inflammation. And it's cheap—about $2 a jar. But that's the problem, too. DMSO is banned from health food stores, and I'll give you my theory why: Do you think drug companies want you to buy $2 jars of DMSO instead of their pricier bottles of aspirin or anti-inflammatories that mess up your gut and force you to spend even more money on antibiotics? No way. It's all about the money.

R O M O

But Dr. Grimes used DMSO I.V.s, amongst other treatments.

"Hey, you think I could get Dr. Grimes's phone number from you?" I asked June.

And a few days later, I had Dr. Grimes on the telephone, listening to him tell me how, even with the countless advances in medicine, mortality rates involving cancer patients had not changed since 1970. Now how could that be? We talked about other medicines, other treatments, other I.V. therapies.

"What would that do for me?" I asked.

"What are you looking for?"

"The toughest thing I have to go through is the trauma of training camp."

"I could put together some I.V.s for you that would help you tremendously in that area. It would help your recovery, help you get rid of inflammation."

But he didn't stop there. Dr. Grimes described the access he had to live cell therapy, imported it from Germany, from a pure strain of protected black sheep that had been all but untouched for thirty or forty years.

"They don't let many people near them so these sheep cannot catch any viruses," he explained.

"What cells would you recommend?" I asked.

Pancreas, adrenals, maybe some mesenchyme, he told me. He rattled off about a dozen. Some, he said, would benefit my brain. This was all I needed to hear. "Well," I finally said, "can you come to training camp and set up shop and give I.V.s and live cell therapy to me and anybody else who wants it?"

Sure, Dr. Grimes said. We discussed dates, times, and cost. For his one week of training camp in Napa, California, with me and the Raiders, I would pay Dr. Grimes $38,000. The good part was that included $12,000 worth of the purest and finest injectable live cell therapy money could buy. To me, it was worth whatever money he charged.

Seven-time Tour de France champion Lance Armstrong put it best. He once said, "When you get a second chance, you're going to go all out." And I felt the Raiders represented a type of second chance for me, another chance to prove I was not as washed up as the Broncos thought.

From the moment I visited the Raiders' training complex in Alameda, California, they made me feel as if I were a part of the team's great tradition. Our only disagreement, however minor it was, came when I told them I wouldn't sign my contract unless I could get number 53, which I had worn since my freshman year at Boston College. Their veteran linebacker, Travian Smith, had worn it since the Raiders drafted him out of Oklahoma in the fifth round of the 1998 draft. Not only did he have it during his first four seasons in Oakland, but he even had "53" tattooed into his arm. I don't know what the Raiders said or did, but I got my number.

During my visit there, the front office made it pretty clear to me that Bill Callahan would be the coach taking over for Jon Gruden, which is exactly how it came down. On March 12, 2002, the Raiders finally made it official and named Bill Callahan as Jon Gruden's replacement and the Raiders' new head coach.

On my next trip to Oakland, I stopped by Coach Callahan's office to talk, get a feel for him while letting him get a feel for me. I told him all these stories about Bill Walsh, George Seifert, and Mike Shanahan, how they set goals, reached them, and established a standard. He wanted to know as much as I would tell him—and then some.

ROMO

He asked how the Broncos handled their off-season training programs, their practices, their game planning. He couldn't get enough inside information about the Broncos or our winning ways from San Francisco. But that was one thing I noticed right away about Coach Callahan: He listened. During his second year in Oakland, some of the players felt he got away from that. But around me, I always felt he listened. "I may not do what it is you would like me to do," Coach Callahan used to tell everyone in our locker room. "But I'll listen to everyone on this team."

What I liked about my new team was that it was a bunch of older guys like me. Quarterback Rich Gannon, wide receiver Jerry Rice, wide receiver Tim Brown, safety Rod Woodson, defensive end Trace Armstrong, defensive tackle John Parrella—experienced veterans, guys who appreciated the game, all aiming for one more ring.

My two closest friends on the team were Trace and John. We laughed together, lifted together, ate together—did most everything together. The other guys started referring to us as "The Three Amigos."

Trace especially shared my passion about training, about getting better, about finding an edge. Nutritionally, he didn't go to the lengths I did and study alternative methods the way I did, but he was more committed than most anybody else I ever met. He also was so honest, so ethical, I called him "The Lawmaker." To Trace, there was right and there was wrong, and during our debates about it he would wrap up our conversations by simply saying, "You know in your heart which is which."

On our flights home after road trips, Trace and I used to share bottles of the finest red wines. Trace loved wine, and I did, too, even if I didn't drink very much of it—just the occasional glass here and there. But I did collect it.

Back when I lived in Milpitas near San Francisco, my neighbor, John Scheff, had a little wine cellar that I admired. One night he brought me over there and handed me a glass of George LaTour. I took a sip and went, *Wow*.

Like everything in my life, Julie and I dove into my newest passion. I built a 200-square-foot stone wine cellar that could hold up to 2,000 bottles. To this day, I have about that much wine, though I rarely drink it. But I'd bring along one nice bottle for the trip back from our road games, when Trace and I would talk football and life.

Trace got to know me better than anybody. But it didn't take the other guys in camp too long to figure out what I was about, either. On our first day in pads, during an up-tempo 9-on-7 drill, our tight end Roland Williams took me on and I nailed him pretty good. Well, that didn't make him very happy. Roland continued trying to block me, and during our tussle, his helmet got jacked up a little and, eventually, popped off his head. I picked it up and threw it about fifty yards. Right away, guys realized my on-field intensity.

They also learned about my attitude. Whenever someone in training camp asked me how I felt, my answer would be, *Great*. No matter how sore, hurting, tired, and fatigued, I always told them I was doing great. I felt that if I told just one of my teammates I didn't feel good, he would admit it, too, because at training camp we were all hurting. "It's a great day to be alive," I would tell my teammates. And it's true. Every day is a great day to be alive.

Dr. Grimes arrived at the Napa hotel that housed our team and checked into the room I had booked for him. He was on call for me morning, noon, and night. It became my own version of two-a-days—much different than the traditional two-a-day training camp practices.

Twice a day, and sometimes even three times, I would go

right over to Dr. Grimes's room, where he would hook me up to vitamin C and glutathione I.V.s to fight the massive amount of stress on my body. Later in the day, after those typical rigorous practices, Dr. Grimes would start me in on those potent DMSO I.V.s. After those thirty-minute drips, my body forgot it was sore. That was the upside.

The downside was that my garlic breath wasn't just bad, it was nauseating. It practically overpowered the more customary smell of Napa's vineyards. Nobody wanted to go near me on the football field. Backs fell down not to have to get near me. Offensive linemen ran backward to avoid blocking me. The guys on the team hated it, but at least they didn't have to live with it.

My hotel room smelled so garlicky, reeked so bad, housekeeping refused to step foot in it any longer. It had become a hazard area. None of the fans or deodorizers in the room worked. Fumigating the room was hopeless. The Marriott was so furious about it, they threatened to make the Raiders pay for new carpeting, new bedding, new wallpaper, new curtains, new everything.

The other problem with the DMSO I.V.s was considerably less funny. While Dr. Grimes was at camp, I had him talk with the Raiders' medical director, Dr. Robert Albo. That was the great thing about Dr. Albo—whenever I wanted to try something or mix together something else, he would go and research whatever I asked him about. When I asked him about all the treatments Dr. Grimes was administering, he had plenty of extra work, but got to it all.

Dr. Albo said he couldn't comment on the live cell therapy. He said he thought there was validity to the vitamin C and glutathione I.V.s. But after his research, he could not endorse the DMSO I.V.s. The Raiders told me those I.V.s had to be halted. So after a week of doing it, I stopped, which was a relief, in a way. I was tired of the rest of the team trying to keep half a mile away from me.

I continued with the live cell therapy in the meantime. From the day Dr. Grimes arrived in Napa, I started undergoing my first treatments. The way they worked surprised even me.

Before he could inject my gluteus with the live cell therapy, he first had to numb the area with a little Xylocaine. Otherwise, it would have been impossible to withstand the pain from a needle the length and thickness of a pencil. Imagine that going into you. Once the area was numbed, Dr. Grimes would inject the live cells. All together I took ten live cell therapy injections.

But during those treatments, I'll admit, I never felt so good in all my life. Dr. Grimes instructed me that the injections would last in my system for six months. But when he left camp, he never warned me about what else might happen.

My body started to break down.

One week after Dr. Grimes headed back to North Carolina, I hurt my neck bad enough that I couldn't practice for a week. Even the DMSO cream I was rubbing on it wouldn't work—that tells you how bad it was. I couldn't take a hit, couldn't turn my neck without discomfort.

It was strange to me how I could feel so good one week, and so bad the next. But then I realized there probably was a correlation. The DMSO I.V.s were so strong, my system couldn't handle them. My suspicions were only confirmed on August 15, in a preseason game against Tennessee, when my lower back went out on me in pregame warmups like never before.

From time to time in the past, I had had some back problems, but not like this. This time, I could barely stand up. This time my consecutive game streak, not to mention my career, was in serious jeopardy. One of the first things I did was seek out the Raiders' senior assistant, Bruce Allen.

"Bruce, I've got to have a chiropractor, somebody for every game—on the road, home, in the locker room, everywhere—so if something happens, he can take care of me," I told him.

Fine, he said. I already had one of my old chiropractors, Mark Lindsay, with me. But now I added Keith Pyne, a phenomenal soft-tissue chiropractor from Phoenix, Robert Rudelic, a stretching specialist from San Francisco and Monte Spicer, a massage therapist. They brought the human element, the human touch.

Yet no doctor can completely neutralize years of pounding on your body. Our strength and conditioning coach, Garrett Giemont, tried to do his part as well, which was not surprising. He did so much for the Raiders organization. Not only was he the strength coach, but he also was Al Davis's personal trainer, he scouted the draft, he improved athletes' speed and strength. He was an NFL renaissance man, which is one reason the first thing Jon Gruden did when he got to Tampa was hire Garrett away from Oakland. Coach Gruden knew Garrett's value. It was immense.

Garrett had me work on an exercise ball, trying to build my core strength. He taught me about the importance of core strength, something I hadn't realized before. It helped, but not enough. Desperate, on August 24, I underwent my first pain-killing Toradol injection as a Raider. As my medical charts with the Raiders show, they never let up the rest of the season.

Date	Comment
08/24/02	Bill got a Toradol Injection prior to the game from Dr. King, as well as some ATP.
09/08/02	Bill got a Toradol Injection prior to the game from Dr. Strudwick.

09/15/02	*Bill got a Toradol and B12 Injection prior to the game from Dr. King.*
10/06/02	*Bill got a Toradol Injection and a B12 Injection prior to the game from Dr. King.*
10/13/02	*Bill got a Toradol Injection and a B12 Injection prior to the game from Dr. King.*
10/20/02	*Bill got a Toradol and B12 Injection prior to the game from Dr. King.*
10/27/02	*Bill got a Toradol and B12 Injection prior to the game from Dr. Strudwick.*
11/03/02	*Bill got a Toradol and B12 Injection prior to the game from Dr. King.*
11/17/02	*Bill got a Toradol and B12 Injection prior to the game from Dr. Strudwick.*
11/24/02	*Bill got a Toradol Injection prior to the game from Dr. King.*
12/02/02	*Bill got a Toradol and B12 Injection prior to the game from Dr. King.*
12/08/02	*Bill got a Toradol and B12 Injection prior to the game from Dr. King.*
12/15/02	*Bill got a Toradol and B12 Injection prior to the game from Dr. Gayle.*
12/22/02	*Bill got a Toradol and B12 Injection prior to the game from Dr. King.*
12/28/02	*Bill got a Toradol and B12 Injection prior to the game from Dr. King.*
01/12/03	*Bill got a Toradol and B12 Injection prior to the game from Dr. Strudwick.*
01/19/03	*Bill got a Toradol and B12 Injection prior to the game from Dr. Strudwick.*
01/26/03	*Bill got a Toradol Injection prior to the game from Dr. King.*

ROMO

Eighteen all together. Eighteen documented Toradol injections. It got to the point where, in my last two years of playing football, I needed those injections to play. I did it, but I didn't like it. Toradol is too hard on your liver. It can cause gastric and intestinal ulcers, as well as decreased blood flow to the kidneys. But I felt I had no choice. In the NFL, there are no sick days. You don't have time to heal properly. So you have to utilize what they give you.

If there was any upside, aside from the fact that I continued playing, it was this: In my consultations with Dr. Albo and my other doctors, I figured I could neutralize the effects with glutathion I.V.s, which help your liver do a better job of breaking down the Toradol. Some doctors might try to dispute that, but most of them have not studied nutrition and alternative medicine extensively. I've had sixteen years of those classes. I don't just read it in a magazine and say, "Huh, that's neat." I get it from books, from doctors, from the foremost authorities in their fields. And I put their knowledge to work.

The Toradol took care of my back pain on gameday, but the discouraging part was I couldn't do anything about my brain. Over the course of the season, it gave me more and more problems, no matter what I tried.

Weeks before I arrived in training camp, I even resorted to a measure that I knew would improve my health and hoped would help with my concussions. I had the silver mercury fillings removed from my teeth. Some people have asked me, "Why would you do that?" Well, mercury is a poison. It is more toxic than lead, cadmium, and arsenic. And that poison, much to my disbelief, was in my mouth. Just as disturbing, it's in a lot of people's mouths, and it shouldn't be.

Dr. Tom Levy, whom I had met at the Cellular Medicine Institute in Denver and who had written extensively on dental toxicity issues, first warned me about the dangers of mercury. It actually penetrates all living cells of the body. Autopsy studies showed a correlation between the number of mercury fillings and mercury levels in the brain and kidneys. It's not like it's some great secret. Countries such as Sweden, Germany, and Denmark had already completely banned mercury fillings.

When I found that out and realized how it might be impacting my brain, I did what I could to have every bit of it removed from my mouth. Immediately. And I didn't stop there. All of a sudden I was on the telephone to family and friends, telling everybody I knew, "If you have silver mercury fillings in your mouth, go and get them out! Now!"

What I discovered during the removal of my mercury fillings was the power of my I.V. therapies. Before I got the fillings on the right side of my mouth removed on a Friday night, I went for an I.V. cocktail of 50 grams of vitamin C and five grams of glutathion. After my mouth surgery, the numbness in my mouth started wearing off as I was driving away from the dentist's office.

The next day, without taking any I.V. cocktails before the surgery on the left side of my mouth, the numbness lasted for two hours. That told me the vitamin C and glutathion killed the toxins contained in the powerful numbing agents as quickly as possible.

Yet I could only do so much for my brain. It had been damaged already. In my hands I now have another medical report that physicians from the University of Pittsburgh's Sports Concussion Program filled out in October 2003, after examining me for my concussions.

During the 2002 football season in Oakland, Mr. Romanowski again reports experiencing several "dings" where his postconcussion sequelae would manifest. The symptom constellation following these injuries was highly consistent with that seen during the 2001 season. Specifically, the patient's most prominent symptoms would include general visual disturbance, feeling as though his vision was "scrambled," noticeable balance difficulties, a mild bifrontal headache, and increased fatigue. Once again, the patient played through these symptoms and essentially either minimized or ignored his symptomatology.

None of these "dings" are noted in my 2002 medical reports, but that's because I didn't want anybody to know about them. When I went to Oakland, I went there with something to prove.

Our second game of the season, September 15 at Pittsburgh, was a match-up against two of the toughest players I had faced in my career. Steelers running back Jerome Bettis was one of the toughest guys I've battled with over the years. He could run over you, outrun you, sidestep you—all at 250 pounds. How many people at that weight are the triple threat that "The Bus" was? Not many.

The Steelers also had Mark Bruener, one of the strongest tight ends I have ever gone against. He was right up there with Mark Bavaro, Howard Cross, Pat Carter, Don Warren, and Tony Gonzalez. By this time in my career, I knew every tight end's strength, weakness, total game. Their skills were put together in a mental black book that contained full scouting reports on every player, and how I fared against each in every game I had ever played.

Even with my brain injuries, there was very little I forgot about those battles—they stood out. And even though Bruener gave me fits in a December 7, 1997, game at Pittsburgh, I got him when we played on September 15, 2002. And we got the Steelers, 30–17. Maybe then I was highlighted in *his* mental black book.

But the games I looked forward to more than any other my

first year in Oakland were the two against Denver. We played the first in the ninth week of the season, at a critical juncture, a Monday night game that would define each team's season. Denver was 6–2: a victory that would have unofficially clinched the AFC West title for the Broncos. We were 4–4, losers of four straight games, and we were on the ropes. Coach Shanahan knew that if the Broncos beat us that night, we were done.

My level of intensity that night was at an all together different level. I briefly knocked running back Clinton Portis out of the game with a rib injury. Then when Shannon Sharpe was running a "7 route" downfield, I hooked on to his arm like I used to do at practice. When I hooked it and came down on him, I knew he was hurt. I could just tell by the way he landed. And he was. A dislocated right elbow.

Shannon thought I purposely injured him because I always wanted to hurt people on the football field. But I never wanted them to land on injured reserve. The Broncos lost Shannon for three games, including a 34–10 game to us, and my thought was, *You let me go, that's what happens to you.* Their season was slipping; ours was just starting.

By the time Denver traveled to Oakland on December 22, we had passed them in the standings and one more victory would have clinched the AFC West title for us. In the days leading up to the game, Broncos quarterback Brian Griese said it was the biggest game of his life. He picked the wrong game for that, though.

We were so pumped for that game, the Broncos had no chance. What stood out to me that day was the number of Broncos carried off the field with injuries. Griese, Shannon, Ed McCaffrey. Go down the line, we got almost all of them. By my count, nine former teammates went down. Yes, a tremendously physical game that we won 28-16.

In the closing seconds, I remember pointing across the field

ROMO

to the Broncos sideline, my war paint smeared across my face, screaming: "You don't get rid of me—ever! I will win! I will always win! I will always come back and haunt you!"

It's amazing how on the field, something got into me, turning me into a person that my family and friends would not recognize. Sometimes, I'd even wonder myself, *Was that really me?* But it was. And by now I was playing to the reputation I had established.

I remember playing the Jets in a Monday night game in December, covering New York tight end Anthony Becht, and kicking his ass. When he ran to the flat, I was leveling him before the football could reach him. When he ran across the middle, I decked him, taking him out of the play. Every time he turned around I'd try to slap him as hard as I could. By the end of the game, a 26–20 Raiders victory, I felt like I had beat up on this kid.

Then, when we played the Jets in the first round of the playoffs, Anthony tried to get his revenge. During the game's first series, after he ran a seam route 30 yards downfield, he leveled me when I wasn't looking. As I got up, I got in his face and yelled, "Never do that to me again! Ever! Or I promise you will not come out of this game alive!"

But as we walked back to the huddle, it occurred to me that Anthony was trying to raise his intensity to a level he did not have. During the game, he jumped offsides twice, got whistled for holding another time, and was no factor during our 30–10 AFC Divisional Playoff win. After the game, I sidled up next to him.

"Anthony, you tried to raise your level of intensity tonight to play me. If that's what you want to do, make sure you do it every game you play."

I respected what he tried to do, but he was messing with the wrong guy.

There were guys who could not maintain the level of intensity that I could on a week-to-week, game-to-game basis. It just wasn't them. But it was me. Early in my career, I had to do it to make my mark. Later I needed it to survive.

For the playoffs, I did what I could to bring our team even closer together. I knew two of our cornerbacks, Charles Woodson and Tory James, were hurting. After missing eight regular-season games, Charles had surgery on December 24 to repair a cracked fibula bone in his right leg. Tory had the same injury and surgery as Charles, and he was further along.

I ordered a $4,000 electromagnetic ring from Canada that Mark Lindsay had told me about. The tire-sized donut supposedly stimulated the cell level and helped broken bones heal faster. Problem was the FDA had not approved it, so the Canadian company had to ship it with a big picture of a dog stuck to the top of the ring, to make it look like it was for some other use.

When the machine showed up at the Raiders' training complex, the players laughed at me to no end.

"Hey, Romo is using dog donut therapy on himself," Charles told me.

"I ain't using something for dogs," Tory told me.

Once they tried it, the jokes stopped. Within two weeks, they were recovered and ready for action. Both played in our AFC Divisional playoff win against the Jets.

Before the playoffs started, I used some of my other contraptions on the players. I brought in a water ionizer and hooked it up to the sink in the locker room. From then on, everyone was drinking ionized water.

Even better, Coach Giemont had introduced me to Michael Pickett, the vice president of CytoSport, an innovative nutritional company in Benicia, California, with two of the best

R
O
M
O

sports recovery drinks on today's market, Cytomax and Muscle Milk. Michael and I grew to share a common passion for better performance and family values. But that season, more importantly, he supplied the CytoSport water jugs for each player to carry his ionized water.

And with alkaline infiltrating our systems, Rich Gannon threw three touchdown passes, we beat the Tennessee Titans 41–24, and Al Davis was headed back to the Super Bowl for the first time in nineteen years, just like I predicted he would be in the first message I left with his assistant, Fudgie Otten.

This was my fifth Super Bowl trip. But in a way, this trip to the Super Bowl site in San Diego felt like going home. We stayed at the Hyatt La Jolla, the hotel the Broncos used during the week of their first Super Bowl victory in January 1998. The Raiders provided two hotel rooms for me: one for my personal use and another for all the I.V. therapies for our team.

Dr. Warren King, the Raiders' medical consultant, helped me order the I.V. materials so we would have enough for the whole week. Any player who wanted one could have had a vitamin C, magnesium, zinc, copper, chromium, or glutathion I.V. To help everybody out even more, I flew in Greg Roskopf to work on the guys' muscle alignments the week of the game. There were no means to which I wouldn't go for a win.

But we had issues that the world's best treatments and doctors could not overcome. We did not have two weeks between Super Bowls, like so many other championship games, and the lack of rest hurt our older team.

Then in San Diego, we did not have very good practices. With each bad practice, Coach Callahan eased up on us a little more, then a little more, hoping that it would turn around in the Super Bowl.

The Friday night before the game, our center Barret Robbins left the hotel at 10:15 and didn't return until Saturday night. Everyone was asking at Saturday's walk-through practice, "Where's Barret?" Nobody knew.

He didn't know where he was. I have no idea how he wound up back at our hotel, to be honest. But he never made it to the game the next day; he was suspended. Subsequently, it was disclosed that Barret had been suffering from bipolar disorder.

For as much of a fog as Barret was in, our team wasn't a whole lot better the next day. Part of the problem was the timing. Instead of going out forty-five minutes before the game, as we always did, the NFL sent us out ninety minutes in advance, because it tells you what to do on Super Bowl Sunday. But before we went out, coaches gave us explicit instructions: keep it toned down.

Well, when I looked around during pregame warm-ups for the Super Bowl, everyone was conserving energy. You're playing the biggest game of your life, what the hell are you conserving energy for? We went back into our locker room and had a spare forty-five or fifty minutes that we ordinarily wouldn't. I went to the San Diego Padres weight room, by myself, and started doing one-armed snatches with 100 pound dumbbells—eight for each arm. I had to do something to get my nervous system firing.

But when I went back to the locker room, nobody else's was. I remember standing in the tunnel, about to charge on to the field, and linebacker Eric Barton asked Coach Giemont, "Can we get fired up now?" At that point, it was too late. We needed to be getting fired up, getting the nervous system going, in pregame warm-ups. Not surprisingly, we came out flat.

We got flattened, too. By halftime, it was 20–3. By the end of the game, the Tampa Bay Bucs had won 48–21, and I experienced my first Super Bowl loss.

Maybe it was easier to accept because I had already been a part of four Super Bowl champion teams. But we didn't deserve

ROMO

the game. And after I went to then Buccaneers safety John Lynch, defensive tackle Warren Sapp, and wide receiver Keyshawn Johnson, in the midst of their celebration, to tell them the same thing. "You guys deserved this," I told each of them. "Enjoy it."

The surprising thing to me now is that I even remember having those postgame conversations. During the game, Tampa Bay's five foot ten, 237 pound blockhead fullback Jameel Cook collided in a hole and he just stung me. Stung me good. It was worse than the results of the two big hits I put on San Diego Chargers' running back LaDainian Tomlinson during the season.

This one from the Super Bowl lasted, as the University of Pittsburgh doctors later noted in my concussion report.

"Mr. Romanowski was fortunate enough to play in the 2002 Super Bowl, during which he sustained a rather discernible trauma. Specifically, during the second quarter of the contest, Mr. Romanowski states that he experienced a rather salient helmet-to-helmet contact from a Tampa Bay fullback. At that point, the patient once again experienced marked levels of dizziness, visual disturbance, and feeling foggy. Interestingly, as was the case with this injury and his prior injuries, Mr. Romanowski essentially denied experiencing any other levels of confusion or anterograde/retrograde amnesia. Moreover, the patient never experienced loss of concussions with any of the aforementioned incidences. The patient stated that the Super Bowl incident took much longer to clear, and that his symptoms seemed to persist for even a month after the injury. During the latter part of the 2002 season, Mr. Romanowski first reported experiencing more chronic presentation of symptoms consistent with post-concussions syndrome. During this time,

he first experienced relatively chronic difficulties with mood. Specifically, the patient reported increased emotionality, moderate anhedonia, increased fatigue, reduced drive, and anergia. In addition to these neurobehavioral symptoms, Mr. Romanowski also reported experiencing some perceived cognitive difficulties, such as difficulties with attention and short-term memory. The patient stated that he would sometimes forget events of his day, walk into a room for no apparent reason, have difficulty reading newspaper articles, etc. At this time, he also began experiencing intermittent sleep deficits and some perceived difficulties with balance. Once again, however, Mr. Romanowski returned to football for the 2003 season."

Of course I did. That's what I was trained to do.

R
O
M
O

13 THE BEGINNING OF THE END

On the first day of training camp the following summer of 2003, during the very first drill, I hit the backside guard, Frank Middleton, on a counter play. I nailed him, and I'll tell you what. I nailed myself. First hit, first drill, first day of camp, I'm dizzy, disoriented. Not good. My head was fuzzy. Every day was getting tougher to get through. The end was near—nearer than I wanted it to be.

My head had always been the hunter, not the hunted, the warhead of my missile. Now, without Romo's "balls to the walls" recklessness, my body was no longer willing to sell out at all costs. So I went conservative. And Romo and conservative cannot coexist.

From then on, I began letting up. Me, letting up. I wasn't going to take anyone on helmet-to-helmet. I couldn't. Instead, I used my shoulders to tackle, something I've never done at any point in my career. Up until then, I had always led with my head. But right in front of me, I was having to change the way I played the game. There was no other choice. Look at what was happening:

First preseason game against St. Louis, concussion.

Third preseason game against Minnesota, concussion.

I could barely make it through a practice, much less a game, without injuring my brain. I tried not to think about it, but I had to. Each game had become like a boxing match—in slow motion. In between games were the equivalent of the bell ringing, with me being sent to my corner, where there was the briefest time to rest from my beat-up career, and then it was right back at it, right back to the enemy I could not defeat.

When I did hit, I wound up inflicting more pain on myself than my opponent. I feared what would happen if I told our trainers, so I confided in Trace instead. "Every time I get a good hit, helmet-to-helmet, I get dizzy and my ears start ringing," I told him. "I'm getting headaches, forgetful. Like I'm just in this cloud. Things are real fuzzy. Even depressed, and that's not like me."

"Romo, you've got to tell them. You've got to tell them what's going on." He was right, of course. So I ignored him some more.

In that Minnesota game, to add to my misery, we sucked. Got our asses kicked. Everybody was pissed off, everybody was on edge, and the following Monday, Coach Callahan was making us pay in practice. He made us wear pads and go through the 9-on-7 drill, the most violent drill of the day. Because we were all on edge, the tempo on this day was at an even higher level, you could just tell. Guys were coming off the ball and slamming into each other, taking out their frustration.

What annoyed me was, at this point of my career, with my brain being more fragile than ever, I had to conserve my aggression during practice. I saved my hits for Sundays. Unlike in the

R
O
M
O

past, I now felt, *Why did I need to hit my own guys when I could hit the other guys on Sundays?* But on this day, we had no choice. The whistles blew, the tensions rose, and we had to suck it up.

On one outside sweep, I engaged with the Raiders' then-tight end Marcus Williams. I managed to get a hit in on the running back but after the play, I felt a push in the back. And I said to myself, *I know that mother didn't just push me in the back, you don't ever friggin' push me in the back.* But sure enough he did.

In return, I jolted him from behind. He turned around and we grabbed and clutched each other. His helmet jarred loose and just as he took a swing at me, I upper cutted him. His punch never landed. Mine did. On his left check. One punch, down he went. Leveled. A six-foot-five, 230-pound tight end reduced to rubble. "Romo!" Coach Callahan shouted, just like Seifert did after I punched Paris in 1990. "Take it in!"

As I headed off the field, all I could think was, *Oh, that friggin' mother. . . . Nobody pushes me in the back. . . . Who does he think he is?* Again, when emotion runs high, logic runs low. I headed straight to the weight room and vented my frustration. But near the end of the workout, I started to realize what I did. And I didn't feel good about it. Reality hit me harder than the punch I landed. *This is a teammate,* I moralized, *and this is not OK.*

I'd never hurt one of my teammates before. When I played for the 49ers, I had gotten into fights three straight summers with Jerry Rice. But I never hurt him, never wanted to. And I had always remembered what Coach Shanahan used to say to us in Denver: "All you end up doing by hitting someone wearing a helmet and shoulder pads is breaking your hand, hurting yourself."

He even would fine us $500 every time a fight broke out. Coach Callahan had done a similar thing with the Raiders. At the start of Raiders' camp that summer, he said, "Any fight is gonna cost you five grand."

And that's what bothered me. He fined me one game check—$58,000—but he didn't fine the fight so much as he fined the outcome, and I didn't agree with that. But there were more punishments awaiting. The next night, Coach Callahan summoned me to his office at ten o'clock, and he got sentimental.

"You have kids, you have a son, you owe it to them to be an example to them, to be a leader to them," Coach Callahan told me. But he also revealed that the team might end up cutting me. For whatever reason, they decided against it.

Maybe it had something to do with the apology I issued to the whole team the next day. "There comes a time in your life when you have to hold yourself responsible for your actions and be a man," I told the Raiders. I replayed the events for them like I replayed them for you, and then I told them: "I've hurt everybody in this room because I hurt a team member. And I have to live with that."

That's who I am on the football field, yes. But sometimes I think about everything I've done—the punching, kicking, spitting, cursing, hurting—and it tears me up. Truly. I can't even count the number of times I've cried thinking about it. Being so mean-spirited was draining, though I didn't realize how much until later in my career. To create the fury and attitude I needed took so much out of me.

Just as draining was the transformation of going from the monster on the field back to being Bill. I remember Steve Wisniewski told me he lived a good one-hour drive from the Raiders' training complex just so he could spend that time in his car unwinding, turning himself from the hated player he was back to the family man he also was, at home.

R
O
M
O

For me it became harder than being Bill, which is who I really am as a person. As a person, I love people. I have a saying now that if you're not expressing peace, love, joy, or happiness, then you're not being yourself. That's who I want to be, a husband and father with peace, love, joy, and happiness in his heart. Off the field, it shows up to anybody who knows me, and even to some who don't. On April 4, 2004, *The Denver Post* ran a reader's letter to the editor that probably surprised those who haven't met me.

About two months ago my son had a "jersey day" at school. The jersey he wanted to wear was from a former Broncos player, Bill Romanowski. We looked everywhere, but our search was unsuccessful.

I am a manager at a restaurant. Two weeks ago, Mr. Romanowski was in for lunch. I asked him if he knew where I could find a Romo jersey for my son. He gave me a number of a company that may have one. He also added that if I did find one, he would be back in a few days and would sign it. I did end up finding a jersey.

Last Wednesday, Mr. Romanowski was in for dinner. Unfortunately, I didn't have the jersey with me. He said: "No problem. I'll be in tomorrow and will sign it for you. What jersey did you find?" I told him it was a visiting Raiders jersey. Being a Broncos fan, I wished I could have found a Broncos jersey. But this was the only Romo jersey in the state.

The next day, Mr. Romanowski did stop by and sign the Raiders jersey for my son. The best part of this story is that he also brought in one of his original Broncos jerseys autographed as well. How cool is that?

It must get tough at times being in the public spotlight with people passing judgments about you without actually knowing you. Whatever bad press Bill Romanowski has had, he has gone above and beyond to make a son and his father proud. Not by being an NFL player with four Super Bowl championship rings, but by doing something that was sincere and totally unexpected. We will remember this for the rest of our lives.

Tom Crumley,
Highlands Ranch

Now this is somebody my critics wouldn't recognize. But then, I don't go home to the critics. I don't kiss them good night, even if I know they're out there.

Before my brain went, it got hit with some verbal jabs that left their own scars. Those were delivered from Shannon Sharpe. After I punched out Marcus Williams, Shannon called me out like I never had been called out before.

"It's wrong, it's totally wrong," Shannon said in the *Denver Post* in August 2003. "But for so long, people talk about 'Romo' and they say, 'Oh, you want a tough guy like this.' Or, 'You want a guy like this in your corner.' Or, 'This is the guy you want to go to war with.' No, you don't.

"There is no code among teammates when you do something like that. There is a code about certain things. You don't talk about people's mothers, you don't talk about teammates' wives or girlfriends. You don't do things of that nature. That is the code you live by in the locker room. But there is no code that says, 'If we get in a fight and you do something to me, I'm not going to take action against you.'

"How many times does a guy have to do something? He

R
O
M
O

does it, then he says, 'I'm sorry' and everybody forgives him. How many times in a 16-year career can a guy do something wrong and then say he's sorry and be forgiven?"

And you know what? I can't believe I'm admitting all this, especially this, but Shannon was right. In return for me dislocating his elbow, he nailed me—with his mouth. He knew before I did that I was playing by my own rules—the Romo Rules that applied to nobody but me. Those rules enabled me to gain an edge, just the edge I was looking for. Anyone going up against me knew they would be getting every ATP molecule I had, and then some. And some of my opponents relished the challenge.

After our final preseason game, August 28 at Dallas, the week after the Marcus Williams' incident, Cowboys coach Bill Parcells found me near midfield after the game. "Romo, I wanted you to know I've got a lot of respect for the career you've had," Coach Parcells told me.

After shaking his hand and thanking him, I turned to walk away, but could not get out of earshot before I heard Coach Parcells playfully shouting out to me. "Hey, Romo. I've still got one good fight left in me," like Coach Parcells had my act all figured out and he was ready to challenge me, even if some other players wouldn't.

Back in the locker room, I had arranged a treat for the Three Amigos. Normally after a game, players are given a boxed lunch with a turkey sandwich, a Snickers bar, and an apple. But I wanted more for me, Trace, and John Parrella. I wanted us to get the most out of every great day. I had given my brother Joe, who lives in Dallas, a couple hundred bucks to go to Del Frisco's, a local steakhouse, to pick us up some filets and creamed spinach.

What a great diversion. Instead of worrying about my brain, Trace and I sat in the back of the locker room and feasted in an atypical postgame fashion, filling our stomachs.

O n September 3, I flipped on my car radio, and the news was the same on every Bay Area station: Raid. BALCO Labs. Steroid scandal.

And my first thought: *Oh, no, was I taking something illegal?*

In October 2003, the FDA released a statement saying it recently had been made aware of it, and after analyzing the product determined that THG is an unapproved new drug. John Taylor, FDA's Associate Commissioner for Regulatory Affairs, said, "Our mission is to protect the American public from this potentially harmful product."

The NFL ban was put into effect on October 6, 2003, but I had stopped taking it long before then, before my last NFL pre-season had even kicked off. And the FDA's statement of THG being "potentially harmful" leaves the second question up in the air—still. Given the ban and the scandal, I doubt we'll ever know. Science, even research science, follows the money. THG hasn't hurt me, physically, not yet at least. And it even might have kept me from getting hurt or worse. But we'll never know that for sure, either.

There's a lot we won't know. But for now, there's a lot we do. In the beginning of November, I received a letter from the NFL saying that I had tested positive for THG—a substance I had stopped using before training camp, the moment I heard rumors they were developing a test for it.

But when I received that letter, I already was finished for the season—another concussion—and my career, in all probability, was over. There was little action the league could take against me. The government, though, was just getting started.

On September 3, 2003, Internal Revenue Service special agents and the San Mateo County narcotics task force raided BALCO. From what I've been told, they didn't find much.

R
O
M
O

The government didn't care. It blitzed BALCO. It subpoenaed forty athletes and coaches connected to BALCO to testify in the same room on the seventeenth floor of the Philip Burton Federal Building that I did.

Eventually, the government indicted Victor, BALCO's vice president James Valente, my former track coach Remi Korchemny, and personal trainer Greg Anderson. Three of them—Victor, James, and Remi—were men I had done some work with. Fair to say that's one reason the grand jury was so interested in my version of the events.

For telling my story, the grand jury granted me immunity. And I told the grand jury the truth.

U p until then, I had been able to handle all the adversity in my career pretty well. But you know what? For the first time in my life, I was struggling with it. Irresponsibly blasting my own teammate. Busting BALCO. Bruising my brain. It became too much to handle, even for me, someone who adversity usually barely affected. And during our season-opening Sunday night game at Tennessee, it only got worse.

On one play, I plowed into Titans running back Mike Green and staggered around. Wobbled back and forth, side to side. I spent so much time in the locker room after the game that Mark Lindsay and Keith Pyne went out to Julie after the game and said, "We're worried about him."

With good reason. Back home that week, I was doing weird things, uncommon things.

I would leave the house one morning, take ten steps out the back door, and realize I forgot my supplement box. Now, that happened as often as I missed a game—which is to say, never. So I would turn around, walk back into the house, and then not remember why I was there. And this was happening again and again, an instant replay.

Other times, I would start driving to the Raiders' training facility and simply forget where I was supposed to be going. On the drive back home one night, I called Julie to check in and see where she was.

"At the Webelos Boy Scout function for Dalton," she said.

"What are you doing there?" I asked.

"Billy, we made these plans weeks ago. I reminded you of them this morning."

My recall was not recalling anything. And yet I still pushed myself on the field for our opening home game against Cincinnati. I don't remember it but my medical report from the University of Pittsburgh says in that game, I "sustained face mask to face mask contact, which resulted in significant levels of dizziness, feeling foggy, visual changes, and general lethargy."

But the next week, we were playing in Denver. How could I not be up for that one? A rematch of the team we took it to twice last season.

And in the first quarter, I struck Clinton Portis with my head and then . . . took a knee. I never had taken a knee. At that point, I could have been taking a knee on my career, all sixteen seasons worth. The only NFL players who ever had played in more consecutive games were defensive lineman Jim Marshall and kicker Morten Andersen.

But even in the end, I was fighting to catch them. I was willing myself to finish the Monday night game.

"Finally, this past Monday evening [09/22/03], Mr. Romanowski was involved in the Monday night football game, and experienced a left frontal blow early in the contest. For the first time, Mr. Romanowski reported experiencing

R
O
M
O

rather salient levels of photosensitivity, in addition to his common symptoms of dizziness, visual tracking problems, balance difficulties, fatigue, frontal headache and increased emotionality. The patient stated that the dizziness was more severe than at any point in his career."

I knew how messed up my brain was. After the Broncos beat us 31–10, I remember sitting at my locker in the bowels of INVESCO Field at Mile High, turning to Trace and whispering, "I don't know if I can do this anymore."

And Trace looked at me and shook his head.

"If you play again, you are a selfish mother. Give it up, Romo. You've got a family that's relying on you."

Walking into our training room, I fessed up to our medical staff. Told them all the problems I was having. Concussions every week. Concussions every game. They arranged for me to stay overnight in Denver, to undergo a brain MRI and brain tests with Dr. Alan Weintraub the next morning.

That night, Julie and I went to dinner at Del Frisco's Double Eagle Steak House in Greenwood Village, about ten minutes from where we used to live. After dinner, the other eight guests at our table ordered ice cream for dessert.

And I remember taking a bite of Julie's and not tasting a thing. My sense of taste, and smell, had gone dead.

To this day, they still have not fully returned.

During a three-week span into mid-October 2003, I made two trips to visit with the University of Pittsburgh's physicians in the school's Sports Concussion Program.

Upon studying my results, Dr. Mickey Collins prepared a report of his impressions and recommendations that he mailed to the Raiders' head trainer Rod Martin, Dr. Albo, and Tom Condon.

*"*First, it is my impression that Mr. Romanowski's case represents a rather chronic presentation of symptoms related to repetitive incidences of cerebral concussion. One purpose of this second evaluation was to ascertain his degree of improvement over a three-week period with no contact or trauma to the head. If the patient's case was a more acute presentation related to this year's injuries, we would likely have seen notable improvements during this three-week period. Conversely, however, it is my impression that Mr. Romanowski's symptom and neurocognitive profile have remained stable with that seen previously. At the current time, the patient continues to exhibit a moderate to severe deficit with reaction time, and milder deficits with aspects of processing speed and visual memory. Little improvement, and some declines, have occurred in terms of Mr. Romanowski's neurocognitive functioning since our last evaluation. Moreover, from a symptom standpoint, the patient remains quite vulnerable to increased physical activity and exertion. This was recently demonstrated by the patient's intense workout, followed by a rather severe presentation of post concussion symptoms, including dizziness, bifrontal headache, feeling slow, increased fatigue, perceived slowed thinking, and possible mild disorientation. Moreover, following this activity, the patient also demonstrated rather significant mood changes consistent with post concussion syndrome. These include increased levels of irritability, anhedonia, and a generally blunted affect. In summary, Mr. Romanowski continues to exhibit clear and at least*

R
O
M
O

moderate signs of post concussion syndrome and related sequelae.

*As outlined in my first evaluation, I feel that Mr. Romanowski has exhibited a progressively insidious presentation of post concussion syndrome starting primarily in 2001 and becoming more chronic over time. Based upon the collected data and his overall history, I feel that the patient will likely be permanently vulnerable to an increased risk of both sustaining concussion and having more prolonged, and progressively more severe, symptomatology related to these events. Though a paucity of data exists examining potential long-term effects of cerebral concussion, I am also concerned about this possibility if Mr. Romanowski were to continue in contact football participation.

*Given the outlined concerns, I feel it is in Mr. Romanowski's best interest to retire from contact football participation."

The odd thing is, I have far less brain injury than I should. Without the supplements I took and the training I did, I believe my injuries would be far more severe. As it is, they are bad enough.

In all my talks with the doctors at Pittsburgh, they said some things that hit me harder than Tampa Bay's fullback. They told me it was impossible to say whether I would end up as slowed as Muhammad Ali.

They informed me that while my frontal lobe tested in the one hundredth percentile—an excellent result—my rear brain tested in the third percentile—a terrible result.

That's where all my concussions were, in my rear brain. The cumulative effects were, to say the least, unnerving.

A recent NFL study revealed that the average impact velocity of a helmet-to-helmet tackle is 20.8 miles per hour. The player being struck, on average, goes from a state of rest to an impact velocity of 16.1 miles per hour.

Think of it as a car crash. On every play. Thirty, forty, fifty times each Sunday. This was how I made my living. By getting into car crashes. And in the end, I came away with the most severe case of whiplash a person could have.

How about that? All that time I had been taking care of my body, obsessing about it, training blocks of hours, spending millions of dollars, and look what happened.

My brain failed me. Or maybe I failed my brain.

ROMO

EPILOGUE:
OF DREAMS AND
DRAGONS

Each and every day I think about being around for Julie, Dalton, and Alexandra for as long as I can. With the recent premature deaths of former NFL stars Reggie White and Sam Mills, I have become especially conscious that what I did to my body and my brain was damaging. To what extent, I don't know. And I don't know if anyone ever will.

My obsessiveness was geared toward extending my career and extending my life. That was the idea of it. People condemned me for it, but I was in charge of what I put in my body and how hard I pushed it, and I thought I knew what worked best. But even I'd admit that it fed right into a vicious cycle. The more my dream became an obsession, the harder I trained. The harder I trained, the better I thought I performed, and the more confident I got. The more confident I got, the more I became intoxicated with power, and the more I took chances. The more I took chances, the more I crossed the line. The more I crossed the line, the more I sold out my integrity.

But the more I sold out my integrity, the more I seemed to be rewarded and the more attention Romo got, whether celebrated or despised. Over time, I lost touch with my values and drifted further away from who I really was. And really, who I really am, at my core, is a small-town kid with big-time dreams. Somehow, my message got lost in translation.

For the longest time, I allowed my career to run me. I refused to pay attention to the obvious signs of physical and mental deterioration. I was afraid to face my increasingly dangerous brain injuries. And I most certainly didn't want to deal with the warped personality Romo had become. Now, even though forced by my circumstances, I can honestly say that I'm embracing the changes I know I need to make.

The longer I played the game I loved, the harder it was to keep up with it. At times, I crossed the line. My story should be a tribute to those who succeed through hard work, an overachiever's celebration of overcoming his limitations. Instead, I have put an asterisk next to my name. I will go on with my life, and yes, I will be even more successful, even with my partially tainted memories.

True, Romo's rules are not obsolete, at least not yet. But Bill Romanowski's rule is to rebuild my integrity and morality while becoming even better than ever. At the same time, I will not discard what has made me successful. I don't automatically forfeit my exceptional work ethic. I don't automatically lose my unmatched passion for excellence.

Clearly, the single-minded pursuit of my own ambitions has unintentionally compromised important relationships in my life. For someone who really hungers for intimacy and friendship, I have too often sabotaged myself and others. This book is, as much as anything else, my personal pledge to my own accountability. If you've ever written your own story, you know that putting things down in black and white really pins

R
O
M
O

you to your own truth. When I slip, I will not only have myself to deal with, but most certainly my family and friends, and I hope many of you who share similar struggles, who will remind me as we run into each other along the way.

I believe I've made it clear that football in no way caused my problems. It was me and the way I made my dreams more important than anything or anyone else. I really wasn't playing the game of football as much as I was playing the game of self-survival.

When I'm able to demonstrate the same drive, the same energy, to my wife and children that I put into football, I'll be the greatest husband and father on this earth. That's my promise, so don't bet against me. Pure love, I've learned, never needs a supplement.

To my wife, Julie, and our children, Dalton and Alexandra, I apologize for not sharing my life with them the way they deserved, not to mention exposing them to undeserved public shame. How many people directed their judgments—meant for me—at Julie over the drug charges that were fully my responsibility? How many people looked at my kids and wondered what kind of parents were raising them?

We are good parents, especially Julie. But others might not see that. My family continues to be victimized by rumor and innuendo. Recently Dalton came home from school and asked point-blank, "Daddy, do you do drugs?"

Now, how do you address the fears of an innocent ten-year-old? Especially when he naturally idolizes his dad?

I struggled to give him the best answer, however imperfect. Very softly I told him, "Daddy took a lot of things to help his body survive the pain of football." And that's the truth, but not the complete version. Both my kids deserve to know about their father and his genuine struggle with his principles and ethics. They deserve to know that I recognize my imperfections, and that my errors, like their own experiments and mistakes, are a part of life. They do not diminish us as human beings. They do not cancel our innate goodness and our obligation to constantly grow and become better people.

> *Dreams and dragons are equal and inseparable allies in the pursuit of human fulfillment.*
> *Dreams test our faith.*
> *Dragons test our convictions.*
> *Without Dreams, we merely exist.*
> *Without Dragons, our Dreams are but empty promises.*

ROMO

AFTERWORD:
PEACE, or,
LIFE AFTER FOOTBALL

I did return to football, but not in the manner in which I was accustomed. After it became clear my season was finished in December, Ed Goren, FOX TV's president and executive producer, called Tom Condon to see if I would have any interest in broadcasting three games during the regular season's last three weeks.

The off-season before, after our Super Bowl loss, ESPN hired me as a draft-day analyst. And you know what? When you are about to go live, there is a little high that hits you. It's not like nailing a quarterback or intercepting a pass or landing a big hit. But there's still a little buzz.

"Hey, we're going live in a minute," the producer yells, and you're shuffling papers, trying to pin down your thoughts, and suddenly the red light goes on. And you're on. I liked it, enough so that I wanted another taste of it.

FOX appointed me its unofficial voice of Arizona, three

straight Cardinals games—December 14 against Carolina, December 21 at Seattle, and December 28 against Minnesota.

To prepare for the games, I started watching game tape, reading newspaper articles, getting as much information as I could about the Cardinals and Panthers. I even attended the 49ers game against Arizona on December 7, when I watched the game from the FOX booth in the press box and bumped into my former linebackers coach and defensive coordinator, Bill McPherson.

"What are you doing here?" Coach McPherson asked, hugging me.

"Working," I told him. "Studying. Getting ready for my next assignment."

"As usual, you look like you're decked out to your eyeballs with your work."

This is how it always is. Whatever I do, I throw myself into. There is no halfway, not with me. And in the hours of preparation work I did for my first broadcast, the Panthers struck me as a team that was going places. They didn't have "I" guys; they were a team. They had a quarterback, Jake Delhomme, who reminded me of Bubby Brister; a safety Mike Minter, who hit as hard as any player in the league; and a defensive coordinator Mike Trgovac, whom I knew from our time together in Philadelphia.

After Carolina beat the Cardinals 20–17, I did an interview with a Carolina radio station that also had on Panthers linebacker Will Witherspoon.

"Will," I asked him on the air, "what's your team's goal for this year?"

"Just keep working, keep improving, week in and week out."

"Wrong!" I said to him. "You've got one goal and one goal only. And that's to win a world championship. You guys have something in that locker room. There's a certain energy. I've

R
O
M
O

seen it five times in my career, the five times my team went to the Super Bowl. Don't be afraid to talk about it. Believe it."

And when I flew back to Oakland and bumped into the Raiders' personnel executive Mike Lombardi at the team's training facility, I told him, as he will confirm to this day: "Mark my words. Carolina is going to the Super Bowl. I can't tell you if they're going to win it or not, but they're going." First the Panthers beat the Cowboys in the wild-card round. Then the Panthers upset the Rams in an NFC divisional playoff. Then they beat the Eagles in the NFC Championship game to get to the Super Bowl in Houston. Before they left for the game, I called the Panthers' special teams coach Scott O'Brien, and left him the following message:

"Scott, I got attached to your team when I did your game. I fell in love with what your team is about. So if I could offer some advice, there're a couple of things I'd love to pass along that I picked up from Coach Walsh. Number one, you're simply playing an away game in Houston against New England.

"Number two with two weeks between the championship game and the Super Bowl, make sure to put in your game plan this week. That way when you get down to Houston, you can refine it. We did that when I was with Denver—put in our game plan the week before we flew to Miami—and the Falcons waited to put theirs in until the week they got down there. So if I can weigh in, those would be two bits of advice I hope can help you in some small way. Good luck."

Lots of help I was, huh? With four seconds left, Patriots kicker Adam Vinatieri booted a 41-yard field goal to give the Patriots a 32–29 win over Carolina. It was a great game, but probably not as exciting as the last one I worked on FOX.

On the final Sunday of the regular season, the Cardinals scored two improbable touchdowns in the final two minutes, the second of which was a 28-yard pass to Nate Poole, whom

Arizona had cut four times. The Cardinals' incredible 18–17 win knocked the Vikings out of the playoffs and set off a celebration in Green Bay, where the Packers seized the last wild-card spot—the one Minnesota thought it had.

After the game, Ed Goren called me personally.

"How do you do it, Romo?" he asked. "How do you end up working the game of the season? What is it about you?"

Ed got me to thinking. In the midst of transitioning from playing football to a new career, I needed to pause and reflect upon my blessings. I guess you could say I've always been fortunate. Good fortune, like winning, followed me from Vernon, Connecticut, to almost everywhere I went.

Even Hollywood.

J ust like I dreamed about being a football player, I've dreamed about making it in Hollywood. During my last off-season, I had a premonition on my way to the track to run sprints. My voice said, "Hollywood needs a new Terminator." A month later, Arnold Schwarzenegger said he was going to run for governor, which meant he was going to be sidelined from his starring role. Then all this stuff started happening.

In May 2004, my agent, Tom Condon, got a telephone call from Adam Sandler's production company, wanting to know if I would have any interest in being cast in *The Longest Yard*, a remake of the 1974 classic starring Burt Reynolds as former NFL quarterback Paul Crewe. Only this time Adam was playing Paul Crewe, with Reynolds being recast as coach Nate Scarborough.

Not long after, I met Adam at the Judy Garland Building on the grounds of Sony Studios in Los Angeles. The first thing we talked about was surfing. He loves it as much as I do, and we've surfed the same spots in Hawaii. After discussing our surfing

ROMO

interests, Adam looked at me and asked, "What do you think about *The Longest Yard*?"

"It would be great, Adam. I'd look forward to the challenge."

"The part is yours if you want it."

Just like that, my acting career was under way. Adam and I spent a Tuesday in Los Angeles doing a reading with the rest of the cast, then the very next day in the waves at Malibu, surfing and discussing the movie. After the reading, I overheard Chris Rock walk up to Adam and say: "You got Ro-man-ow-ski! How did you get Ro-man-ow-ski?'"

Simple enough. I'm just trying to enjoy the incredibly blessed life that football has enabled me to have, living a new dream. While my former teammates spent the summer at training camp, I spent it playing Guard Lambert, one of the middle linebackers on the prison guards' football team. Our team was a sadistic group that included Brian Bosworth, Stone Cold Steve Austin, Kevin Nash, Conrad Goodie, Michael Papa John, and Bill Fichtner.

On our first day of shooting in Santa Fe, New Mexico, Mark Ellis—whose company, Reel Sports, hired football players after putting them through tryouts and a training camp before filming began—warned us how hard this was going to be.

All I could think was, "You've got to be kidding me! They're treating everyone like a bunch of babies!" It drove me crazy. Suddenly I felt like I was unretired.

When I walked into the locker room, it was training camp all over again. I taped up my wrists and my fingers the exact way I would do it before every NFL practice. I put on the same pads that I wore for sixteen NFL seasons, the same cleats, the same gloves, the same wrist gear, the same Number 53 jersey, the same everything. Beneath my eyes, I even put on the same slashes of black war paint. And the rush of adrenalin was racing through me, the same as always. I went out there wanting to hit people, but careful not to be too aggressive. But to be truthful, you just can't fake football.

Almost immediately I noticed similarities between football practices and movie shoots—or at least football movie shoots. Actors got sore, their bodies broke down. Actors needed to fuel their bodies the same way football players do, so I had Michael Pickett of CytoSport—the Bay Area nutritional company that I consult with—send out palettes of Muscle Milk, the fastest-growing protein drink on the market today. For the rest of our shoots, we had three full-time people on the set, mixing up protein shakes, with the whole cast drinking them.

When wrestler Stone Cold Steve Austin pulled a hamstring early in the filming while doing some drills, I had another idea. These guys needed trainers. To get the best performance, the actors had to have the best treatments. So, naturally, I worked with the movie's executive producer, Barry Bernardi, to bring Nelson Vetanzi, Robert Rudelic, Tim Adams, and Mark Lindsay on board. Everyone was blown away by their expert advice and especially the fact that our movie set had turned into a training ground for excellence.

Meanwhile, I was getting to meet new and interesting people. Every night we would gather in the hotel lobby and hang out. There was no pressure like there was in the NFL—I knew I could have a glass of wine that night and not worry about losing my job in practice the next day. I could show up at 95 percent, instead of 100 percent, because that 95 percent was 150 percent of what the director needed. So I could relax, connect with people, and develop relationships so they could see what I was about. It was during these "hang" times that I realized how much I missed the friendships I could have had in the NFL locker room.

One was Brian Bosworth, whom I once had openly criticized before my senior season at Boston College. As I got to talk

R
O
M
O

to him, I realized I had preconceived ideas of him, just as people have them of me. Brian was a serious guy, and the more I talked to him, the more I respected him. Injuries cut short his football career, so he never got to live his football dream, and I felt badly for him. He told me it took its toll on him, leaving him initially depressed and lost.

When I thought about how I had criticized him, I knew how wrong I was. I only did it because a part of me wanted to be just like him—with the headlines, with the attention, with the spotlight on what he was doing. Talking to him made me realize that if I can get inside a person, like I can get inside an acting role, then I'll be able to understand him. Then prior judgments play no part, which is how it should be. I was beginning to become better at being a friend.

Another person I got to know pretty well was Adam Sandler. On our first day of football training camp, we talked about our families, and I told him how the greatest gift my parents gave me was being there. When I said it, I noticed Adam had a little tear in his eye. He said he recently had lost his father, and not a day goes by when he didn't think about him and wished he could give him a call. It told me how real Adam was, and I only saw more examples of it.

When I was out on the road in San Francisco promoting *The Longest Yard,* Adam left me a message, saying, "Romo, heard you're doing a great job. Just want to let you know how much I appreciate your work." That wasn't necessary, but it was awfully nice to be recognized. I've learned to take moments out of my day to do the same. Why wait until someone important is in our past to tell them how we feel today?

Adam and I hit it off so much he wrote another movie, *Benchwarmers,* a feel-good baseball movie that stars Rob Schneider, David Spade, and John Heder, and is slated to be released in 2006. He asked me to play Coach Karl, an angry baseball coach whose only objective is to humiliate the opposition. Hmmmm, how did I get this role?

Hollywood can be a small world, as can New Orleans. When I was down there in December 2004 to film a part for another movie, *Pool Hall Prophets,* starring Ving Rhames; Freddie Prinze, Jr.; and Rosalyn Sanchez, I walked into my hotel and bumped into Sean Penn. I introduced myself, but he didn't know who I was. The more I pushed him in our conversation the more he opened up. He liked me enough that he invited me to meet him at Commanders Palace that night at 10:30 P.M.

We spent the next seven hours, into the early morning, talking about improving relationships and growing and changing as a person. One thing I learned about Sean that night was, if he's your friend, he'll do anything for you; he's that loyal. It showed two weeks later, when I was scheduled to fly back to New Orleans with Julie. We were driving to the Oakland airport that morning to fly to New Orleans when I listened to my voicemails from the night before. Sean had called from his home in northern California to offer a ride to New Orleans on his private plane. Right then, knowing we had a day of connecting flights ahead of us, Julie and I turned our car around and headed home. Sean extended a nice gesture, and we were fortunate enough to be able to take advantage of it.

During one of our conversations, Sean turned me on to a performance coach, Phil Towle, fresh off helping the heavy metal band Metallica get back on track. "He's another guy that can talk our game, who would be interesting for you to meet. He can help you."

We all had dinner one night in San Francisco and since then, I'm happy to say, Phil has helped me in so many areas—to be a better husband, a better father, and a better professional in the business world. He has helped me make the transition back from Romo to Bill Romanowski. He is always finding a way to move something forward and improve upon it, whether it's my acting career, this book, or relationships. As you would expect, my passion for personal growth has extended from the playing field to life itself.

By now I've made some nice connections and I'm just going to try to bring to Hollywood what I brought to the NFL. Once again, I'm in a position to make an impact on society. That's quite a challenge. It's like starting over in peewee football with the goal to get to Hollywood's NFL. Right now I may be at the bottom of the acting pile, but you can bet that's not where I'll wind up. We're blessed with talents, and we should deliver on them.

During a break in the shooting for *The Longest Yard,* Burt Reynolds walked right over to me with his own inspirational message. He threw his arm around me. "Hey, sonny," he said. "You're going to be a big star in this business."

He should've added, ". . . if you survive this shoot." In one scene, Adam Sandler faked a pitch to his left, rolled around to the right, and I came off full speed and nailed him, head to head. Adam had a stand-in do his part; I didn't. And I had to do this four times, and you know me. I didn't let up at all. I annihilated him.

Man, it knocked me for a loop. I was dizzy, woozy, frightened. The last thing I wanted was to let anybody know that I got wounded on a movie set—by a stand-in quarterback, no less.

To be honest, up until that point, I held onto the fantasy of returning to the NFL. But now I knew there was absolutely no way whatsoever I could ever do it again. It definitely was over. After we finished shooting the scene, I went back to my trailer, sat down, and tried to rest and regain my senses.

A couple of weeks later, there was another scene in which I spot Adam Sandler in the locker room and I say, "I'll see you on the field!" as I bang my head against a metal locker to scare him.

I didn't even think about how it might affect me; I just did it. Rammed my head right into the metal locker. As soon as I did, I started getting a little bit dizzy. I had to reshoot the scene seven more times—with seven more headbangers. By the end of it, I was praying, "Please don't have me do this again."

While I sometimes hold on to the unrealistic hope that one day these lingering side effects will disappear, I'm reminded in even the simplest of ways that they just won't. When we were filming *Benchwarmers* in Los Angeles, I brought my family to Six Flags Magic Mountain, as a little break. I thought it would be fun to take my children on the roller coasters. But by the time we got finished with four roller coaster rides, I felt like I had just finished with another NFL game. I was sick to my stomach, dizzy, disoriented.

Part of me says I went too far with it, as I had done in other ways, but as usual, I'm going to try to somehow, some way, turn this personal challenge into a positive. My crisis has forced me to search for a cure for brain injuries. My partner, Tom Incledon, and I have devloped a line of supplements called "Pure Romo Nutrition," specifically a high-powered mix of nutrients for improving mental performance called "Neuro Path." Since I started using it in the winter of 2004, it has enabled me to get through my workouts without any dizziness, without any headaches, without some of the problems I experienced in my last few NFL seasons. Of course, I'm not ramming myself into any more opponents or lockers, either.

Eventually I believe we'll come up with a cure for concussions, so that other players are not prevented from playing the game the way I am. And I don't want anybody else enduring what I have.

My sense of taste, like my career, is almost history. My sense of smell is all but gone. Sometimes I find myself slurring some of the simplest words in our language.

R
O
M
O

Despite all the physical and mental scars it left on me, it was worth every side effect. Playing linebacker in the NFL, I never had to work a day in my life. It meant so much to me. It's not easy knowing I won't have any more football. Julie loved the fact I played it; she loved watching me out there. And my children were starting to really understand that their dad played football for a living. Their friends thought it was cool.

Now that I can focus more on my family, my real challenge with both of my children is to provide a stronger role model. I want to teach them to respect themselves as healthy young people so that their relationships will come from positions of strength. With Julie, it is about respecting her as an equal instead of relegating her to the chief of my pit crew. I'm not entitled to have favored status in our family.

I'm beginning to take the time to know who I really am. Reputation is more about what others form about us. As I've said, there was a time when I fed on what other people thought. But I can't live on image forever, especially when it's not a complete picture. And especially since there are not many requests for wild and crazy linebackers in my current business projects and private life.

That being said, there is plenty of room for my intensity and ambition. There will always be my next dream. And I will always be in pursuit. I recognize now, though, that I've become my most important obstacle to happiness and fulfillment. I'm my own biggest dragon. Aren't we all? So what I'm doing is working the hell out of my insides. Training my mind and emotions, if you will, with the same relentlessness I gave to being a warrior.

I'm fascinated with psychology and philosophy. I want to do whatever I can to make the world a better place, whether from my supplemental nutritional aids or as a public figure. In order to be effective, not to mention principled, I've got to clean up my own personality.

Hey, maybe I got it backward! At least I'm getting it. That's what history is for. Remember, this off-season for Bill Romanowski is forever. I aim to get my priorities straight and have much more fun doing it. I've got much, much work to do. But that's never been the problem. I just need to be patient with myself, which is hard for me.

It's interesting how I end my phone messages with the affirmation, "Peace." I know it's important to me, but I still don't honestly know what peace really means.

I hope I'm about to find out.

R
O
M
O

POSTSCRIPT

What is it about the "difference makers" among us? You know them: the ones never satisfied with "what is." Do they simply take advantage of possibilities that do not exist for the average individual? Or do they just have a more compelling vision of what they want to be?

As I've often witnessed, their passion accelerates into obsession, propelled by a will that exceeds natural ability. And, because they never quite trust when enough is enough, they cannot relent for a millisecond, lest they lose their ongoing battle with fear of failure.

To the Bill Romanowskis of the world, addiction to the impossible is often more desirable than having life pass them by. "Whatever it takes" becomes more crucial than "whatever the consequences."

Pioneers of human potential cannot break new ground unless they go where the rest of us have never been. They discover so that we may learn. They experiment so that we don't have to make the same mistakes. They risk and we watch, appreciating the cost of insatiable commitment, urging them on from the safety of our apprehension to take risks ourselves.

We take from their self-sacrifice, but when we determine that they have crossed *our* judgment line, we are quick to condemn and discard. We partner in their glory, reject when they threaten what we're comfortable with.

Whatever your predeterminations, *Romo: My Life on the Edge—Living Dreams and Slaying Dragons* has forced you to think about yourself, your values, and most certainly about whether you are cheating your life and God-given talents. With Adam Schefter, Bill has brought us beyond the customary "memoirs of a jock-hero." As he did every down of his sixteen-year pro-football career, he has left us with every drop of his disquieted soul.

You've decided where you stand . . . not just with Bill . . . but with YOURSELF!!

—Phil Towle, August 2005

POSTSCRIPT

APPENDIX A:
ROMO'S RECOMMENDATIONS

Football and I have a mutual love affair, and as you know, there are few who have taken their football as seriously. While my controversial actions may have sometimes tainted my image, I honestly trust that over time my unmatched devotion to being the best will ultimately define Bill Romanowski, human being.

While my place in NFL history is being sorted out, I'm already full-on with my next set of dreams. You've already heard about my Hollywood aspirations. Now let me tell you about my plan to share the immense body of knowledge I've accumulated over sixteen years of learning from the best experts and studying innovative procedures, techniques, and supplements.

Remember, I am never possessive about what I learn. I've always felt especially good helping others achieve their success. I invested over one million of my own dollars to help myself and others maximize their performance. In short, I don't think there's anyone better qualified at knowing, firsthand, what works and what doesn't.

Over the course of my career, I've figured out the basic goals of supplementation. Each athlete's program varies a little based on what he or she feels after taking their supplements, but the basic program that I think everyone should take focuses on four goals.

1. Generating energy.
2. Minimizing inflammation.
3. Recovering quickly.
4. Growing.

Generating energy. You've got to generate all the energy you can to compete with other athletes. Energy comes from burning carbohydrates and forming ATP bonds, also called adenosine triphosphate. ATP is like cash for your body. Just like cash, money talks when it's ATP; you can spend it anywhere and everywhere. Every cell from your brain to your Achilles thrives on it, and ATP is what makes you quick, strong, and mean when you have to be.

You can't take ATP by itself and instantly have energy. I know because when I was playing in Denver and Oakland I tried it, and it didn't make much difference. You can't take any supplement and have instant energy. Foods and supplements are broken down into their most minute parts to enter your body, so big molecules like ATP are not directly absorbed. You've got to eat and drink and otherwise set the stage for the energy production.

There are lots of supplements to choose from, but only a handful really work. The process of burning carbs for ATP and burning ATP during workouts and games is combustive. You burn a calorie and three things happen: energy, which is the good part; waste, which has to be hauled off by your breath, circulation, or sweat and moved out of your body; and damage.

Damage is, of course, the bad part. It's the part that limits your energy production. If you eat the right mix of proteins, healthy fats, and carbs you will still do damage but won't make as much energy as you would if you also have rich levels of antioxidants. Every time you burn a calorie, you injure some part of your body in the process. This damage is called oxidative stress, and it's offset or neutralized by antioxidants. Generating as much energy as you can involves eating the right kinds and proportions of carbs, proteins, and healthy fats, but to minimize the damage it also requires antioxidants.

Minimizing inflammation. This is a must if you're going to train, compete, excel, and be a better athlete every time you hit the gym or take the field.

Each time you move you damage something. Roll over in bed and something tears. Micro-tears are happening from the movements it takes to read this book; turn this page and you'll have injured your fingers and the connective tissues in your wrist and arm in a very small and easily repaired way. But do a leg workout like the ones I used to do with Tim Adams or play a three-hour football game, and you'll have more than micro-tears and more inflammation than you want or need.

Any physical damage to your body, great or small, is dealt with by your immune system. Your immune system routinely triggers the inflammatory response to fix and repair torn or injured tissues. It does so by releasing inflammatory chemicals, which are part of the healing and growing process.

If you want to wear out early in your workouts or during competition, ignore this important fact and you'll go down. If you want the stamina it takes to train and play with the big boys and girls, then take a supplement routine that focuses on minimizing inflammation. The less excess inflammation, the longer you'll last and the sooner you'll recover.

Recovering quickly. The goal of every elite athlete. You could say that certain athletes are elite because they do recover more quickly than others.

Play-by-play is one aspect of recovering quickly, but a slower, more grueling aspect is getting over the soreness from heavy lifting, a big sprint, or running day, and the pounding you give and get in a game. The whole pharmaceutical industry is looking for the next best anti-inflammatory that can take away muscle and joint soreness to your mother's and grandmother's arthritis, and NFL players are glad they are doing this research because we're some of its best customers.

When I got to San Francisco, I was introduced to state-of-the-art anti-inflammatories, Feldene, Indocin, Naprosyn, and a pill that had the anti-inflammatory power of six aspirin, Motrin—the prescription strength kind, not the over-the-counter ones you can buy now.

These drugs work by inhibiting an enzyme that makes inflammatory chemicals in the body. I also found that certain foods, like omega-3 oils, ginger, and certain supplements do this better. I tried dozens of anti-inflammatories and supplements with the same goal in mind and I found the few that work well—or at least that worked for me.

Growing. This is what it's all about. Growing physically, mentally, and emotionally. They're not the same, but they do require some of the same nutrients.

Physically you grow by producing energy; burning that energy produces flash fires or a holocaust of activity that breaks you down more than ever before, releasing inflammatory chemicals to start the growth and healing phase, and healing as aggressively as possible by stimulating the release of gallons of growth factors.

You do this by having high levels of antioxidants in your body, which insulate you from the damage of calories burning for energy, minimizing the inflammatory response, stimulating the healing phase quickly to help recover, and pitching and prolonging the release of growth factors as high and long as possible.

The last phase, taking certain nutrients on a regular basis, can enhance releasing growth factors.

These goals require a handful of supplements. That means you'll take four handfuls a day, in addition to the macronutrient foods and meal supplement shakes. In general, I think developing athletes at the junior high and high school level should concentrate on the first and second goals. They have nature on their side when it comes to recovery and growing. However, if you really want to know which specific nutrients you need, I recommend blood testing by a competent professional. This way, you find out exactly which nutrients are needed and you avoid guessing.

College athletes should develop energy and anti-inflammatory programs and add recovery and growth agents. They should be training and playing hard enough to need help and support in all four phases.

Athletes who aspire to become elite and play in semipro or professional leagues need to eat an ideal diet, train hard, use as many innovative techniques as they can, and sleep whenever they are not training, eating, or playing.

But always remember: Training is why you grow, eating is how you grow, but sleeping is *when* you grow. Sleep as much as you can when you're striving for the top and take all four phases of supplements to be sure you've got everything you need to make it happen.

Every athlete is different and you will no doubt add to or leave out one or two of these supplements because you'll find that you feel a little better when you do. Yet the basics are the basics, and you won't get as far in your sport if you don't take them as you would if you did.

So here, through my years of work with doctors, through my own experiences of research, and through the knowledge I have built, are the programs that I would recommend to athletes at various stages.

• *Program I*—for young athletes competing in high school sports.

To generate energy start by eating the way you know you're supposed to eat. Don't take supplement or meal replacement shortcuts. There is no substitute for a balanced diet. If you don't like vegetables, tough! Eat 'em anyway or find a way to get them down. You're not going to beat the guy across the line, field, or court if he's eating them and you're not.

Eat 0.8 grams of protein per pound of body weight per day. Food is better than a shake, but you can take about 30 grams of your protein in a shake made with whey protein, fresh or frozen fruit, and a teaspoon to a tablespoon of a healthy oil, like olive oil or better yet an omega-3 oil like flaxseed or fish oil. Drink this between meals so you don't dampen your appetite. Avoid the ready-to-drink brands that have a lot of carbs or additives. A simple whey powder, oil, water, frozen berries or other fruit, and a blender is all you need. Don't worry about tasting the oil, you won't; but it will add to the value and help keep your insulin stable.

Don't forget water. Water is the primary nutrient. It will not only keep you out of trouble, but it might keep you off the bench.

Take a multivitamin with antioxidants and minerals. One pill or capsule is not likely to contain all the agents or potency you'll need to maximize protection and 'gin up those mitochondria. Choose a multi that requires three or more pills or capsules (I prefer capsules for better digestion and absorption) each day. You don't need individual antioxidants if you're eating well, and there are not enough vitamins made to help protect you if you're not. To minimize inflammation take omega three oils. Shoot for 2 grams of EPA and 1 gram of DHA (not DHEA! That's an adrenal hormone. Be aware and don't take the wrong thing). Take this amount of oil twice a day with a meal.

To speed recovery, take a B complex vitamin and a gram of vitamin C. You can take them both with meals or with a small snack at bedtime which ever you choose. Don't take vitamin C right after working out or it will cause more harm than good.

To grow take a zinc and magnesium mineral supplement and some calcium. Zinc will boost your hormone levels if they're not already through the roof and the magnesium will help your muscles relax and recover more quickly. Calcium works its wonders in many ways. I suggest you take 30 mgs of a chelated zinc, like zinc gluconate or aspartate, 1 g of calcium gluconate or citrate and 800 of magnesium glycinate with a snack before bed. If you take too much magnesium you'll get diarrhea. Don't sweat that, just back off 200 mgs and know you're maxing out, which is a good thing.

• *Program II*—for aspiring professionals and advanced college level athletes.

To generate energy, eat like you should have or better than you did in high school. Eat five or more times a day, balancing each meal with 1 gram of protein for every pound of body weight. Eat or drink lean or clean (whey derived isolate) protein with healthy carbs derived from vegetables and oils, the polyunsaturated kinds from nuts and seeds.

Use the convenience of protein shakes to supplement your diet. Use 30 grams of whey protein in water, with or without fresh or frozen fruit. Eat a meal, drink a shake, eat a meal, and drink a shake. Do that as many times as you can if you want to gain weight, do three meals and two shakes if you want to maintain weight, and three modest meals and one shake—fresh fruit—if you want to lose weight.

Take a basic program of antioxidants, including 400 IU of vitamin E and 500 milligrams of C twice a day, with a mixed carotene, multivitamin, and mineral supplement to cover your trace mineral and B complex needs twice a day. Breakfast and supper are the ideal times to take this basic formula so you can absorb it and so you won't forget it.

Take amino acid supplements before working out, including 5 grams of leucine and taurine and 1 gram each of glutamine, and acetyl-L-carnitine. Drink sixteen ounces or more of water to help absorb these proteins.

Take the same amino acid mixture plus 5–15 grams of Creatine, 200 milligrams of alpha lipoic acid, and 1 gram of flax oil after training or practice. Don't worry about Creatine and cramping. Research shows it actually gets more water into the muscles and reduces muscle cramps.

To minimize inflammation take 1.5 grams of glucosamine chondroitin or MSM (no need to take both) along with the omega-3 oils EPA and DHA. Take 2 grams of EPA in addition to the flax, an EPA oil you're taking after working out, and 1 gram of DHA, fish oil, twice a day with meals. This much oil might require a digestive enzyme or two. If you have gas after dosing or see droplets in the toilet water after elimination take one or two digestive enzymes containing "lipase" with each dose of supplemental oil.

To speed recovery take 400 milligrams of alpha glyceryl phosphoryl choline a day, along with the antioxidant resveratrol or green tea extract. Both are potent antioxidants that can help you bounce back from tough workouts and wake up feeling your best. Take 30 milligrams of a chelated zinc like zinc gluconate or aspartate, 1 gram of calcium gluconate or citrate, and 800 milligrams of magnesium glycinate with a snack before bed. If you take too much magnesium you'll get diarrhea. Don't sweat that, just back off 200 milligrams and know you've maxed your capacity to absorb this valuable mineral. Take these along with 100 milligrams of B6 at bedtime to help you sleep and grow.

To grow even more, take 2 grams of arginine, 1 gram of acetyl-L-carnitine, 1 gram of glutamine, and 1 gram of lysine at bedtime, and take 4 grams of glycerol phosphoryl choline before bed. This will make the most out of your growth factor secretion and activity.

• *Program III* for professional and advanced college-level athletes.

Ideally at this level, you get your body tested and determine exactly what your needs are. Research scientist and nutritionist Thomas Incledon, PhD(c), RD, LD/LN, RPT, NSCA-CPT, CSCS, CFT (www.thomasincledon.com), has developed exceptionally effective testing protocols for athletes that examine hundreds of markers in blood, urine, stool, and saliva. The results from this type of testing allow people at any level to know exactly what their body needs. This way you don't waste time or money taking things that you don't need. For the professional athlete, this is extremely valuable so you optimize your performance and maximize your playing career.

To generate energy eat like a professional. Balance your insulin by eating six or more precisely balanced meals and meal replacement drinks of 40–50 grams of protein, 40–120 grams of carbohydrates from fruits and vegetables, and 30 grams of healthy fats like omega oil supplements, nuts, and seeds. You can set this up so that you eat four meals and drink three shakes (made with high-quality whey and branched chain proteins in isolate form) each day. Mix your drinks with water and chase it with an equal amount to insure absorption and avoid dehydration. Flavor it with fruit and add a tablespoon of omega-3 and/or CLA (conjugated linoleic acid). Use olive oil in a pinch but don't get lazy, get a cooler and carry your oils and liquid proteins with you to take before and after training and practice.

To generate energy take a basic formula of antioxidants and energy converting cofactors, including 400 ius of vitamin E, 500 milligrams of vitamin C, a mixed carotene, and a multivitamin and mineral to cover your basic needs. Take these twice a day at breakfast and supper.

Take amino acid supplements before working out, including 5 grams each of leucine and taurine, and 1 gram each of glutamine, and acetyl-L-carnitine, thirty minutes before working out or practice. Drink 16 ounces or more of water with these supplements.

Take 1 gram of DL and L phenylalanine, 200 milligrams of DMAE (2-Dimethylaminoethanol Bitartrate), 200 milligrams of panax ginseng, and a B complex vitamin fifteen to twenty minutes before training or practicing.

Take 5 grams of leucine and taurine, and 1 gram each of glutamine and acetyl-L-carnitine, plus 5 grams of Creatine, 200 milligrams of alpha lipoic acid, and 1 gram of flax oil after training or practice. Drink plenty of water.

To minimize inflammation take 5 Wobenzyme (or its equivalent) enzymes two times a day between meals and at bedtime. Take a ginger product like Zyflamend with 100 milligrams of ginger, 150 milligrams of rosemary, and 100 milligrams of turmeric twice a day. Keep up with the omega-3 oils, taking 2 grams of EPA and 1 gram of DHA three times a day with meals or in meal replacement protein shakes.

To speed recovery take 1 gram of acetyl-L-carnitine, 400 milligrams of alpha lipoic acid and 200 milligrams of phosphatidyl serine twice a day. Take 30 milligrams of a chelated zinc, 1 gram of calcium gluconate or citrate, and 800 milligrams of magnesium glycinate with a snack before bed. If you take too much magnesium you'll get diarrhea. Don't sweat that, just back off 200 milligrams and you'll be fine.

To grow take 2 grams of arginine, 1 gram of acetyl-L-carnitine, 1 gram of glutamine, 1 gram of lysine and take 400 mg of glycerol phosphoryl choline before bed. This will make the most out of your growth factor secretion and activity.

Take di-indolin to block the uptake of estrogen from your gut and tribulis terrestis (I think the Bulgarian brand is probably the best available) to maximize testosterone effect. Take the testosterone analog, tongkat ali, to get the most out of those receptors.

There will always be the next best supplement. But these are the ones I've found to be helpful and reliable. Be careful of someone wanting to sell you the "greatest." Use the Internet to find the science that supports the claims. Take a new supplement by itself for the first few days and expect to feel something. If you don't find a lot of science to support the manufacturers' or distributors' claims and you don't feel the promised effect, you might want to use that "money back" guarantee most supplements carry.

These are some of my initial ideas, which have popped into my head since I decided to retire. But there are more. I'm committed to seeing if there is a way for pro athletes to get improved health care, better structural care, and better nutritional testing than they are getting. It's good now, but it could be even better.

There's a story I once heard of an Arabian prince who has one of the world's most exclusive collections of custom-made cars. But because he loves to drive them hard, he scoured Europe to find the most experienced and masterful mechanics to maintain them. He pays his mechanics very well to keep his stable of cars running to their optimum potential.

Maybe pro sports teams will get the same idea as the Arabian prince and hire the best team of people—sports scientists, trainers, medical doctors, chiropractors, nutritionists, acupuncturists, soft-tissue therapists, and massage therapists—to help maintain the health of its stable of athletes. They're paying hundreds of millions of dollars to these athletes—might as well treat them like the pricy investment they are.

And I have some ideas that could help. Right now there is a rigid policy allowing absolutely no hormone replacement in sports. But the kind of stress and training that most pro athletes live with day in and day out cause too many stress hormones, such as cortisol and adrenaline, to be produced.

These stress hormones are "catabolic," meaning they tear tissue down and make athletes much more vulnerable to injuries and moody behavior. When these stress hormones are overproduced, they actually lower the kind of hormones that help build muscles, bones, and connective tissue.

These tissue building "anabolic" hormones, such as testosterone and DHEA, are often alarmingly low in many pro athletes. Over time, this can shorten their careers because of repetitive injuries and a much slower healing time.

My vision is that, one day, athletes will be allowed to be monitored for natural, bio-identical hormone levels and be allowed to do just enough hormone replacement to stay within normal healthy ranges. Outrageously high levels of artificial hormones never are safe, and that is not what I'm recommending at all.

What I'm recommending is something to keep hormones within normal, healthy ranges so athletes can stay healthier longer and recover from injuries faster. Team doctors and league officials could easily monitor those levels. Everyone would be better off.

The bottom line is that athletes are not going to be able to fully take away the trauma and the damage they're doing to their bodies. But they can minimize it as much as possible. I'd like to help. In other ways, I already am.

My postcareer emphasis always will continue to be on better performance. It's just that it's not my athletic performance any longer. It's all about helping other athletes.

Already I feel like I'm on the type of playoff roll we got on in San Francisco, Denver, and Oakland. With the help of Thomas Incledon, a scientist at Human Performance Specialists, Inc., we've developed a new supplement line called Pure Romo. (For more information, go to www.PureRomoNutrition. com.)

We've produced it to change people's lives. I have no doubts, absolutely none, that it will. Our product line is going to be professional-grade supplements, unavailable in most stores, but available to anyone looking to take their game to the next level, be it a professional athlete or business person. Try it and watch your workouts and your focus go through the roof. You can't believe this stuff; I couldn't the first time I tried it.

From here on in, our mission will be to continue developing products that will help athletes recover, help the trauma in their body, help their bodies function at a higher level, help their brains function at the highest level. They will be able to use the types of supplements I sought out for sixteen years.

Eventually science will come up with a cure for concussions. Of course, I intend to be right in the middle of the action. I can't help but believe that our misfortunes and our mistakes make us better teachers. I owe my game whatever I can give back, especially to the healing and restoration of our bodies and brains.

Football is a sport whose brutality is a big part of its popularity and its mystique. Our most celebrated and successful players play "all out," giving every ounce of themselves, often without regard to the physical and emotional side effects. They are excellent role models for what it takes to be great.

But we need to take better care of our wounded. We need to find better ways to help them stay healthy to begin with, to prevent dangerous and permanent injuries without compromising the drama of what makes the NFL the best sport in the world.

I don't want anyone to have to learn the hard way and go through what I did. Still, I do challenge future athletes to train with even greater intensity than I gave, because that's what turned this average talent into a Pro Bowl performer.

I'll pledge to continue my exhaustive research into improved training methods, safety, and healthy supplemental nutrition. And I expect all of you to do your best in whatever you do. That's your obligation. Meanwhile, I'll try to continue to raise my bar toward even higher standards.

One such example is my new innovation, The Dream Capsule. Imagine visualizing your dreams, writing them down, and placing them in a capsule you carry on a necklace wherever you go. It would be a constant reminder of the responsibility you have to how you want to use your God-given talents.

Dreams are what make us live, what push us to our highest potential. I get so excited about whatever moves us. And I pledge to do whatever I can to help you get to where you want to go.

And don't forget the dragons. Those fire-breathing, often self-imposed obstacles to our success. Without them, we wouldn't discover how great we can be. I can't wait for you to share your dreams and dragons with me at www.ofdreamsand dragons.com.

APPENDIX B:
MY INJURY HISTORY

The following is a list of my injuries during my sixteen years of playing in the National Football League. All of the injuries have been reported and documented with each team I played for.

SAN FRANCISCO 49ERS

July 1988 training camp—Left groin pull 8/3/88

Neck strain 7/17/88

1988 regular season—Left mid-biceps tendon strain 11/10/88

Kicked in the right occipital region; was stunned and suffered a concussion; had continuous headaches throughout the later part of the season due to concussion 12/11/1988

Right wrist (navicular bone broken); still does not have full range of motion and surgery is still necessary to repair it.

Left 5th finger tendon tear (loss of motion)

Left thumb sprain

Right thumb sprain 11/22/88

Left calf contusion 9/11/88

Left hamstring strain 11/9/88

July/August 1989 training camp—Left knee strain 8/19/89

Left/right quadricep strain 8/28/89

1989 regular season—Left hamstring strain 9/4/89

Left cervical-brachial pain 9/17/89

Left finger sprain (proximal) 10/4/89

Lower back strain10/8/89

Hit to the right lower ribs (sprain) 10/22/89

Hit to the left elbow, contusion of the olecranon process 10/29/89

2nd hit to the left elbow, contusion of the olecranon process 11/6/89

Right hamstring strain 11/13/89

Left calf strain 11/19/89

Right elbow strain 12/26/89

1989 playoffs (January 1990)—Anterior thigh contusion 1/6/90

Left thigh contusion 1/14/90

1990 off-season training—Pain in the medial olecranon border of left elbow; apparent loose bodies

July 1990 training camp—Right hamstring contusion

Stinger to the upper part of trapezius

1990 regular season—Left acromioclavicular injury 9/23/90

Left shoulder AC sprain 9/23/90

Left acromioclavicular joint injection 10/21/90

2nd acromioclavicular joint injection 11/7/90

Concussion while making a tackle (dazed, lightheaded and continued headaches during the rest of the football season) 12/3/90

Right upper anterior chest pain (fell on right arm while

tackling opposing player), contusion, and muscle strain associated with injury 12/17/90

Hyperextension of the left wrist

Hyperextension of the left knee

Left contusion/strain to quadriceps

Weakness in supraspinatus/external rotators

C6 root versus upper brachial plexus stretch injury

1990 playoffs (January 12, 1991)—Left shoulder pain, neck was extended and rotated to the left side, numbness and pain to his deltoid 1/12/91

Neck stinger 1/7/91

Neck stinger 1/20/91

Hyperextension of the left knee 1/20/91

Hyperextension of the left wrist 1/12/91

1991 off-season training—Left AC pain, continued left wrist pain, weakness in the supraspinatus and external rotators. Cervical lordosis in the mid segments.

1991 training camp—Sacro pain

Right calf contusion

Right metacarpophalangeal sprain

1991 regular season—Right knee strain 9/2/91

Brachial plexcompression/pinched nerve 9/22/91

Left knee bone bruise

Left medial parapatellar pain

Concussion—dazed with a dull headache, head precautions were taken 9/29/91

Headaches continued throughout the season

Right acromioclavicular joint contusion 9/29/91

Right lateral thigh contusion 11/3/91

Right lower leg contusion 12/1/91

Neck/shoulder pain radiation of pain and numbness in the deltoid region associated with making a tackle of an opposing player 1/12/91

1992 off-season training—Continued left wrist pain, neck pain and residual headaches.

1992 training camp—Stinger to neck (numbness of right arm) 8/5/92

> Right hamstring strain 8/7/92

1992 regular season—Right lumbar facet syndrome 9/17/92

> Right elbow contusion 9/27/92
>
> Right calf contusion 10/4/92
>
> Celiac/solar plexus syndrome 11/1/92
>
> Left thigh contusion (anterior) 11/1/92
>
> Left thigh contusion (lateral) 11/9/92
>
> Concussion with motor loss 12/19/92
>
> Right thigh fasclitis 12/19/93

1992 playoffs (January 1993)—Stinger of the left deltoid 1/3/93

> Right rib contusion 1/8/93

1993 off-season training—Continued pain in left wrist, residual headaches and neck pain

> Left ankle sprain 4/15/93

1993 training camp—Concussion with a loss of consciousness for approx.10 seconds; nausea, vomiting and blurred vision also experienced 7/22/93

> Low back pain—strain to the left L5 facet, facet synovitis 7/28/93

1993 regular season—Hyperextension of left elbow 12/93

> Neck stinger 9/93
>
> Left shoulder strain
>
> Right shoulder strain
>
> Contusion of left elbow
>
> 2nd neck stinger 11/93
>
> Continued headaches associated with concussions

1993 playoffs (January 1994)—Stinger with pain in the left shoulder pain with cervical and left rotation 1/10/94

Right Rib contusion 1/7/94

1994 off-season training—Left elbow surgery to remove loose bodies of cartilage 2/94

1994 training camp—Right hamstring strain 7/19/94

Left eye abrasion bleeding in medial portion of the eye

Nasal abrasion 7/29/94

Left eye double vision 7/29/94

Right groin strain 7/30/94

1994 regular season—Right hip strain 9/12/94

Right lateral quadriceps contusion—struck on the thigh with during full contact struck with helmet 10/9/94 and /24/94

Blow to right thigh, contusion 11/20/94

Took a severe blow to the head while attempting to make a tackle; concussion was noted; failed conversation test on the field 10/24/94

Left hamstring strain 12/4/94

Left hamstring strain 12/12/94

Left hip contusion 12/18/94

PHILADELPHIA EAGLES

1995 off-season training—Continued left wrist pain; headaches associated with past concussions.

1995 training camp—Right hamstring strain 7/22/95

Right shoulder strain 8/7/95

Low back pain associated with a low back strain 8/30/95

1995 Regular Season—Left thigh contusion 9/4/95

Left knee strain 9/4/95

Left quad strain 9/6/95

2nd left knee strain 9/7/95

Left thumb sprain 9/11/95

Right hamstring strain 9/27/95

Broken left thumb 9/17/95

Right hip flexor strain 10/8/95

Right knee strain 10/12/95

Stinger 12/18/95

2nd neck and trapezius stinger 12/21/95

Left shin bone bruise 12/24/95

Abrasions and contusions to right and left forearms from playing on artificial turf

DENVER BRONCOS

1996 off-season training—Continued pain in broken left wrist, headaches associated with numerous past concussions

1996 training camp—Left thigh strain

Contusion to right thigh

1996 regular season—Dislocation of right middle finger 11/2/96

Right patellar tendon tendonitis 12/1/96

Acute cerebral concussion (hit in the head with opponent's helmet during a full-contact tackle) 9/29/96

Right torn patellar tendon (played with this injury throughout the rest of the season)

1996 playoffs (January 1997)—

1997 off-season—Surgery of the right patellar tendon showed there was a tear; fluid drained and a bursectomy performed. Patellar tendon was repaired with a metal anchor. Extensive physical therapy was needed in order to regain strength and mobility of right knee, right quadriceps, and right hamstring

1997 training camp—Trauma to left ring finger determined to be an acute sprain (7/97)

Anteromedial right knee pain 7/97

Left knee patellar tendonitis 4/97

APPENDIX B

1997 Regular Season—Left ring finger sprain 12/27/97

Poked in left eye, eye contusion 11/16/97

Left knee strain 4/97, 7/97

Right quad contusion 9/97

Neck stinger 11/97

Left wrist strain 10/97

2nd dislocation of middle finger 11/97

Right knee quadriceps strain 11/20/97

1998 off-season training—Continued pain in left wrist and left ring finger, headaches associated with past concussions

1998 training camp—Right patellar tendon strain 7/98

Left talus bruise 8/98

Stiffness in ulna 8/98

1998 regular season—Right latissimus/serratus strain 9/6/98

Right proximal adductor10/5/98

Right groin contusion—kicked in groin while making a tackle 10/98

Right clavicle contusion 11/98

Right groin pain 12/98

Chronic right knee pain, pain with flexion 12/98

1998 playoffs (January 1999)—1st concussion sustained while making a direct-impact hit on opposing player. Hit head to running back's body. Dazed and dizzy. Same series 2nd concussion sustained while tackling running back to avoid scoring. Got up stumbling and was dizzy 1/17/99

1999 off-season training—Continued pain in left wrist; headaches more frequent, with occasional nausea after training.

1999 training camp—Jammed left wrist 7/29/99

1999 regular season—Left elbow pain and swelling 9/26/99

Concussion—direct hit to head while making a tackle on a run play 9/26/99

Left ankle calcaneous and cuboid ligament sprain 11/7/99

2000 off-season training—Continued pain in left wrist; headaches are more frequent with occasional nausea after training

2000 training camp—

2000 regular season—Cervical strain 9/2000

    Elbow Inflammation 12/2000

2001 off-season training—Continued pain in right elbow

    Surgery of right elbow to remove multiple loose bodies of cartilage measuring up to 12mm in size 1/10/2000

    Pain in left patella tendon—MRI revealed chronic patellar tendonitis, osteoarthritis in the medial compartment. Defect in the posterior and medial aspect of the medial femoral condyle. 1/28/2000

    Pain in left wrist and continued headaches, lightheadedness, and some nausea when training hard

2001 training Camp—

2001 regular season—Direct blow to the left iliac crest while trying to recover a fumble 9/23/2001

    Hip pointer, another direct helmet blow to left iliac crest, significant bruising and swelling 10/07/2001

    MRI showing that there is a tear of the internal oblique muscle attachment to the iliac crest and a tear in the traverse abdominis muscle attachment. Played the rest of the season with this injury.

2002 off-season training—Continued pain in left wrist; headaches associated with past concussion in addition to feeling dizzy at times with excessive training

OAKLAND RAIDERS

2002 training camp—Neck cervical muscle strain 7/30/02

    Left lumbar musculoskeletal condition 8/17/02

    Left lumbar spondylolysthesis 8/24/02

APPENDIX B

2002 regular season—Right neck strain happened while struck in the helmet while practicing 9/4/03

 Neck cervical muscle strain 9/09/92

 Right ankle sprain 10/19/02

 Concussion—direct blow to head while making a tackle 12/08/02

2002 regular season (January 2003 Super Bowl)—Concussion 2nd quarter, helmet-to-helmet hit with Tampa Bay fullback 1/2003

2003 off-season training—Left elbow pain; MRI shows loose bodies in the olecranon fossa 1/30/03

 Right ankle pain—MRI shows posterior tibialis tenosynovitis 1/30/03

 Surgery of the left elbow—removal of extensive debridement of loose bodies also shows degenerative osteoarthritis 3/21/03

2003 training camp—Patella infrapatellar bursitis 8/01/03

 Concussion—first hit in training camp taking on guard Frank Middleton 7/23/03

 Concussion 8/08/03

 Concussion 8/14/03

 Concussion 8/22/03

2003 regular season—Concussion 9/07/03

 Concussion 9/14/03

 Concussion 9/22/03

Put on injured reserve October 2003 due to repeated concussions from blows to the head. Still feeling the affects of postconcussion syndrome. Has no sense of taste or smell; has residual headaches and dizziness when working out.

ACKNOWLEDGMENTS

Let me admit up front that acknowledgments are tougher than the fourth quarter of a pressure-packed championship battle. What challenges me the most is that I will fail some of you out there. The truth is that I know now that everyone who crosses my path for even the slightest moment has the power to influence me if I let it happen. So, named or not, you know what you've done to impact my life and I sincerely appreciate you for your contributions.

Thank you to John Steed, Mike Power, Glen Schmelter, and Jim Bell for creating a rich scrapbook of fond memories.

How do I even begin to thank all my coaches for their help over all these years? To Coach Dunn, for changing my life and believing in me and my dreams.

Jack Bicknell, Red Kelin, Bill McPherson, Greg Robinson, and Larry Coyer for their signficant contributions to my career and this book.

Thank you to Coach Bill Walsh, Coach George Siefert, and Coach Mike Shanahan—the Lords of My Rings. I can't imagine any player in history being blessed with the collection of coaches I had.

Thanks also to coaches Rich Kotite, Ray Rhodes, Bill Callahan, Bob Zeman, Jim Vicharella, Joe Vitt, Frank Bush, Frank Pagac, Emmitt Thomas, Chuck Bresnahan, Danny Smith, Bud Carson, Lynn Stiles, Richard Smith, John Teerlinck and George Dyer.

Team owners Eddie DeBartolo and Jeff Lurie.

Strength coaches Wes Emmerit, Jerry Attaway, Jim Williams, Mike Wolf, Rich Tuten, Garrett Giemont, Greg Saporta, Chris Pearson, and Mike Durand.

Equipment managers Bronco Hinek, Ted Walsh, Doug West, Chris Valenti, Richard and Bobby Romanski.

And for all the winning I was a part of, none of it would have been possible without the great teammates I've had at every level, from the Shamrocks to the NFL.

Then there were high-performance specialists. Remi Korchemny and Dan Pfaff. Tim Adams, special friend and advisor. We pushed each other relentlessly. My team of medical advisors—Dr. Dean Raffelock, Dr. Mauro DiPasquale, and Dr. Chris Renna—were just three of the men who helped train and educate me so that I could help train and educate others. I can't thank you enough—ever. The same goes for Greg Roskopf and Craig Buehler, who know my body better than I know it myself. Their knowledge and friendship will always be special to me.

Thank you to Ron Carducci, for being my private sounding board.

Dr. Lindsay, Dr. Pyne, and Nelson Vetanze, chiropractors and soft tissue specialists by trade, but linebackers to me.

The training and public relations staffs for the San Francisco 49ers, Philadelphia Eagles, Denver Broncos, and Oakland Raiders provided me with a steady stream of medical reports, stories written about me, and much of the information I needed to piece together my sixteen-year career. For this, and everything they did, thank you. A special thank you to Lindsy McLean, Otho Davis, Steve Antonopulos, Rod Martin, and Randy Shrout and their assistants for putting me back together time after time.

Broncos owner Pat Bowlen and his wife, Annabel. You cared for me, Julie, and the kids as people first. We're friends forever.

Attorneys Harvey Steinberg and Jeff Springer, who are so good in their field that somebody should write their professional stories.

So many others helped us with research that was indispensable. Jody Woodman, Ann Depperschmidt, and Rene Mahan. Ira Miller was the ultimate 49ers resource. Cindy Marshall had to listen to hours and hours of me—a worse fate than some of the tight ends I covered.

Bruce Allen, the Raiders' top personnel man while I was there, helped me so much near the end. He is a superior man and football excecutive.

Trace Armstrong, Bubby Brister, and Riki Ellison, my dearest friends in pro football.

Al Davis, for the unforgettable talks about "the game."

And to the best in the business, my agent, Tom Condon, and his partner, Ken Kremer, who were always there for me through the good and the bad.

Thank you Adam Schefter for a year and a half of unparalleled persistence, work ethic, and devotion to most likely the most difficult person you've ever had to write with. Thanks for your skills and, most importantly, our friendship.

A huge thank you to Basil Kane for pushing this project through. Mauro DiPreta for getting it and getting me—believing more than any other editor could. Joelle Yudin, who pushed back every deadline to satisfy my ever-changing schedule and mind.

ACKNOWLEDGMENTS

To Greg and Michael Pickett, it's great to be a part of your championship CytoSport team.

Current Oakland Raider GM Michael Lombardi, whose office became a safe passage for my emotional exit from the sport that was my life.

To my friend and mentor Victor Conte, thank you for showing me the power of the courage of conviction in the face of controversy.

To my in-laws, Barbara and Donald Lagrand, thank you for your persistent love and devotion to our family. Mama, your phone number will always be 911 on our speed dial.

To Dad and Mom, role models who have enjoyed each other's company for fifty years. For instilling a work ethic second to none and providing unconditional love for all your children.

To my brothers, Mike and Joe, and my sisters, Sue and Patricia, thanks for rallying around my dreams sometimes at the expense of yours. I promise to get closer to each of you and your families.

My coauthor has the same relationship with his parents, Shirley and Jeffrey Schefter, who offered unmatched support, as always. Thank you to someone special—Leigh Wald, for putting up with Adam.

Thank you to my children, Alexandra and Dalton, the two greatest gifts a father could have and for making me aware that my greatest blessing is to be your dad.

And alongside every successful man is an even stronger successful woman. My wife, my soulmate, my love, Julie. You are my most important dream come true.

—Bill Romanowski, June 7, 2005